JAPANESE

H. J. Ballhatchet
and
S. K. Kaiser

TEACH YOURSELF BOOKS
Hodder and Stoughton

An audio-cassette has been produced to accompany this course and is available separately via all good bookshops or, in case of difficulty, direct from the publishers.

For further details please write to the publishers at the address given on page iv, enclosing an SAE and quoting Teach Yourself Books (Dept. S/Cass.).

British Library Cataloguing in Publication Data

Ballhatchet H. J.
Japanese.
1. Japanese language. Grammar
2. Spoken Japanese Language
I. Title II. Kaiser, S. K.
495.6′82421

ISBN 0 340 49245 7

First published 1989
Third impression 1991

Typeset by Cotswold Typesetting Ltd, Gloucester.
Printed in Great Britain for the educational publishing division of Hodder and Stoughton Ltd, Mill Road, Dunton Green, Sevenoaks, Kent by Clays Ltd, St Ives plc.

This volume is available in the USA from:
Random House Inc.,
201 East 50th Street, New York, NY 10022

Contents

Acknowledgments

We would like to thank Ms Tomoko Aoyama of the University of Queensland for her help and advice; responsibility for any mistakes, however, lies with us. We would also like to thank Yoshitaka Kobayashi, Riko Sherratt, Shinya Sugiyama, and Hiroko Tayama for taking part in the recording.

The publishers and authors would also like to thank the following for granting permission to reproduce material in this book: p. 43 Kobori Jūken Ltd.; p. 83 Rōto Seiyaku Ltd.; p. 84 Tōkyō Yomiuri Kyojin Gun; p. 106 Higashi Nihon Ryokaku Tetsudō Ltd.; p. 107 Teito Kōsokudo Kōtsū Eidan; p. 130 Unayoshi; p. 147 Nihon Goodyear Ltd.; p. 172 Happo-en; p. 185 Watanabe Ltd.; p. 201 Bayer Yakuhin Ltd.; p. 231 Japan Airlines.

How to use this book

You are advised to read the General Introduction with care as it contains information that will be useful in learning the language, including an outline of how Japanese sounds are pronounced. You may find it useful to keep referring back to it as you work through the first few units.

Contents of a unit

Each unit starts with a brief description of what it contains.

Kaiwa

Set in a wide variety of everyday situations, the dialogues (**kaiwa** in Japanese) form the core of each unit. They are generally divided into two or more sections, each preceded by a few sentences to set the scene. For the first four units, these sentences are in English, and after that in non-conversational Japanese. This will provide you with an opportunity to develop an understanding of this style, too, and a basis on which to go on to study written Japanese should you decide to do so.

English translations accompany the first two **kaiwa** to ease you into the Japanese text; thereafter, only new vocabulary is given, with cross-references to explanations of new structures and language and society information.

True or false?

These serve to test your understanding of the **kaiwa**; do not attempt them until you have developed a good grasp of the dialogue. If you find that your answer does not match the key, try working out where you went wrong by going over the **kaiwa** again.

Structures

In order to get an idea of the points covered in a new unit, you may wish to read through this section first of all, but you may find it easier to look up structures as you are referred to them in the **kaiwa** vocabulary. New structures are often given in pattern form: for example, **A wa B desu** (*A is B*). An explanation will follow, telling you about things like the relation between A and B, what kinds of words can be used in these positions, and how to form the negative of the new pattern. This approach is adopted here because of its suitability in illustrating differences in word order to Western students of Japanese. You will also see structures expressed in the form of, for instance, **[noun] o kudasai** *please give me* [*noun*]. Among other things, this is again useful for illustrating differences in word order between English and Japanese. When example sentences are very straightforward, we have not given an English equivalent.

Renshū and the key to the exercises

The exercises (**renshū**) provide you with an opportunity to produce your own sentences on the basis of structures mastered in the unit. Checking your results against the key will help you to identify any problems in your understanding of new structures.

Language and Society

The language of a people is intimately connected with its social organisation and way of thinking, customs and habits; these are especially important for the understanding of a culture like that of Japan, which does not share a common heritage with the West. In this section, various pieces of information relating to the way of life of the Japanese people are given, often in combination with phrases or expressions that will be useful in such situations. Attention is also drawn to uses of language and non-verbal behaviour (body language), enabling you to grasp the meaning implicit in the ways people react in the **kaiwa**, and acquire an insider's use of the language.

Use of this course with the cassette

The cassette tape available with this course contains pronunciation exercises, the **kaiwa** of all units, plus some practice material. Pay particular attention to the pronunciation exercises at the beginning, as they lay the foundation for a good pronunciation – mistakes are difficult to correct later on!

When starting a new unit, it is perhaps best if you listen to the **kaiwa** once or twice to get a very general impression of the new material. Then you should read the explanation of what the unit contains, work out what the setting is (given in Japanese from Unit 5), and read through the vocabulary, Structures and Language and Society sections before going back to the cassette. Repeat this process until you have a good grasp of the new unit. Try and check your command of the new material by first speaking along with the tape, then stopping the tape at the relevant points to take over a **kaiwa** part at a time yourself.

Do not attempt the true or false questions or the taped practice material until you have mastered the new unit and finally check your understanding by doing the **renshū**.

General introduction

Japanese is not a difficult language to learn, especially at the basic level. To begin with, pronunciation is easy, which makes it eminently suitable for self-study. The language is best suited to explanation based on sentence patterns or 'structures'; these are especially useful for the learner since new sentences can often be formed simply by substituting other words or expressions. This is possible because in Japanese you need not worry about making words agree in terms of distinctions between masculine/feminine or singular/plural as in languages such as French or German. New structures are listed in the vocabulary after each **kaiwa** (dialogue) with a cross reference if a further explanation is given. The following abbreviations are used: S = Structures, LS = Language and Society.

Japanese compared with European languages

Japanese is unrelated to Indo-European languages, so naturally there are a number of basic differences. It will facilitate your study of the language if you keep such differences in mind; you should therefore read the following with special care.

Word order

In English, verbs precede their objects (*I saw a man*), but in Japanese they normally follow their object, coming last in a sentence. Subjects (*I* in the English sentence), and even objects (*man*), are often optional in Japanese, so a Japanese sentence may consist of a verb only (**mita** can mean *I saw him/her/it* etc.). It is therefore possible to say that Japanese depends more on the context than English. Word order differences deserve special attention in the Japanese equivalents to

English relative clauses and comparative sentences. Thus, *Yesterday I saw a man who had red trousers* turns out something like the following in Japanese word order: *Yesterday red trousers had man saw. He is bigger than I* normally has the order of *he than I bigger is.* Note, however, that except for the verb (which is always at the end of a sentence), Japanese word order is more flexible than English word order.

Particles

Relations between parts of speech, which in English and other European languages are indicated by means of case endings or prepositions, are expressed in Japanese by 'particles', which are attached directly ***after*** the word they mark. In the structure notes this is indicated as, for instance **[place] e** *to* [*place*], which gives three pieces of information in this case: (1) **e** is equivalent in meaning to *to*; (2) *to* comes in front of a noun in English whereas **e** is attached after the noun in Japanese; and (3) the noun used with **e** in this structure indicates a place.

Speech levels

Japanese uses different forms of verbs (and occasionally, other words) for formal and informal levels of speech. Units 8, 16 and 18 specifically deal with this, but relevant information is given in various other places too, as this is an area that requires special attention by English speakers.

Writing system

For reasons of economy of space, this book does not introduce the Japanese writing system (which is notorious for its complexity); instead, romanised script is used.

The system used here is usually called the modified Hepburn system, which is better suited for English speakers than the **kunrei** system officially used in Japan, although the differences are not great.

A few words on the nature of the Japanese writing system may be useful for the learner: Japanese is written in a mixture of Chinese characters (imported some 1500 years ago) or **kanji**, as they are called in Japan, and **kana**, two syllabaries derived from **kanji**. Roughly speaking, **kanji** are used for those parts of the language that convey ***meaning***, while **hiragana** (the cursive variety of **kana**) are used for elements indicating the ***functions*** of words (particles, tense-endings and such like). The second, square-looking set of **kana**, (**katakana**) is used in a way akin to our italics to give prominence to words. **Katakana** are particularly common for words of Western origin (for words of Chinese provenance, **kanji** are of course used), words depicting a sound (Japanese has a rich inventory of these – see Unit 12), and, traditionally, the texts of telegrams.

Pronunciation and syllable structure

The impression created by the sounds of Japanese on Western ears, often described as 'monotonous' or 'staccato', is largely caused by a combination of two factors: there is no clearly perceivable stress on sections of words or sentences, and syllables are uttered at equal length and speed. *YokoHAAma* or *SuZUUki* are English versions of Japanese words that sound quite different in the original; in careful pronunciation, more like **Yo-ko-ha-ma** and **Su-zu-ki**, without any section lengthened or stressed. (However, see below about Japanese accent.) These segments are in fact Japanese syllables.

Short and long syllables

Japanese differentiates between long and short syllables, and in order to make yourself understood it is vital that you distinguish these carefully in your pronunciation; all syllables in the above examples happened to be short, but this is not so, for instance, in the place-names **Tōkyō** and **Kyōto**, which may be cut up into **To-o-kyo-o** and **Kyo-o-to**. In slow, careful pronunciation a long syllable takes twice as long to pronounce as a short syllable (although at higher speeds the ratio is more like 60% longer). A short syllable in Japanese may be regarded as a basic unit of pronunciation.

Syllable structure

A Japanese syllable consists of a vowel alone (**a**, **i** etc.), a combination of a consonant + vowel (e.g. **ka**, **ta**), or consonant + glide + vowel (**kya**, **cha**); these syllables can in principle be lengthened by doubling the short vowel. There are also syllabic consonants, which are either used to double the consonant (other than **n**, **m**) in a non-initial syllable (**to-te-mo→to-t-te-mo**), or 'syllabic **-n**', which is used to double the consonants **n** and **m**, but also occurs at the end of another syllable or between other syllables without doubling them: **sa-n**, **sa-n-kai** (see the section on consonants below for pronunciation of syllabic **-n**).

The following table contains the basic Japanese syllable structure:

a	ka	ga	sa	za	ta	da	na	ha	pa	ba	ma	ya	ra	wa	-n
i	ki	gi	shi	ji	chi		ni	hi	pi	bi	mi		ri		
u	ku	gu	su	zu	tsu		nu	fu	pu	bu	mu	yu	ru		
e	ke	ge	se	ze	te	de	ne	he	pe	be	me		re		
o	ko	go	so	zo	to	do	no	ho	po	bo	mo	yo	ro		
	kya	gya	sha	ja	cha		nya	hya	pya	bya	mya		rya		
	kyu	gyu	shu	ju	chu		nyu	hyu	pyu	byu	myu		ryu		
	kyo	gyo	sho	jo	cho		nyo	hyo	pyo	byo	myo		ryo		

Vowels

Japanese vowels are pure and clipped; the strong contraction of the throat that takes place at the beginning of English words starting with a vowel is almost unnoticeable in Japanese. Long vowels have the same quality as short ones; they are simply longer in duration.

Consonants

Most consonants are similar to English consonants, although **k**, **g**, **s**, **z**, **t**, **d**, **p** and **b** are all pronounced without the noticable puff of air that accompanies the English sounds in accentuated position. Special attention is needed for the syllabic **-n**.

As the consonant in a consonant + vowel combination (**na** etc.), **n** causes no difficulties; however, syllabic **-n** requires some attention as its pronunciation changes according to the sound following it:

1 Before **p**, **b**, **m** it is pronounced **m**:

an-pi (pron. a**m**pi)
an-bai (pron. a**m**bai)
an-ma (pron. a**m**ma)

2 Before **t**, **ts**, **d**, **n**, **ch**, **j** it is pronounced **n** (the same sound as in ***na*** etc.):

antei, annai, enchō

3 Before **k** and **g** it is pronounced **ng** (as in English *si**ng**er*):

ginkō, shingō

4 Before all other sounds, or at the end of a word, it is pronounced as a nasal **n**. This sound is like the nasal in French 'Jean', but as it constitutes a separate syllable in Japanese the preceding vowel is ***not*** nasalised. Before vowels and **y**, this syllabic nasal is marked by an apostrophe to distinguish it from the **n** in **na**, **no** etc. Compare the following pairs:

kani	kan'i
kanō	kan'ō
kanyū	kan'yū

Syllable combinations to watch

Sound combinations that are difficult to distinguish for English speakers include the following:

1 **kiya** versus **kya** etc. Whereas **ki-ya** is a combination of two syllables pronounced consecutively, **kya** is a single syllable. Pronounce the following pairs:

kiyaku	kyaku	biyōin	byōin
shiyōnin	shōnin	riyaku	ryaku
jiyūka	jūka	riyōshi	ryōshi

2 **Single versus double consonants** Doubling means 'holding' the consonant for a syllable's length. Compare the following pairs:

a-ka	a-k-ka	a-na	a-n-na
Ma-sa-o	ma-s-sa-o	a-ma	a-n-ma
ma-ta	ma-t-ta	ta-ne-n	ta-n-ne-n
i-chi	i-t-chi		

Despite the spelling convention, **tch** represents simply a doubling of **ch**.

3 **Single versus double vowels** Recall that a double vowel is a syllable longer. In the romanisation used in this book, macrons are used over the short vowel for doubled **a** (**ā**), **o** (**ō**) and **u** (**ū**), whereas the double **e**-sound is written **ei**, and double **i**, **ii**. (In loanwords from English and other Western languages, however, **ē** and **ī** are used; **ē** is also used for the few items where **ee** occurs in Japanese spelling, such as **ē** (*yes*).) Pronounce the following sets of words with long and short vowels:

asa	āsā	seki	seiki	(NB pronounced sēki)
kita	kiita	koko	kōko	kōkō
suki	sūki			

Whispered vowels

In Standard Japanese, which is based on the Tokyo dialect, a short **i** or **u** occurring between unvoiced consonants (**k**, **s**, **t**, **h**, **p**) becomes unvoiced too, making it scarcely audible (like a whisper), or even appearing totally absent:

k(i)sha	*train*	k(u)sa	*grass*
sh(i)ki	*the seasons*	s(u)koshi	*a little*
ch(i)kara	*strength*	ts(u)ki	*moon*
h(i)kōki	*airplane*	f(u)ton	*quilt*
p(i)ttari	*exactly*	p(u)rin	*pudding*

Unvoicing of the same vowels often takes place at the end of a word as well, although it is optional:

h(i)tots(u)/h(i)totsu	*one*
f(u)tats(u)/f(u)tatsu	*two*
mitts(u)/mittsu	*three*
yotts(u)/yottsu	*four*
its(u)ts(u)/itsuts(u)	*five*
ikimas(u)	*I (etc.) go.*
Hādo des(u)	*This is (Mr) Herd.*

Foreign words

Japanese has a large stock of words that were originally introduced from China, the so-called Sino-Japanese vocabulary. Many terms associated with modern technology, such as **denwa** (*telephone*) and **hikōki** (*airplane*) are of Chinese coinage. The bulk of Sino-Japanese words, however, were brought to Japan long ago and may be said to play a role comparable to words derived from Latin or Classical Greek in present-day English.

For example, the difference in usage found between English words such as *to begin/to commence* or *of the night/nocturnal* has its parallels in expressions like **hajimeru/kaishi suru** and **yoru no/yakan no**, the second word being used in formal language or as a technical term.

In the wake of the impact of Western civilisation on Japan, there has been an influx of words from European languages like Dutch, Portuguese and German over the past few centuries (e.g. **pan**, *bread*, from Portuguese; **bīru**, *beer*, from Dutch; and **karute**, (*patients'*) *card*, from German), but since the Second World War foreign loanwords have been taken almost exclusively from American English. It is important to make a habit of pronouncing these in the Japanese way, if communication is not to be seriously impaired. For example,

suteki *steak*   konpyūta *computer*   supīkā *loudspeaker*

Often shortened forms are used:

biru *building*   wāpuro *word processor*

Many English-type expressions are actually coined in Japan, often using truncated forms of English words in new combinations (**pansuto** 'panty stocking', i.e. *panty hose*).

Loanwords are generally adapted to Japanese syllable structure and sounds by inserting vowels between consonant clusters and after final consonants:

Christmas	ku-ri-su-ma-su	*lamp*	ranpu
mat	ma-t-to	*Tom*	Tomu

Exceptions are words or names ending in *-n* and *-ng*, which become (nasalised) **-n** in Japanese:

Jane	Jēn
tongue	tan (in food sense, used at the butcher's, in restaurants etc)

There are some syllables (not contained in the table) that are restricted to use in Western loanwards, such as **je** (**Jēn**, *Jane*), and **ti** (**tī**, *tea*).

Accent

The Japanese accent consists of differences in pitch, that is to say some syllables are relatively higher or lower than others. To our ears, these differences are rather slight in comparison to the quite marked stresses of English, and therefore difficult to pick up. Below are some examples of Standard Japanese accent (in dialects, you will often hear different accents for the same words):

Kyo-o			-ko-ha-ma		-ho			-yo-o-na	
	-to	Yo		Ni		-n	sa		-ra

Particles attached to these words will be at the same level of pitch as the last syllable. Different endings attached to verbs and adjectives may bring about a change in accent, for example:

	ta-ra-shi				ta-ra-		
a-		-i	*is new*	a-		shi-ka-t-ta	*was new*

The Japanese accent may be said to provide a natural sentence melody rather than distinguish items of vocabulary; failure to apply it correctly will not normally impede communication. While the higher/lower relations are almost exactly opposite between Standard Japanese and the dialects of Western Japan, this does not greatly seem to impede mutual understanding.

In this book, no accent markings are given, but many dictionaries indicate the accent of individual vocabulary items according to various systems. Although accent will differ greatly by area in Japan, do try to attempt to develop an ear for the subtle ups and downs in the speech of native speakers whenever you have the chance: this will give your Japanese the final polish.

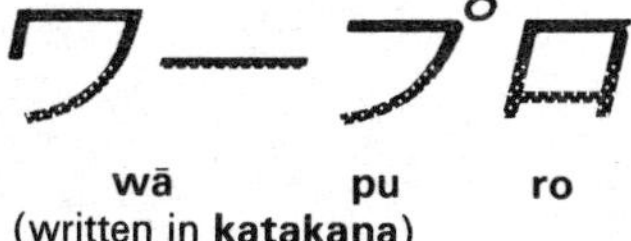

wā pu ro
(written in **katakana**)

a ta ra shi i
(written in **hiragana**)

List of people in the book

The Herd family:

Tom Herd, a middle-aged British businessman in charge of the Tokyo end of a European trading company; **Jill**, his American wife who teaches English at a Tokyo language school; **Ken**, their sixteen-year old son, attending an international school in Tokyo.

The Anzai family:

Anzai-san, Tom Herd's dentist, a middle-aged Japanese; **his wife**, currently engaged in looking after the family full-time; **Michiko**, their sixteen-year old daughter, attending a Tokyo high school; **Tarō**, their ten-year old son, attending a Tokyo primary school.

Yamada-san, Tom Herd's secretary, a woman in her late twenties.

Tanaka-san, a former pupil of Jill Herd, a female company employee in her early twenties.

Suzuki-san, a senior employee of Yamanaka Māketingu, a Japanese firm based in Sendai, a middle-aged man who is a long-time business associate of Tom Herd.

(This list is given to clarify the sex, age, status and inter-relationships of the various characters in the book, since this affects the sort of Japanese which they use to each other.)

1 Kanai desu *This is my wife*

In this unit you will learn how to form some basic Japanese sentences. You will find out how to introduce and address people, identify things and ask simple questions. There is also information about words dealing with countries, nationality etc.

東京
Tō kyō

Kaiwa

Tom Herd and his wife have gone into a Tokyo coffee shop. Tom thinks he recognises someone sitting at a table reading a newspaper:

Tom	Shitsurei desu ga . . .
Anzai	A, Hādo-san! Shibaraku desu ne.
Tom	(*to Anzai*) Sensei, (*gestures in Jill's direction*) – kanai desu.
Jill	Jiru to mōshimasu. Hajimete o-me ni kakarimasu.
Anzai	Anzai desu. Hajimemashite.
Tom	Anzai-sensei wa boku no ha-isha-san desu.
Jill	Dōzo yoroshiku.

Tom	Excuse me, but . . .
Anzai	Well, Herd-san! It's been some time since we've met.
Tom	Sensei, – my wife.
Jill	My name is Jill. How do you do.
Anzai	I'm Anzai. How do you do.
Tom	Anzai-sensei is my dentist.
Jill	Pleased to meet you.

a/ā *well!, ah!*
[name]-san form of address ● LS2
shibaraku desu ne ● Unit 2 LS2

sensei (here) form of address ● LS2
kanai *(my) wife* ● LS2
desu *is* ● S1
Jiru to mōshimasu. Hajimete o-me ni kakarimasu./ Hajimemashite. ● LS1
[noun] wa ● S1
boku *I*
boku no [noun] *my [noun]* (used by men only)
[noun] no [noun] ● S6
ha-isha *dentist* (**ha** *tooth* + **isha** *doctor*)
dōzo yoroshiku ● LS1

Tom and Jill join Anzai-sensei, and they talk a little:

Tom	Kanai wa Eigo no sensei desu.
Anzai	Ā, sō desu ka. Hādo-san wa Igirisujin desu ne. Okusan mo Igirisujin desu ka?
Tom	Iie, Igirisujin de wa arimasen. Amerikajin desu.

Tom	My wife is a teacher of English/English teacher.
Anzai	Oh, is that so? You're (a) British (person) aren't you, Herd-san. Is your wife British too?
Tom	No, she isn't British. She's (an) American.

Eigo *English (language)* ● LS4
sensei *teacher*
sō desu *that is so*
[sentence] ka? ● S2
Igirisujin *British (person)*
[sentence] ne ● S3
okusan *(your/his) wife*
[noun] mo ● S4
iie/ie *no*
de wa arimasen negative of **desu**
Amerikajin *American (person)*

True or false?

1 Anzai-sensei wa Tomu-san no ha-isha desu.
2 Jiru-san wa Eigo no sensei de wa arimasen.
3 Jiru-san wa Igirisujin desu.

They all get up to go, leaving the newspaper on the table. Tom notices an umbrella on the floor and picks it up:

Tom	(*to Anzai*) Kore wa sensei no kasa desu ka?
Anzai	Hai, watashi no desu. Dōmo.
Jill	Shinbun mo sensei no desu ka?
Anzai	Iie, sore wa watashi no de wa arimasen.

Tom	Is this your umbrella?
Anzai	Yes, it's mine. Thanks.
Jill	Is the newspaper yours too?
Anzai	No, that's not mine.

kore *this* ● S5
kasa *umbrella*
hai *yes*
watashi *I*; **watashi no [noun]** *my* [*noun*] (used by both men and women)
dōmo *thanks*
shinbun *newspaper*
sore *that* (*by you*)

Tom and Jill then take Anzai-sensei to a special fair of imported goods which Tom has helped to organise at a nearby exhibition centre.

Anzai	Sore wa doko no chīzu desu ka?
Jill	Kore desu ka? Kore wa Furansu no chīzu desu.
Anzai	Sore kara, are wa nan desu ka?
Jill	Ā, are wa Igirisu no jamu desu.
Anzai	Nan no jamu desu ka?
Jill	Ichigo no jamu desu.
Anzai	Zenbu tabemono desu ka?
Tom	Iie, sō de wa arimasen yo. Hora, are!
Anzai	Ā, Rōrusu-roisu desu ne.

Anzai	Where is that cheese from?
Jill	Do you mean this cheese? This is cheese from France/French cheese.
Anzai	And then, what is that?
Jill	Ah, that's jam from Britain/British jam.
Anzai	What sort of jam is it?
Jill	It's strawberry jam.
Anzai	Is it all food?
Tom	Oh no, that's not so. Look at that!
Anzai	Why, it's a Rolls Royce!

Furansu *France*
doko? *where?/what place?*
doko no [noun] [*noun*] *of what place*

chīzu *cheese*
are *that (over there)*
nan? *what?*
Igirisu *Britain*
jamu *jam*
ichigo *strawberry*
zenbu *all*
tabemono *food*
hora! *look!* (informal way of getting someone to look at something)

True or false?

4 Anzai-sensei no shinbun desu ka? Hai, sō desu.
5 Doko no chīzu desu ka? Amerika no chīzu desu.
6 Nan no jamu desu ka? Ichigo no jamu desu.

Structures

the particle **wa**

1 A wa B desu

Things or persons are identified in Japanese by using this pattern, which means *A is B*. The particle **wa** marks the thing or person (**A**) which is identified by means of **B**; **desu** (*is*) then completes the sentence.

Kore	wa	kasa	desu.	*This is an umbrella.*
Watashi	wa	Igirisujin	desu.	*I am British*
Sensei	wa	Amerikajin	desu.	*The teacher is (an) American.*

The negative equivalent of this pattern is formed by replacing **desu** with **de wa arimasen**. Alternative forms are **ja arimasen**, **de wa nai desu**, and **ja nai desu**. All are commonly used and you should be able to recognise them.

Kore	wa	kasa	de wa arimasen.	*This is not an umbrella.*
Watashi	wa	Amerikajin	de wa arimasen.	*I am not (an) American.*

When **[A] wa** is understood, it is frequently omitted to avoid unnecessary repetition. For example, see the following sequence of sentences, both statements about **A**, with **watashi wa** omitted in the second sentence:

Watashi wa Amerikajin de wa arimasen. Igirisujin desu. *I am not (an) American. I am British.*

2 *The question particle* ka?*:* A wa B desu ka?

A statement of the type seen in **1** can be made into a question by attaching **ka?** to the end of the sentence. In speech, questions are normally accompanied by rising intonation similar to that used in an English question. (Note that no change in word order is necessary in Japanese, unlike English.)

Sensei wa Amerikajin desu. *The teacher is (an) American.*
Sensei wa Amerikajin desu ka? *Is the teacher (an) American?*

This type of question is often called a 'yes/no question', as it calls for an answer beginning with *yes* (**hai**) or *no* (**iie**).

Hai, (sensei wa) Amerikajin desu.
Iie, (sensei wa) Amerikajin de wa arimasen.

[A] wa will again be omitted in an answer.

か
the particle **ka**

3 *The sentence-final particles* yo *and* ne

Both of these are attached to the end of sentences to provide emphasis.

Yo is used to alert the listener to the situation indicated by the sentence to which **yo** is attached, very much like an exclamation mark in English (the intonation in Japanese can be either rising, as in a question, for weak emphasis, or falling, but not as much as in English, for stronger emphasis):

Watashi desu yo. *It's me!*
Kore wa jamu desu yo. *This is jam!*
Sō ja arimasen yo. *Oh no (that's not so)!*

Ne is used to solicit agreement from the listener, rather like *isn't it* in

English (intonation can be slightly rising, or falling, especially in its lengthened form **nē**).

> Kore desu ne. *You mean (it is) this (one), don't you?*
> Okusan wa Igirisujin de wa arimasen ne. *Your wife isn't British, is she?*

4 *The particle* mo*:* A wa B desu. C mo B desu

Consider once again our basic pattern:

Yamada-san wa	sensei desu.	*Mr Yamada is a/the teacher.*

If you want to go on to substitute another person, C, for A, **wa** is replaced by **mo** (*too, also*). You can make this statement into a question by adding **ka?**.

Watashi	mo	sensei	desu.	*I am a teacher, too.*
Okusan	mo	sensei	desu ka?	*Is your wife also a teacher?*

The answer to the question could be the following:

> Hai, (kanai mo) sensei desu.
> Iie, **kanai wa** sensei de wa arimasen.

Note that with the answer *Yes*, the repeated **[A] mo** is optional; when the answer is *No*, **[A] mo** cannot be used and it is usual to give **[A] wa**.

5 *Words used to point at things (or sometimes persons)*

Where we use the words *this* or *that* in English, Japanese has three words: **kore**, **sore** and **are**:

> **Kore** for items closer to the speaker than the listener: *this*
> **Sore** for items closer to the listener than the speaker: *that*
> **Are** for items at a distance from both: *that over there*

Thus, if you enquire about an item that is on the salesperson's side of the sales counter you would ask:

Sore wa nan desu ka? *What is that?* (Lit *That is what?*)

If the salesperson wants to confirm which item you referred to by **sore**, he might sometimes point at it (or pick it up) and ask back:

Kore desu ka? (*You mean*) *this one?*

6 *Combining nouns with* no*:* A wa X no B desu

No can be used to extend our basic pattern **A wa B desu**. Compare the following pairs of sentences:

Kore wa Kore wa	 Igirisu no	jamu desu. jamu desu.	*This is jam.* *This is British jam.*
Kanai wa Kanai wa	 Eigo no	sensei desu. sensei desu.	*My wife is a teacher.* *My wife is an English teacher.*
Kore wa Kore wa	 watashi no	kasa desu. kasa desu.	*This is an umbrella.* *This is my umbrella.*

In the second sentence of each pair, the noun **(X)** before **no** is providing further information about the noun after **no**. **No** can join any two nouns, leading to various English equivalents depending on the types of nouns involved:

(*a*) Where **X** stands for a person, **no** will indicate either ownership, if **B** is a thing, or, if **B** is a person too, it will indicate a personal relationship between **X** and **B**:

Watashi no Rōrusu-roisu *My Rolls Royce*
Tomu-san no sensei *Tom's teacher*

(It might help you to get used to the word order if you think of **no** as equivalent to *'s* in English, though its use is much wider.)
(*b*) If the first noun is a place noun, it shows the place of origin of the second noun:

Furansu no jamu *French jam*
Igirisu no kasa *An English umbrella*

(*c*) If **X** is any other type of noun, it will describe the contents or make-up of **B** where **B** is a thing, or **B**'s area of specialisation where it is a person:

Nihongo no shinbun	*A Japanese newspaper*
Ichigo no jamu	*Strawberry jam*
Eigo no sensei	*A teacher of English*

The difference between (*a*), (*b*) and (*c*) becomes clearer when **A wa X no B desu** type sentences become information-seeking questions. The place of **X** is taken by the question words **dare?** (*who?*), **doko?** (*where?*), and **nan?** (*what?*), becoming respectively **dare no?** (*of who, whose*), **doko no?** (*from where, where from*), **nan no?** (*of what*):

(*a*) Kore wa dare no kasa desu ka?
Whose umbrella is this?

(*b*) Kore wa doko no jamu desu ka?
Where is this jam from? (Lit *This is jam from where?*)

(*c*) Yamada-sensei wa nan no sensei desu ka?
What does Mr Yamada teach? (Lit *What is Mr Yamada a teacher of?*)

In the case of (*a*) and (*b*) only, and where the second noun (**B**) is ***not*** a person, **B** is commonly abbreviated where understood:

Talking about cheese:	Kore wa Furansu no desu.
Talking about umbrellas:	Sore wa watashi no de wa arimasen.

Renshū

You will need to read through the Language and Society section before working through questions **1**, **2**, **3** and **5**.

Here is a list of some of the teachers employed at the language school where Jill Herd works, giving their names and countries of origin:

Michel Barre	France	Helmut Gläser	Germany
Jill Herd	America	Carla Santos	Spain
Lucia Verde	Italy	Mā Xun	China

1 Using this list as a basis, complete the following to produce sentences giving the nationality of each teacher:
Rei (*example*): Hādo-san wa Amerikajin desu.

(*a*) Bāru-san
(*b*) Gurēza-san
(*c*) Santosu-san
(*d*) Berude-san
(*e*) Mā-san

2 Again using the list as a basis, produce sentences in a similar order giving what each person teaches: (Assume that they all teach their respective native languages.)
Rei: Hādo-san wa Eigo no sensei desu.

3 Here are some more of the teachers:

John Brown Australia	Karl Schmidt Austria	Pablo Torres Mexico

Produce pairs of sentences similar to the following, using first **wa**, and then **mo**:
Rei: Yamada-san wa Nihongo no sensei desu.
Tanaka-san mo Nihongo no sensei desu.

(*a*) Hādo-san
(*b*) Gurēza-san
(*c*) Santosu-san

4 At the trade fair there are also the following items: German cameras, Italian handbags, British umbrellas, and strawberry ice-cream. Complete Anzai-sensei's questions and Jill's replies:

Anzai Sore wa (*a*) no kamera desu ka?
Jill (*b*) desu ka? (*c*) no desu.
Anzai Are wa Igirisu (*d*) handobaggu desu ka?
Jill Iie, (*e*) wa Igirisu (*f*) handobaggu (*g*). Itaria no (*h*).
Anzai Kasa (*i*) Itaria no desu ka?
Jill Iie, kasa wa Igirisu (*j*) desu.
Anzai Sore wa (*k*) no aisukurīmu desu ka?
Jill (*l*) aisukurīmu desu.

5 Give the Japanese equivalent for this conversation:

Tom	This is my French teacher.
Michel	My name is Barre. How do you do.
Tanaka	I'm Tanaka. How do you do.
Tom	Mr Tanaka is a German teacher.
Michel	Pleased to meet you.

Language and Society

1 *Introducing people*

As you will have noticed from the conversation passage, the **(A wa) B desu** pattern is used for introductions:

Kanai desu. *This is my wife.*

This may be preceded by the name of the person to whom **B** is being introduced, just as we say in English: *Tom, meet my wife.*

Tomu-san, – kanai desu.

In reply, the set phrase **hajimemashite** (or its more formal equivalent **hajimete o-me ni kakarimasu**, both literally meaning *I meet you for the first time*) is used by the person introduced, normally after repeating his/her own name:

Jiru desu. Hajimemashite. *I am Jill. How do you do.*
Jiru to mōshimasu. Hajimete o-me ni kakarimasu. *My name is Jill. How do you do.*

The phrase **dōzo yoroshiku** can be used after **hajimemashite**, etc., or in its place; it may also be used in reply to the introduction.

The above expressions are accompanied by bows (where Westerners are involved, often handshakes ***and*** bows). Between professional people of any kind, an exchange of namecards (**meishi**), which are again tendered with a bow, is extremely common; such people are advised to have namecards made, preferably with a Japanese version of their name and position on one side and the English on the other.

2 *Forms of address and reference*

The Japanese equivalent of *Mr/Mrs/Ms/Miss* is **-san**; this is always attached to someone's name (surname or given), it cannot be used on its own. Neither can **-san** be used with one's own name or in reference to members of one's family.

Teachers, medical doctors and MPs are customarily addressed and referred to by **-sensei** (*teacher*) attached to their surname (teachers of any kind enjoy a very high social status!). **Sensei** can also be used on its own to address persons of the above description in the sense of *you*:

Kore wa **sensei no** kasa desu ka? Is this ***your*** *umbrella?*

You has no direct equivalent in Japanese; instead, a variety of words are used, depending on the relative status levels and degree of intimacy of those involved. The problem of which word to use can, however, be avoided by using **[name]-san** and **[name]-sensei** in situations where one ***has*** to express the idea of *you* as in the sentence above, and otherwise, by quite legitimately abbreviating that part (**A wa**) of the sentence:

Hādo-san desu ka? *Are you Mr Herd?*

Okusan is another word that can be used for both address and reference. Depending on who is being addressed (the wife herself or her husband), the following sentence can have two meanings:

Okusan wa sensei desu ka? Are ***you*** *a teacher?/Is* ***your wife*** *a teacher?*

As a question about a third person it could also mean *Is* ***his*** *wife a teacher?*

Oku-san clearly incorporates **-san**. Just as **-san** cannot be used to refer to members of one's family, so **okusan** cannot be used by a husband with reference to his own wife. **Kanai** is used only when talking about one's own wife, although it, too, would not be used by a husband when addressing his own wife directly. For this purpose he would use his wife's given name (often without **-san**), **omae** (*you there*), or perhaps **kimi** (intimate *you*), while wives generally call their husbands **anata** (*you*).

In Japanese, given names are used much less than in English; instead, surnames are used, normally with **-san** attached (except when referring to a member of one's family or group, when the surname is used on its own: wives sometimes refer to their husband as Anzai, etc.). On the other hand, you will note a tendency to use the given name of foreigners rather than their surnames.

Male friends use **-kun** to address/refer to each other rather than **-san**; **-kun** is also used in the case of boys, and when men address or refer to men junior to them. Junior members of a family are generally addressed/referred to by their given name (**Tarō**, etc.), sometimes with the diminutive **-chan** attached.

3 *Countries, peoples and languages*

If you add **-jin** (*person*) to the name of any country, you get the name for a person from that country; if you add **-go** (*word/language*), you get the name for its language (note exceptions such as Australia, where the language is obviously English; incidentally, *Australian English* would be called **Ōsutoraria-Eigo**).

Australia	Ōsutoraria	Ōsutorariajin	Eigo
China	Chūgoku	Chūgokujin	Chūgokugo
France	Furansu	Furansujin	Furansugo
Germany	Doitsu	Doitsujin	Doitsugo
Italy	Itaria	Itariajin	Itariago
Spain	Supein	Supeinjin	Supeingo

Note especially the following:

Britain	Igirisu/ Eikoku	Igirisujin/Eikokujin	Eigo
Japan	Nihon/ Nippon	Nihonjin/Nipponjin	Nihongo/Nippongo

Lastly, for foreign countries, foreigners and their languages in general:

gaikoku	gaikokujin/gaijin	gaikokugo

2 Resutoran wa tōi desu ka? *Is the restaurant far?*

In this unit you will learn how to ask and answer questions about where things are, and how adjectives work in Japanese. There is also some information about everyday greetings between acquaintances.

Kaiwa

Jill has been invited out to lunch by Tanaka-san, a friend who is also an ex-pupil. They meet as arranged:

Jill	Tanaka-san, – konnichi wa. O-genki desu ka?
Tanaka	Hai, o-kage-sama de. Sensei wa?
Jill	Totemo genki desu. Demo, Nihon no natsu wa atsui desu ne.

Jill	Tanaka-san, hello. Are you well?/How are you?
Tanaka	Yes, thanks for asking/I'm fine, thank you. And you, sensei?
Jill	I'm very well. But aren't Japanese summers hot!

konnichi wa *hello/good day* ● *LS2*
genki na *healthy, well* ●S1, 2
o-genki desu ka? ●LS1
o-kage-sama de *thanks for asking*
totemo *very* ● S2
demo *but, however* (at the beginning of a sentence)
natsu *summer*
atsu.i *hot* ● S1,2

As they set off in the direction of the restaurant, Jill begins to feel very hungry:

Jill	Resutoran wa tōi desu ka?
Tanaka	Iie, ano takai biru no tonari desu.
Jill	(*rather unenthusiastically*) Furansu ryōri desu ka?
Tanaka	Ē . . . Jā, Nihon ryōri wa ikaga desu ka? Asoko wa totemo oishii Nihon-ryōriya desu.

Jill	Is the restaurant far?
Tanaka	No, it's next to that high building.
Jill	Is it French cuisine/a French restaurant?
Tanaka	Yes . . . Well then, how about Japanese cuisine? Over there is a very good Japanese restaurant.

resutoran *restaurant* (specialising in Western-style food)
tō.i *far*
ano [noun] *that* [*noun*] (*over there*) ● S3
taka.i *high*
biru *building*
[noun] no tonari *next to, neighbouring* [*noun*] ● S5
ryōri *cooking, cuisine*
ē *yes* (less formal than **hai**)
ja/jā/de wa, . . . (at the beginning of a sentence) *well then/if that's so, . . .*
ikaga? *how?*
[noun] wa ikaga desu ka? *How about/Would you like* [*noun*]*?*
asoko *over there/that place* (*over there*) ● S4
oishi.i *delicious; good* (of restaurants, etc.)
[noun]-ya *shop etc. dealing professionally in* [*noun*] ● LS3
ryōri-ya *eating place, restaurant*

True or false?

1 Tanaka-san wa genki desu.
2 Ano Nihon-ryōriya wa oishii desu.

Jill and Miss Tanaka have decided on the Japanese restaurant and are now eating. Suddenly, Jill's face takes on a strange expression:

Tanaka	Sensei, – daijōbu desu ka?
Jill	Kono hen na mono wa nan desu ka?
Tanaka	Tako desu. Ikaga desu ka?

Jill	Tako! Amari oishiku arimasen ne. . . . (*in a low voice*) O-tearai wa doko desu ka?
Tanaka	Sugu soko desu.

Tanaka	Sensei, – are you all right?
Jill	What's this strange thing?
Tanaka	It's octopus. How is it?/How do you like it?
Jill	Octopus! It's not very tasty, is it. Where is the ladies' toilet?
Tanaka	It's just there.

daijōbu na *all right*
kono [noun] *this [noun]*
hen na *strange*
mono *thing*
tako *octopus*
amari [negative] [*not*] *very* ● S2
o-tearai *toilet* ● LS4
sugu *immediately/just*
soko *there/that place (by you)*

True or false?

3 Jiru-san wa daijōbu de wa arimasen.
4 Tako wa oishii desu.

Structures

おいしい
o i shi i

1 A wa [adjective] B desu

As in English, adjectives can go either before or after the noun they are describing. First we will look at adjectives before nouns:

Kore wa **oishii** chīzu desu *This is delicious cheese*
Sore wa **hen na** tabemono desu *That is strange food*

There are two types of adjective in Japanese, one which ends in **-i** before nouns, and one which ends in **na** before nouns. We will call these **-i** and **na** adjectives, and they will be identified in vocabulary lists as in the following examples:

-i adjective: **atsu.i** **na** adjective: **genki na**

Other common **-i** adjectives include:

atataka.i	*warm*
samu.i	*(atmospheric) cold*
tsumeta.i	*cold (to the touch, or emotionally)*
ōki.i	*big*
chiisa.i	*small (used for young, i.e. small, children)*
waka.i	*young (teenagers, adults)*
atarashi.i	*new*
furu.i	*old (opposite of* **atarashii**, *not of* **wakai**)
i.i	*good, all right*
waru.i	*bad*
haya.i	*quick, early*
oso.i	*slow, late*

Many **na** adjectives are of foreign, primarily Chinese, origin. Common ones include:

benri	na	*convenient, useful*
shizuka	na	*quiet, peaceful*
shinsetsu	na	*kind*
yūmei	na	*famous*
kirei	na	*pretty, clean, neat*
taisetsu	na	*important*
hontō	na	*true*
taihen	na	*serious, awful*
hansamu	na	*handsome*

Na adjectives taken from Western languages such as English and French are often used to enhance the vocabulary of the advertising copy-writer:

ereganto na resutoran	*an elegant restaurant*
shikku na burausu	*a chic blouse*

2 A wa [adjective] desu

Note what happens to each type of adjective when it comes at the end of a sentence in normal polite speech:

Tanaka-san wa wakai desu.	*Tanaka-san is young.*
Suzuki-san wa hansamu desu.	*Suzuki-san is handsome.*

While the **-i** adjective remains exactly the same, the **na** adjective drops **na** before **desu**.

The two types of adjective also behave differently when forming the negative:

(*a*) **-i** adjectives. To turn an **-i** adjective into the negative, for example in order to say that British summers are ***not*** hot, you have to actually change its form:

Nihon no natsu wa atsu	i desu.	*Japanese summers are hot.*
Igirisu no natsu wa atsu	ku arimasen.	*British summers are not hot.*
Oishi	i desu ka?	*Is it tasty?/Does it taste good?*
Iie, oishi	ku arimasen.	*No, it isn't/doesn't.*

-i desu is replaced by **-ku arimasen**, or alternatively **-kunai desu**:

Igirisu no natsu wa atsu	kunai desu.
Oishi	kunai desu.

There is only one exception to this. **ii desu** becomes:

yo	ku arimasen
yo	kunai desu.

(*b*) **na** adjectives. To turn a **na** adjective into the negative, for example in order to say that Miss Yamada is not pretty, all you need to do is put **desu** itself into the negative:

Tanaka-san wa kirei desu.
Yamada-san wa kirei de wa arimasen/ja arimasen.

Note: (*i*) Before nouns, two **-i** adjectives, **ōkii** and **chiisai**, commonly have alternative **na** forms – **ōki na** and **chiisa na**: i.e., you can say either **ōkii resutoran** or **ōki na resutoran**; **chiisai o-tearai** or **chiisa na o-tearai**.

(*ii*) **Totemo**, and the less colloquial **taihen** (here acting as an adverb not as a **na** adjective), can both precede a positive adjective to mean *very*:

Igirisu no jamu wa totemo oishii desu. *British jam is very tasty.*
Jiru-san wa taihen shinsetsu na sensei desu. *Jill is a very kind teacher.*

When an adjective is in the negative, however, **amari** must be used:

Fukuda-sensei wa amari wakaku arimasen. *Fukuda-sensei is not very young.*
Kore wa amari benri de wa arimasen. *This is not very useful.*

3 *Words to indicate which thing/person*: kono, sono, ano

While **kore**, **sore** and **are** always stand by themselves, **kono**, **sono** and **ano** have a similar meaning, but are always in front of nouns: **kono jamu** (*this jam*): **sono Rōrusu-roisu** (*that Rolls Royce, by you*); **ano sensei** (*that teacher, over there*); **ano hito** (*that person* [**hito**], *over there*; *he/she*)

Kono jamu wa taihen yūmei desu.
Ano shinbun wa dare no desu ka?

4 *Indicating place*: koko, soko, asoko

These words are parallel in meaning to **kore**, **sore** and **are**:

koko for places closer to the speaker than the listener: *here/this place*
soko for places closer to the listener than the speaker: *there/that place*
asoko for places at a distance from both: *over there/that place over there*

To ask questions, **doko?**, meaning *where?/what place?*, is used. With the help of these and other place words, we can extend our basic **A wa B desu** pattern to indicate where **A** is. For example:

Hoteru wa koko de wa arimasen. *The hotel* (**hoteru**) *is not here.*
Fukuda-sensei wa doko desu ka? *Where is Fukuda-sensei?*
(Fukuda-sensei wa) resutoran desu. *He is in the restaurant.*

Jiru-san mo soko desu ka? *Is Jill there too?*

(Note that here **soko** refers to the place associated with/mentioned by the listener rather than physically closer to him/her. This is another function of the **so-** words.)

Similarly, we can indicate where **B** is:

Asoko wa yūmei na resutoran desu. *Over there is a famous restaurant.*

If you are not sure where you are, you might ask:

Koko wa doko desu ka? *Where is here?/Where are we?*

There is another series of words referring to place which you will hear. These are **kochira**, **sochira**, **achira**, and **dochira?**. They act either as a more formal equivalent of **koko**, etc., or to mean *this way/in this direction*, etc., according to context:

O-tearai wa kochira desu. *The toilet is here/this way.*

They can also be used to address or refer to people politely:

Dochira-sama desu ka? *Who is this?* (*on the telephone*)
Kochira wa Kimura-san desu. *This is Kimura-san.*

(For another use of **-sama** with people, see Unit 16 Language and Society 1.)

5 *Words to indicate position:* **tonari,** *etc.*

In Japanese, these words act as nouns. Where in English we would say *next to X*, in Japanese you say **X no tonari**. Other common position words are:

chikaku	*nearby*
mae	*in front*
naka	*inside*
ushiro	*back, behind* (*i.e. behind buildings, people, etc., rather than in front of them*)
ura	*reverse/other side, behind* (*i.e. behind in sense of rear side, of buildings, etc. but not of people*)
ue	*on top, above*
shita	*underneath*

Resutoran wa kissaten no chikaku desu. *The restaurant is near the coffee shop* (**kissaten**).
Jiru-san wa Tomu-san no ushiro desu. *Jill is behind Tom.*
Jiru-san wa kissaten no ushiro/ura desu. *Jill is behind/at the back of the coffee shop.*

Note that *next to this thing/that thing*, etc. is **kono/sono tonari**, etc., not **kore no/sore no tonari**, e.g.:

Shinbun wa ano zasshi no shita desu. *The newspaper is under that magazine.*
Shinbun wa ano shita desu. *The newspaper is under that thing over there/under there.*

Renshū

1 Complete the following sentences by filling in the blanks from the choices you are given below:
Rei: Jiru-san wa . . . . . na Amerikajin desu. *D* kirei

(*a*) . . . . . kissaten wa . . . . .
(*b*) Tanaka-san wa . . . . . Nihonjin desu.
(*c*) . . . . . wa . . . . . kasa desu.
(*d*) . . . . . wa . . . . . na hoteru desu.
(*e*) . . . . . no sensei wa taihen . . . . .

A taihen atarashii; *B* yūmei; *C* kono; *D* kirei; *E* ano Igirisujin; *F* sore; *G* shinsetsu desu; *H* asoko; *I* ōkii desu; *J* wakai.

2 Use the words given to make short conversations as in the example, replying positively first, and then negatively. Do this with a partner if possible.
Rei: Asoko, oishii, resutoran.→Asoko wa oishii resutoran desu ka?
Hai, taihen oishii desu.
Iie, amari oishiku arimasen.

(*a*) Sore, shizuka na, hoteru.
(*b*) Are, furui, Rōrusu-roisu.
(*c*) Koko, yūmei na, kissaten.
(*d*) Kore, atatakai, sūpu (*soup*).
(*e*) Sore, hayai, kuruma (*car*).

kuruma

3 You are in a bad mood. Complain about the following, using the negative forms of adjectives:
Rei: the jam you are eating→Kono jamu wa oishikunai desu.

(*a*) the cool beer (**bīru**) you have ordered
(*b*) the handsome Frenchman you had a blind date with
(*c*) the automatic umbrella which takes an hour to open
(*d*) the restaurant with the over-enthusiastic jazz band
(*e*) the coffee-shop with the dirty tablecloths

4 Practise the position words by explaining the location of objects in your room, and of shops, etc. in your local shopping centre:
Rei: Jamu wa tēburu no ue desu. *The jam is on the table* (**tēburu**).
If possible, do this in question and answer form with a partner:
Rei: Kissaten wa doko desu ka? *Where is the coffee-shop?*
Indo-ryōriya no tonari desu. (*It's*) *next to the Indian restaurant.*
You will find some relevant vocabulary in Language and Society 3. Other words which might come in useful are **enpitsu** (*pencil*), **todana** (*cupboard*), **yūbinkyoku** (*post-office*).

5 Give the Japanese equivalent for this conversation:

Tom Where is the hotel?
Suzuki It's that way.
Tom Is it far?
Suzuki No, it's not very far. It's near the station (**eki**).
Tom Is it a famous hotel?
Suzuki Yes, it's very famous.

駅
eki

Language and Society

1 *The use of* o- *in front of words*

This makes a word polite, and will generally be found in front of certain words, such as those for traditional items of food and drink, or for things which were traditionally regarded as unclean, such as money:

o-tearai *toilet*
o-kane *money*
o-sake *sake/alcohol*

Women tend to use **o-** in this way more than men, particularly if they want to emphasise their femininity:

o-niku	*meat*
o-sakana	*fish*

In polite speech, **o-** is also found in front of a wider range of words to indicate that they are connected to the person being spoken to, or (more rarely) to some third person of high status:

o-namae	*your name*
o-shigoto	*your work, business*
o-tegami	*the letter* (*you wrote, or which I am going to write to you*)
o-hanashi	*the talk* (*which you gave*)/*the conversation* (*I had with you*)

Similarly, note that **o-** is only used in the following exchange to refer to the health of the person being spoken to, not to the speaker's health:

O-genki desu ka?	*Are you well?/How are you?*
Hai, genki desu.	*Yes, I'm fine.*

With some words you will find **go-** used instead, with the same effect:

go-shujin	*your husband*
go-hon	*your book*
go-jūsho	*your address*

This **go-** is also the first syllable of **gohan**, the word used for both a meal and for rice in its cooked state, as opposed to **o-kome**, the uncooked state in which you actually buy it.

2 *Everyday greetings*

The following greetings are normally used by acquaintances on meeting:

Ohayō gozaimasu	*Good morning*

This is used by people when they meet for the first time in the morning, at home, on the way to work, or as the working day begins.

Bar hostesses will therefore use it to greet each other as they come to work in the evening.

Konnichi wa	*Good day* (*Used from mid-morning and during the afternoon*)
Konban wa	*Good evening* (*Used after it begins to grow dark*) (**konban** *this evening, tonight*)

If it is some time since you last met, you may add **Shibaraku desu ne** or the more feminine **o-hisashiburi desu ne**, with the meaning *It's a long time since we met*, as occurs in the **Kaiwa** to Unit 1.

3 *The use of* -ya *after nouns*

This usually indicates the shop where the noun is sold, or the person who sells it:

niku ¦ ya	*butcher's shop/butcher's*
sakana ¦ ya	*fishmonger's shop/fishmonger*
saka ¦ ya	*wine shop/wine merchant* (*note the change in the final vowel of* **sake**)

Ryōriya (*restaurant*), formed using **ryōri** (*cooking*), is slightly different from this basic pattern (as is, for example, **sushiya**, a restaurant specialising in **sushi**). Note that **ryōriya** is the word used when you want to specify that an establishment produces a particular national cuisine:

Nihon-ryōriya
Indo-ryōriya
Furansu-ryōriya

Also note that there are exceptions, such as **kissaten**.

4 *Words for 'toilet'*

As in other languages, there are several words for this in Japanese, of varying degrees of delicacy. **Benjo** would only be used by men and is nowadays regarded as a rather unrefined term, having been replaced by **toire**. Women would probably use either **o-toire** or **o-tearai**. It is not unusual for public lavatories to lack both paper and hand-drying facilities, but you can buy small packets of tissues (**tisshu**), and may well be given them, by your bank for instance.

3 Shī dī ga takusan arimasu ne
Haven't you got a lot of compact discs!

In this unit you will learn two similar patterns to express the idea of *there is* and *I have*, and see that **arimasu** is normally used about objects only, while **imasu** is used for living things. You will also become familiar with set phrases used when entering someone's house.

家 **ie**

Kaiwa

Michiko has met Ken at the station. They are now on their way to her house.

Ken	Daibu arimasu ka?
Michiko	Iie, sugu desu. Asoko ni tabakoya ga arimasu ne? Sono ura desu yo. (*After turning two corners*) Are ga watashi-tachi no ie desu.
Ken	Rippa na ie desu ne.
Michiko	Iie, tonde mo nai.

The two enter the entrance hall (**genkan**).

Michiko	Tadaima!
Okusan	O-kaeri nasai! (*Mrs Anzai comes to the entrance hall*)
Michiko	Okāsan, kochira wa Ken-san desu.
Okusan	Hajimemashite. Yoku irasshaimashita.
Ken	Ken desu. Yoroshiku.
Okusan	Dōzo, o-agari kudasai.
Ken	O-jama shimasu.

daibu *a great deal*
arimasu *there is* ● S1, 2; *to exist; to have* ● S3
daibu arimasu ka? *Is it far to go?* (Lit. *Is there a great deal?*)
tabako-ya *tobacco shop* (● Unit 2 LS3)
watashi-tachi no *our* ● S4
[noun] ga ● S2
ie *house*
rippa na *fine, impressive*
tonde mo nai *not at all* (expression of modesty)
tadaima *I'm home* ● LS1
o-kaeri nasai! *welcome back*
okā-san *mother* (form of address) ● Unit 16 LS1
yoku irasshaimashita *thank you for coming*
o-agari kudasai *please come in*
o-jama shimasu set phrase used when entering someone's house

True or false?

1 Michiko-san no ie wa tabakoya no tonari desu.
2 Michiko-san no ie wa chiisai desu.

Michiko is showing Ken about the house – now they are going up the stairs to the second floor.

Ken Michiko-san no heya wa?
Michiko Watashi no heya wa nikai ni arimasu yo. – Soko ni otōto no heya ga arimasu.
Ken Otōto-san wa imasu ka?
Michiko Iie, ima uchi ni imasen. – Kore ga watashi no heya desu.
Ken Kawaii heya desu ne. A, shī dī ga takusan arimasu ne.
Michiko Watashi wa sonna ni takusan arimasen. Otōto wa motto arimasu yo.
(*Ken is looking down into the garden from Michiko's window*)
Ken Are wa inugoya desu ne . . . o-taku ni wa inu ga imasu ka?
Michiko Ee, kawaii pūdoru desu yo. Naporeon . . . !
Naporeon Wan!
Ken A, honto ni kawaii desu ne. Petto wa hoka ni imasu ka?
Michiko Iie, imasen.

heya *room*
nikai *first floor, upstairs*
otōto *younger brother*
ima *now*
uchi (*my/our*) *house; the inside*
kawai.i *lovely, cute*
shī dī (*CD*) *compact disc*
takusan *many, a lot*
sonna ni *so, that much*, etc. ● Unit 4 S6
motto *more* ● Unit 8 S7
inugoya *dog's house, kennel*
o-taku *your house*
inu *dog*
pūdoru *poodle*
Naporeon (*Napoleon*) dog name
wan *woof*
honto ni (=hontō ni) *really*
petto *pet*
hoka ni *apart from this, in addition*
imasu=arimasu *there is* (but used with living things only) ● S1, 2, 3

True or false?

3 Michiko-san no otōto-san wa ima uchi ni imasen.
4 Michiko-san wa petto ga takusan imasu.

Structures

the particle **ni**

1 A wa B ni arimasu/imasu

In Unit 2 we saw that **A wa B desu**, where **B** is a place, tells you the whereabouts of **A**. **Desu** identifies **A** with the place indicated by **B**, in the same way that it identifies two things or two persons when **B** is not a place.

For indicating location, there is an alternative pattern, involving the verb **arimasu**. Used with **ni** (*at/in/on*), it has the meaning of *to be at/in/on*. Compare the following pairs of sentences:

Honya wa soko	desu.	(Lit *The bookshop is that place*)
	ni arimasu.	(Lit *The bookshop is located in that place*) ***The bookshop is there.***

Watashi no heya wa nikai	desu.	(Lit *My room is first floor*)
	ni arimasu.	(Lit *My room is located on the first floor*)
		My room is on the first floor.

Notice that only a literal translation can capture the difference between the two versions; an idiomatic English translation will often be the same.

When **A** is inanimate (a thing or plant), **arimasu** is used, while **imasu** is normally used instead of **arimasu** if **A** is animate (a person, animal or insect):

Otōto wa nikai ni imasu. *My brother is upstairs.*
Inu wa niwa ni imasu. *The dog is in the garden.*

2 B ni A ga arimasu *(B=place)*

It is possible to have the location (**B ni**) at the beginning of the sentence; in this case, **A wa** is changed to **A ga**, as **A wa** tends to be confined to the beginning of a sentence, whereas **A ga** has no such restriction. Compare the following pairs of sentences:

Tabakoya **wa** asoko ni arimasu. ***The*** *tobacco-shop is over there.*
Asoko ni tabakoya **ga** arimasu. *Over there is* ***a*** *tobacco-shop.*
Inu **wa** niwa ni imasu. ***The*** *dog is in the garden.*
Niwa ni inu **ga** imasu. *There is* ***a*** *dog in the garden.*

As can be gleaned from the differences in the translations (*the*/*a*), **wa** is attached to an **A** that is already known or understood (either in the form of common knowledge, or because it has been mentioned earlier on in the conversation), whereas **ga** is attached to an **A** that the speaker notices for the first time. For **A ga B desu**, see Unit 10 Structures 4(*a*).

Where the situation implies a contrast between two different **A**s, then **wa** in **A wa B ni arimasu/imasu** can additionally signal the notion of contrast, even if only one **A** is actually mentioned. (See also Unit 10 Structures 4(*b*).)

Inu wa niwa ni imasu. Neko wa ie ni imasu. *The **dog** is in the garden, the **cat** in the house.*
Inu wa niwa ni imasu. *The **dog** is in the garden* (*wherever the cat may be*).

3 *Existence/possession with* B (ni) wa A ga arimasu/B (ni) wa A ga imasu

These patterns literally mean *as far as B is concerned, there is an A*, or *B has an A*.

When **B** is a person, possession or ownership is indicated (note that all the elements except **arimasu** can be omitted):

			Arimasu.	(*I*) *have* (*some*).
		Takusan	arimasu.	(*I*) *have a lot.*
	Shī dī ga	takusan	arimasu.	*There are many CDs*/(*I*) *have many CDs.*
Watashi wa	shī dī ga	takusan	arimasu.	*I have many CDs.*

	O-kane ga	amari	arimasen.	(*I*) *don't have much money.*
Otōto wa		takusan	arimasu.	(*My*) *brother has lots.*

When **A** is a person too, the idea of *having* friends (**tomodachi**), relatives, etc. is expressed. Notice that **arimasu** can be used as well as **imasu**, even though **B** is animate. **Ni wa** can be used instead of **wa**.

Watashi (ni) wa	tomodachi ga	takusan	arimasu.	*I have many friends.*
Watashi (ni) wa	tomodachi ga	amari	arimasen.	*I don't have many friends.*
Watashi (ni) wa	otōto ga		imasu.	*I have a younger brother.*

B will not always be a person; it could be a place, as in the following example:

Kono hoteru wa tenisu-kōto ga arimasu ka? *Does this hotel have a tennis court?*

4 [noun]-tachi

-tachi can be attached to certain personal nouns to indicate the plural:

watashi	(*I*)	watashi-tachi	(*we*)
kanojo	(*she*)	kanojo-tachi	(*they*)
hito	(*person, persons*)	hito-tachi	(*persons*)

When attached to people's names (with **-san**), the resulting meaning is somewhat different:

Anzai-san-tachi *Mr/Ms Anzai and those with him/her (often the Anzai family)*
Ken-san-tachi *Ken and his group*

Renshū

1 Change the order of elements and the particle as shown in the example in order to change the meaning from *there is an A there* to *the A is there.*

Rei: Asoko ni tabakoya ga arimasu.→Tabakoya wa asoko ni arimasu.

(*a*) Koko ni hon ga arimasu.
(*b*) Niwa ni inu ga imasu.
(*c*) Soko ni watashi no shī dī ga arimasu.
(*d*) Doko ni Michiko-san ga imasu ka?

2 Produce sentences as shown in the example by building up the elements given, and adding the appropriate particles (you should practise each sequence several times, keeping in mind that all the sentences you produce in this exercise, whether short or long, will be considered complete sentences in Japanese).

Rei: arimasu; takusan; o-kane; watashi.→Arimasu; Takusan arimasu; O-kane ga takusan arimasu; Watashi wa o-kane ga takusan arimasu.

(*a*) Imasen; amari; tomodachi; otōto.
(*b*) Arimasu; takusan; shī dī; heya.
(*c*) Arimasu; nikai; heya; watashi no.
(*d*) Imasu; niwa; inu; ōki na.

3 Say the following in Japanese, paying attention to the choice between **wa** and **ga**, and **arimasu** and **imasu**:

(*a*) There is (some) money here.
(*b*) The tobacco-shop is here.
(*c*) The books are over there.
(*d*) Over there is a dog.
(*e*) Michiko is over there.

4 With a friend, practise the various phrases used when (*a*) entering and (*b*) leaving people's homes as their guest (read the relevant sections in Language and Society first).

Language and Society

1 *Greetings between family members leaving and returning home*

(*a*) *Outgoing person:* **Itte kimasu** or **itte mairimasu** (the latter is more polite).
(*b*) *Remaining family member(s):* **Itte irasshai/itte'rasshai.**
(*c*) *Returning person:* **Tadaima.**
(*d*) *Person(s) at home:* **O-kaeri nasai.**

(*c*) is normally said (or exclaimed if no one is within sight) as soon as the returning person has stepped inside the house at the front or back entrance. The order of (*a*) and (*b*), and (*c*) and (*d*) can be reversed, as it may be the person at home who notices someone return, prompting him to say (*d*), to which the reply then would be (*c*). Visitors sometimes partake in this exchange together with the relevant family members.

2 *Greetings between visitors and hosts at arrival and departure*

Arrival:	*Host*	Dōzo, o-agari kudasai.
	Guest	O-jama shimasu/shitsurei shimasu
Departure:	*Guest*	O-jama shimashita/shitsurei shimashita.
	Host	Mata dōzo. (*Please come again.*)
	Guest	Arigatō gozaimasu. (*Thank you.*) Ja, shitsurei shimasu (*please excuse me; good-bye*).
	Host	Sayōnara.

Japanese entrance doors are often kept unlocked when guests are expected, so people arriving without being escorted by a member of the family will often open the **genkan** door and call out for attention: **gomen kudasai!** (the standard reply to that is normally just **hai!**).

3 The **genkan** or entrance area in a Japanese house is generally at a lower level than the rest of the house, so that you have to step up in order to enter the living area (**o-agari kudasai** literally means *Please step up*). If invited in, you take off your shoes and your host(ess) will strategically place a pair of slippers so that you can step up into them as you enter the house proper.

An advertisement for new houses

4 Bīru demo nomimashō ka? *Shall we have a beer or something?*

In this unit you will be introduced to a wide range of ordinary verbs and some new particles, along with more on **wa**. You will also find some words and phrases which will be useful in wining and dining.

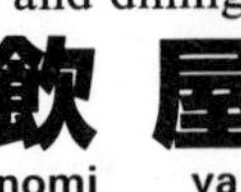

Kaiwa

Tom has just finished a long discussion with Suzuki-san, a business associate from Sapporo.

Tom	Sā . . . , bīru demo nomimashō ka?
Suzuki	Un, nomimashō. Doko ka ii tokoro ga arimasu ka?
Tom	Ē, chikaku ni totemo ii nomiya ga arimasu.
Suzuki	Ja, soko ni shimashō.

(*They arrive and sit themselves at the bar.*)

Mama-san	Irasshaimase.
Tom	Nan ni shimasu ka?
Suzuki	Sō desu ne. (*to proprietress*) Bīru o kudasai.
Tom	Boku mo bīru da.
Mama-san	Wakarimashita. . . . (*produces beer and begins to pour*) Hai, dōzo.
Tom & Suzuki	(*raising their glasses*) Kanpai!

sā *well* (often used, as here, as a preliminary to inviting someone to do something)
[noun] demo *[noun] or something* ● Unit 10 S3
nom.u (nomimasu) *to drink* ● S1
nomimashō *let's drink*
nomimashō ka? *shall we drink?* ● S2

un *yes* (only used in fairly informal situations)
doko ka *somewhere* ● S8
tokoro *place*
nomiya *drinking place, bar, pub* ● Unit 6 LS2
suru (shimasu) *to do*
[noun] ni suru *to decide on/have [noun]* ● Unit 8 S2
nan/nani ni shimasu ka? *What will you have?*
mama-san *proprietress (of a bar)*
irasshaimase stock greeting used to a customer entering a shop, bar etc. ● LS
[noun] o kudasai *please (give me) [noun]* ● S3 and Unit 8 S5
Boku mo bīru da *That'll be beer for me too*
wakarimashita Lit *I have understood* ● Unit 5 LS3
Hai, dōzo *Here you are* (often used when giving people what they have asked for)
kanpai! *cheers!*

True or false?

1 Nomiya wa chikaku ni arimasu.
2 Suzuki-san wa bīru o nomimasen.

日 Ni
本 hon
語 go

Suzuki	Maiban koko de nomimasu ka?
Tom	Iie, sonna jikan wa arimasen yo!
Suzuki	Sonna ni isogashii desu ka?
Tom	(*complaining almost to himself*) Isogashii, isogashii! Hiruma wa kaisha de hataraku. Yoru wa uchi de Nihongo o benkyō suru.
Suzuki	Sore wa taihen desu ne.
Tom	Mā, tōbun wa shikata ga arimasen. Suzuki-san wa?
Suzuki	Māmā desu.
Tom	Kondo wa itsu made Tōkyō ni imasu ka?
Suzuki	Raishū made desu.
Tom	Ja, mata aimashō.
Suzuki	Hoteru no denwa bangō o oshiemashō ka?
Tom	Hai, o-negai shimasu.
Suzuki	(*producing card with details of the hotel printed on it*) Kore desu.
Tom	(*searching in all his pockets*) Are? Pen ga nai na . . .

Suzuki Boku no pen de dōzo.
Tom A, dōmo. (*writes down number, and automatically puts pen in his pocket*)
Suzuki Anō . . . , sore wa boku no pen desu ga . . .

maiban *every evening* ● Unit 5 S6
[place] de ● S3
sonna [noun] *that sort of [noun] (by you/that you are thinking of)* ● S6
jikan *time*
isogashi.i *busy* (**isogashii, isogashii!** ● S4)
hiruma *daytime/during the day*
kaisha *company/the office*
hatarak.u (hatarakimasu) *to work, labour*
yoru *night-time/at night*
[noun] o ● S3
benkyō *study/work* (in the educational sense)
 benkyō suru *to study/work*
mā *well* (here an expression of resignation)
tōbun *for the time being*
 tōbun wa ● S5
shikata ga arimasen *there's no alternative/it's inevitable*
māmā desu *it's so-so*
kondo *this time*
itsu *when?*
[time] made *until [time]* ● Unit 7 S3
raishū *next week*
mata *again*
a.u (aimasu) *to meet*
denwa bangō *telephone number*
oshie.ru (oshiemasu) *to teach/inform*
o-negai shimasu stock phrase used when making a request (Lit *I humbly request*) ● S3
are? *What's this?*
nai plain negative of **aru** ● S4
[sentence] na/nā informal variant of **ne**, used primarily by men
Boku no pen de dōzo *Please (write it) with my pen*
 [instrument] de ● S3
anō . . . *excuse me . . .* (device for getting someone's attention)

True or false?

3 Tomu-san wa yoru kaisha de benkyō shimasu.
4 Suzuki-san wa raishū made Tōkyō ni imasu.

Structures

1 *Verbs*

So far, the only verbs you have met are **arimasu** and **imasu**. In the conversation for this unit we introduced several more verbs, and gave their present tense plain form in the vocabulary lists. (The present plain forms of **arimasu** and **imasu** are **ar.u** and **i.ru**, and of **desu**, **da**.) This form is the simplest form which a Japanese verb can have, and is the one that is used to list verbs in dictionaries. Polite (**-masu**) forms such as **arimasu** are the norm in ordinary adult conversation, and we would advise you to use such forms, except when talking to children (or to yourself). In both the latter cases, plain forms, such as **aru**, would be appropriate; they will also be found in the non-conversational Japanese which is used to set the scene of the **kaiwa** from Unit 5 onwards. More information on formal and informal Japanese occurs throughout the book. In the meantime, it is a good idea to learn both the plain and the **-masu** form whenever you encounter a new verb.

Almost all Japanese verbs fall into one of two groups. The first group, which we shall call **–iru/–eru** verbs, have a present plain form ending in either **-iru** or **-eru**. Their **-masu** form is obtained by dropping the **-ru** and adding **-masu**. In the vocabulary lists they are therefore identified by means of a dot before the **-ru**. Some common **–iru/–eru** verbs are:

oshie.ru	oshiemasu	*teach, inform*
tabe.ru	tabemasu	*eat*
i.ru	imasu	*there is (animate), stay*
mi.ru	mimasu	*see*

The second group, which we shall call **-u** verbs, obtain their **-masu** form by dropping the **-u** and adding **-imasu**. In the vocabulary lists they are therefore identified by means of a dot before the **-u**. Some common **-u** verbs are:

ar.u	arimasu	*there is* (*inanimate*)
wakar.u	wakarimasu	*understand*
owar.u	owarimasu	*finish*
kir.u	kirimasu	*cut*
nom.u	nomimasu	*drink*
yom.u	yomimasu	*read*
hatarak.u	hatarakimasu	*work* (*i.e. labour*)
kak.u	kakimasu	*write*
oyog.u	oyogimasu	*swim*
a.u	aimasu	*meet*
ka.u	kaimasu	*buy*

Note that **kir.u** looks like an **-iru/eru** verb but is not, as the position of the dot shows. Also note that **-u** verbs ending in **-su** and **-tsu** obtain their **-masu** form as follows:

hanas.u	hanashimasu	*speak, talk*
mats.u	machimasu	*wait for*

The only 'irregular' verbs are **suru**, **shimasu** (*to do*), and **kuru**, **kimasu** (*to come*).

A number of 'action' nouns, like **benkyō**, can be turned into verbs with the addition of **suru**. Others are **ryokō** (*travel*), **kenbutsu** (*sightseeing*), and **kaimono** (*shopping*). Almost all the nouns which work like this are of foreign origin, either Chinese-derived like the ones above (with the exception of **kaimono**), or Western derived, such as **dansu** (*dance*) or **tenisu** (*tennis*). They will be identified in the vocabulary lists by the addition of **suru** in brackets.

As you have already seen, whether in the plain or the **-masu** form, Japanese verbs stay the same whatever the subject, and the subject is often left out if understood. We have already had the negative of the **-masu** form (e.g. **arimasen**); the negative present plain form is introduced in Unit 6 Structures 1. In terms of tense, verbs ending in

-masu or in the present plain form refer to habitual actions, general truths, or the definite future, according to the context:

Tomu-san wa maiban benkyō shimasu. *Tom studies every evening.*
Yokohama wa Tōkyō no chikaku ni arimasu. *Yokohama is near Tokyo.*
Raishū mata kakimasu. *I am going to write again next week.*

2 *The suggesting form of the verb:* -mashō

This is used when suggesting a course of action:

Sā, tabemashō. *Well, let's eat.*
Raishū mata hanashimashō. *Let's talk again next week.*

Followed by the question particle **ka**, it occurs when in English we would use either *Shall I . . . ?* or *Shall we . . . ?*, according to the context:

Machimashō ka? *Shall I wait?*
Owarimashō ka? *Shall we stop?*

This is a polite form, but there is a plain form too, which we will come across in Unit 13 Structures 6.

3 Y de X o shimasu

O indicates that the noun which it follows is the object of the verb, or of **kudasai/dōzo**:

Jiru-san wa maiban shinbun o yomimasu. *Jill reads the newspaper every evening.*
Kōhī o nomimashō ka? *Shall we drink some coffee?*

[Noun] o kudasai (or, more formally, **o-negai shimasu**) is used when asking for something; when offering something to someone else, **dōzo** should be substituted.

Pen o kudasai/o-negai shimasu. *A pen, please.*
Shinbun o dōzo. *Please take a look at the newspaper.*

Note that **matsu** takes **o**:

Michiko-san o machimashō. *Let's wait for Michiko.*

On the other hand, **au** takes **ni**:

Tomu-san wa raishū mata Suzuki-san ni aimasu. *Tom will meet Suzuki-san again next week.*

In the conversation, we introduced two uses of the particle **de**. The first use is after place nouns, when it indicates where the action of the sentence occurs. **Ni** is also used after place nouns, but this is only with a very limited number of verbs, most commonly **aru** and **iru**, which are concerned with static location rather than with action:

Tanaka-san wa doko ni imasu ka? *Where is Tanaka-san?*
Tanaka-san wa doko de kaimono shimasu ka? *Where does Tanaka-san shop?*

Note that verbs such as **au**, **matsu**, and **benkyō suru** all work as verbs of action rather than of static location:

Eki de aimashō. *Let's meet at the station.*

The other use is to indicate the instrument by means of which an action is performed:

Fōku de tabemashō. *Let's eat with forks* (**fōku**).
Kēki o naifu de kirimasen ka? *Won't you cut the cake* (**kēki**) *with a knife* (**naifu**)*?*

Linked to this function of **de** is its use to indicate a means of communication, as in the following:

Nihongo de hanashimashō. *Let's speak in Japanese.*
(as opposed to **Nihongo o hanashimashō.** *Let's speak Japanese.*)

Jiru-san wa maiban shinbun de Amerika no nyūsu o yomimasu. *Every evening Jill reads the news* (**nyūsu**) *about America in the newspaper.*
(as opposed to **Jiru-san wa maiban shinbun o yomimasu.** *Every evening Jill reads the newspaper.*)

4 *Plain forms of adjectives*

Like verbs, adjectives have plain forms; they occur at the end of sentences whenever the use of plain forms is appropriate. (Adjectives before nouns have the same form whatever the level of speech.)

In the case of **-i** adjectives, all that happens in the plain form is that **desu** is omitted, as when Tom was complaining to himself in the **Kaiwa**, or as in:

A, kawaii! *How sweet!*
Igirisu wa samui. *Britain is cold.*

Na adjectives use the plain form of **desu**, **da**, instead of **desu** itself; in informal spoken Japanese, however, **da** is frequently avoided at the end of sentences, especially in women's speech (Unit 8 Language and Society):

Kore wa taisetsu da. *This is important.* (*male speaker*)
Kore wa taisetsu yo. *This is important.* (*female speaker*)

In the case of the negative, the plain ending for both types of adjective is **nai**. This replaces **arimasen**, and the **-i** adjective **-nai desu** alternative, and is in fact the plain form of **arimasen** (Unit 6 Structures 1):

Kono hoteru wa amari yokunai. *This hotel isn't very good.*
Ano nomiya wa shizuka ja nai. *That bar isn't peaceful.*

5 *The contrasting use of* wa

This use of **wa**, which is linked to its main function of indicating the topic of a sentence, was introduced briefly at the end of Unit 2 Structures 2. The contrast can be explicit:

Jikan wa arimasu. Shikashi, o-kane wa arimasen. *I have time; however* (**shikashi**), *I don't have money.*

When only one element is mentioned, the contrast is implied:

A: Chikaku ni resutoran ga arimasu ka? *Is there a restaurant nearby?*
B: Nomiya wa takusan arimasu ga . . . *There are lots of bars (but no restaurants).*

You also saw this in the **Kaiwa**:

Tōbun wa shikata ga arimasen. *It's inevitable for the time being (but things should get better in the future).*

6 *This/that sort of:* konna, sonna, anna

Again, these words are parallel in meaning to **kore**, **sore** and **are**; they go in front of nouns in the same way as **kono**, **sono** and **ano**. The question equivalent is **donna**:

Konna handobaggu wa ikaga desu da? *How about this type of handbag?*
Watashi wa anna tokoro de wa tabemasen! *I don't eat at places like that (associated with neither of us)!*
Donna kamera o kaimasu ka? *What sort of camera will you buy?*

Konna ni, **sonna ni**, etc. are found with adjectives and verbs, and indicate *to this/that/what extent*:

Atsui desu ne. Amerika no natsu wa konna ni atsui desu ka? *Isn't it hot! Are American summers this hot (hot to this extent)?*
Watashi wa sonna ni hatarakimasen. *I don't work that much (to the extent that you work/that you think I work).*

7 Nan/nani?: *what?*

Nan and **nani** are different ways of pronouncing the same word. The choice is quite irregular. Before **ga**, **o** and **mo** (Unit 6 Structures 8) for instance, **nani** is used, while before **no**, **de** (and **da/desu**) **nan** is used. Before **ka** (Structures 8) and **ni** , both will be heard, although **nani** is preferred on formal occasions. (See also Unit 9 Structures 8 for combinations of **nan(i)-[counter]**.)

Tōkyō de nani o kaimasu ka?
Kono kēki o nan de tabemashō ka?

8 [Question word] ka: dare ka, doko ka, nan(i) ka, itsu ka

This has an effect similar to adding *some-* in English, **dare ka** being *someone*, **doko ka** *somewhere*, **nani ka** *something*, and **itsu ka** *sometime*.

Note that **o**, and usually **ga**, are omitted after [question word] **ka**:

> Dare ka imasu ka? *Is there someone (anyone) there?*
> Nani ka tabemashō ka? *Shall we eat something?*
> Raishū mata doko ka de aimashō. *Let's meet again somewhere next week.*

Renshū

1 You are trying to cheer up a depressed friend. Join each noun in list A to a verb in list B, adding the appropriate particle, and putting the verb into the suggesting **-shō** form.
Rei: (1)+(*e*): bīru o nomimashō.

A	B
(1) bīru	(*a*) taberu
(2) terebi (*television*)	(*b*) yomu
(3) hanbāgā	(*c*) kaimono-suru
(4) Tōkyō	(*d*) oyogu
(5) shinbun	(*e*) nomu
(6) umi (*sea*)	(*f*) miru

2 Complete by putting particles into the gaps, as appropriate.

(1) Tomu-san wa maiban nomiya (*a*) bīru (*b*) nomimasu ka?
(2) Kono pen (*c*) denwa bangō (*d*) kakimashō.
(3) Doko (*e*) Jiru-san (*f*) aimasu ka?
(4) Shinbun (*g*) kudasai.
(5) Eigo (*h*) hanashimashō. (*Note that there are two possible answers.*)

3 You are quarrelling with a friend. One of you contradicts everything the other says, using **sonna ni + the negative**.
Rei: (koko) (totemo) (shizuka na)

A: Koko wa totemo shizuka desu ne. *It's very quiet here, isn't it.*
B: Iie, sonna ni shizuka ja arimasen. *No, it isn't that quiet.*

(*a*) (Kono bīru) (totemo) (tsumetai)
(*b*) (Michiko-san) (taihen) (kirei na)
(*c*) (Ken-san) (yoku) (benkyō suru) (**yoku** *well, often*)
(*d*) (Suzuki-san) (o-sake) (takusan) (nomu)

4 When Tom and Suzuki next meet it is the afternoon, so they decide to go to a coffee shop. They both order **burendo**, a blend of different types of coffee. Adapt the first half of the dialogue at the beginning of this unit to fit the new situation, leaving out the **kanpai!**

5 Give the Japanese equivalent for the following short dialogues:

Tanaka Do you study English every evening?
Yamamoto No, I haven't the time!

Jill Is there a good butcher's somewhere?
Michiko There is a good butcher's next to the wine shop.

Ken Let's meet sometime.
Michiko Shall I tell you my telephone number?

Language and Society

Eating and drinking out in Japan

There is a great variety of places to eat and drink in Japan, from the very expensive and formal to the cheap and informal. Many display incredibly realistic plastic versions of their wares which will help you if you cannot read the menu, although in Western-style establishments knowledge of **katakana** alone (and a good phonetic imagination) will get you a long way. Do not be surprised if you are greeted with a chorus of **Irasshaimase** (*Welcome*) from the staff as you enter; there is no need to reply.

Here are some useful words and phrases:

mōningu	*morning*	setto ('set' – *special deal of food + something to drink*)
ranchi	*lunch*	
keki	*cake*	

At a Japanese restaurant, the equivalent of **setto** would be the **teishoku**. For instance, a **tenpura teishoku** would consist of **tenpura** + rice + soup + pickles + Japanese tea.

To call for attention: (Chotto) sumimasen. / (Chotto) o-negai shimasu. } *Excuse me, please*

Here are some possible dialogues:

Waiter	Nanmei-sama desu ka? *How many are you?*
You	Hitori/futari (etc.) desu. *One, two, etc.* (For counting people, see Unit 9 Structures 7)
Waiter	O-nomimono wa? *What would you like to drink?*
You	Bīru/kōhī/(o-)mizu/wain (o) kudasai. *Beer/coffee/water/wine please.*

At most establishments, the bill will automatically be placed on your table once your order has been fulfilled, and you should pay at the cash-register (**reji**) near the exit as you leave. To ask for the bill, however, say:

Kanjō o o-negai shimasu. *The bill* (**kanjō**) *please.*
Ikura (desu ka)? *How much?* (*male speaker*)
O-ikura (desu ka)? *How much?* (*female speaker*)

メイン ディッシュ MAIN DISHES

17. クラブミート コロッケ Crabmeat Croquette with Tomato Sauce	¥2,000
18. 海老フライ タルタルソース添え Fried Prawns with Tartar Sauce	2,000
19. ナマズのバターソテー ガーリック風味 Sautéed Fillet of Catfish Garlic Butter	2,000
20. 貝柱のフライ Fried Sea Scallops with Tartar Sauce	1,900
21. 伊勢海老と貝柱のクリーム和え パイケース入り Lobster and Sea Scallops in Pie Case	2,300
22. 魚介類のピラフ Seafood Pilaff	1,400
23. ビーフピラフ Beef Pilaff Japanese	1,300
24. ハヤシライス Hashed Beef with Rice	1,500
25. チキンカレー Chicken Curry with Rice	1,300
26. 海老のカレー Shrimp Curry with Rice	1,400
27. ビーフ カレー (カレーにはチャツネのご用意もございます。) Beef Curry with Rice (Chutney is available upon request.)	1,500
28. 魚介類のスパゲッティ Seafood Spaghetti à la Maison	1,500
29. スパゲッティ ミートソース Spaghetti Bolognaise	1,200
30. スパゲッティ チキン入り冷製トマトソース Spaghetti with Chicken, Cold Tomato Sauce	1,400
31. 野生のめん鳥網焼き トマト添え Broild Game Hens with Tomato	1,800

A Western-style menu

5 Rondon de kaze o hikimashita
I caught a cold in London

In this unit you will learn how to talk about past experiences, and find out how verbs of motion work in Japanese. You will also encounter various time expressions, and two ways of joining sentences. There will be some information on souvenir-giving, and on feminine sentence endings.

Kaiwa

Tanaka-san wa sengetsu Yōroppa e itta. Nishūkan gurai ryokō shite, ototoi kaetta. Soshite, kesa Jiru-san ni atta.

Jiru	Dō deshita ka, Yōroppa wa?
Tanaka	Totemo yokatta desu.
Jiru	O-tenki wa?
Tanaka	Samukatta desu.
Jiru	Sore wa zannen deshita ne.
Tanaka	Demo, kirei desu ne; toku ni Itaria wa.
Jiru	Sō desu ka? Watashi wa Itaria e itta koto ga arimasen.

sengetsu *last month*
Yōroppa *Europe*
[place] e *to, in the direction of [place]* ● S1
itta plain past form of **ik.u** (*to go*) ● S2
nishūkan gurai *for about two weeks* ● Unit 8 S8
shite -te form of **suru** ● S4
ototoi *the day before yesterday* ● S6
kaer.u *to go/come back, return (to the place where you live or otherwise belong)*
[sentence] soshite, [sentence] *[sentence] then/and [sentence]*
kesa *this morning*

Dō deshita ka, Yōroppa wa? *How was it, Europe I mean?* ● LS2
deshita past form of **desu** ● S2
yokatta desu past form of **ii desu** ● S5
tenki *weather*
Sore wa zannen deshita ne *That was a shame/What a shame*
zannen na *disappointing*
zannen deshita past form of **zannen desu** ● S5
toku ni *especially*
Watashi wa Itaria e itta koto ga arimasen *I have never been to Italy*
[verb (past plain form)] koto ga aru ● S3

True or false?

1 Tanaka-san wa sengetsu Yōroppa kara kaetta.
2 Jiru-san wa Itaria e itta koto ga aru.

Tanaka-san wa Yōroppa de shashin o takusan totta. Soshite, Jiru-san ni sono shashin o miseru.

Jiru Kore wa doko no shashin desu ka?
Tanaka Ēto . . . Rōma no shashin desu. Rōma wa sonna ni samukunakatta desu. (*Tsugi no shashin o dasu.*) Koko wa doko datta kashira? (*Jiru-san ni miseru.*)
Jiru A, natsukashii wa. Rondon no yūmei na Okkusufōdo Dōri desu.
Tanaka Omoidashimashita. Hoteru kara basu de itte, o-miyage o iroiro kaimashita.
Jiru Rondon wa dō deshita ka?
Tanaka Tanoshikatta desu ga, mainichi ame deshita. Asoko de kaze o hikimashita yo.

shashin *photograph*
tor.u *to take*
shashin o tor.u *to take a photograph(s)*
[person] ni *to [person]* ● S1
mise.ru *to show*
ēto . . . *let me see . . .*
Rōma *Rome*
samukunakatta desu past form of **samukunai desu** ● S5
tsugi no [noun] *the next [noun]*
das.u *to take out, produce*
datta plain past form of **desu**
kashira? *I wonder?* ● Unit 6 S3

A, natsukashii wa *This brings back memories*
natsukashi.i [noun] *dear old/good old [noun]*
[sentence] wa (feminine) ● LS4
Rondon *London*
Okkusufōdo Dōri *Oxford Street*
omoidas.u *to remember*, in the sense of *to recall something forgotten*
omoidashimashita *past* **-masu** *form of* **omoidas.u** ● S2
[place] kara *from [place]*
basu *bus*
[vehicle] de *by [vehicle]* ● S7
o-miyage *souvenir* ● LS1
iroiro *various, all sorts of*
mainichi *every day*
ame *rain*
kaze o hik.u *to catch a cold*

True or false?

3 Tanaka-san wa Jiru-san ni Rōma no shashin o miseta.
4 Tanaka-san wa Itaria de kaze o hiita.

Structures

1 [noun] e/ni/kara: *indicating direction of action*

In Unit 3 Structures 1 and 2 we saw **[place] ni** being used with **aru** and **iru**, verbs indicating a 'state', or the way things are, to specify a static location. With verbs indicating movement ***to*** or ***towards*** (rather than location ***in***) a place, **ni** or **e** will specify the direction of the movement:

Tomu-san wa raishū Kyōto e/ni ikimasu. *Tom is going to Kyoto next week.*
Ken-san wa itsu Igirisu e/ni kaerimasu ka? *When is Ken returning to Britain?*

When the action is directed at a person rather than a place, for example in showing or giving things to people, **ni** is used rather than **e**:

Michiko-san wa okāsan ni Ken-san no tegami o misemashita. *Michiko showed Ken's letter to her mother.*

To indicate where an action comes from, **kara** is used:

Tomu-san wa itsu Kyōto kara kaerimasu ka? *When will Tom come back from Kyoto?*

2 *Past form of verbs*

To put any **-masu** form verb into the past, all you need to do is turn **-masu** into **-mashita**:

tabe.ru	tabemasu	tabemashita
ik.u	ikimasu	ikimashita
suru	shimasu	shimashita

Suzuki-san wa bīru o takusan nomimashita. *Suzuki-san drank a lot of beer.*
Nani o mimashita ka? *What did you see?*

The past form of **desu** is **deshita**. You can put the negative **-masen** form of any verb into the past just by adding **deshita**. Similarly, the past of **de wa arimasen** is **de wa arimasen deshita**:

oshie.ru	oshiemasen	oshiemasen deshita
ka.u	kaimasen	kaimasen deshita
kuru	kimasen	kimasen deshita

Kyōto e ikimasen deshita. *I didn't go to Kyōto.*
Jiru-san wa tako o tabemasen deshita. *Jill didn't eat the octopus.*
Sore wa Rōma no shashin de wa arimasen deshita. *That wasn't a photograph of Rome.*

The past plain form of **-iru/-eru** verbs is formed by substituting **-ta** for **-ru**:

mise.ru	miseta
oshie.ru	oshieta
tabe.ru	tabeta
i.ru	ita
mi.ru	mita

The past plain form of **-u** verbs, however, depends on the consonant preceding the **-u**, as you will see from the following groupings:

ar.u wakar.u tor.u kir.u	atta wakatta totta kitta	
nom.u yom.u	nonda yonda	also asob.u asonda (*to play*) yob.u yonda (*to call/invite*)
hatarak.u kak.u hik.u	hataraita kaita hiita	(*note, however, the exceptional* ik.u itta)
oyog.u	oyoida	
hanas.u das.u	hanashita dashita	
mats.u	matta	

Verbs like **a.u**, which have a vowel in front of the **-u** rather than a consonant, go like this:

a.u ka.u	atta katta

The two irregular verbs behave like this:

suru kuru	shita kita

The plain past form of **desu** is **datta**. The plain present and past forms of the negative will be dealt with in the next unit. Information about some particular uses of the past tense in Japanese is given in Language and Society 3.

3 [Verb (past plain form)] koto ga arimasu

This structure is used to refer to experiences in the past:

A: Tako wa dō desu ka? *How* (**dō**) *do you like octopus?*
B: Nihon ryōriya de tabeta koto ga arimasu. Oishikatta desu. *I've had it at a Japanese restaurant. It tasted good.*

Note that in questions it is equivalent to English *Have you ever . . . ?*, and with **arimasen** rather than **arimasu** at the end, to *I* (*etc.*) *have never . . .* :

A: O-sake o nonda koto ga arimasu ka? *Have you ever drunk sake?*
B: Hai, (nonda koto ga) arimasu. *Yes, I have* (*drunk it*).
Iie, (nonda koto ga) arimasen. *No, I haven't.*
A: Michiko-san no otōto wa hansamu desu ne. *Michiko's younger brother is handsome isn't he?*
B: Zannen desu ga, atta koto ga arimasen. *It's a shame, but* (=*unfortunately*) *I've never met him.*

Koto is a noun meaning (*abstract*) *thing*. You will meet other constructions in which **koto** follows the plain forms of verbs in Unit 13 Structures 4 and Unit 14 Structures 1, 2, and 5.

4 *Joining sentences with the* -te *form and* ga

(*a*) The **-te** form is made by changing the vowel at the end of the past plain form from **-a** to **-e**:

oshieta	oshiete
owatta	owatte
nonda	nonde
kaita	kaite
shita	shite

The **-te** form of **da** is **de**.

The **-te** form has many uses, and is similar to the *-ing* form of the verb in English in that it has no tense and cannot form a full sentence by itself. A very common use is in joining sentences which form a consecutive sequence of events. Thus the sentences:

Suzuki-san wa maiban nomiya e ikimasu.
Nomiya de o-sake o takusan nomimasu.

can be made into one by putting **ikimasu** into its **-te** form, **itte**:

Suzuki-san wa maiban nomiya e itte, o-sake o takusan nomimasu. *Every evening Suzuki-san goes to a bar and drinks a lot of sake.*

Similarly,

Tanaka-san wa shashin o dashimashita. Shashin o Jiru-san ni misemashita.

becomes

Tanaka-san wa shashin o dashite, Jiru-san ni misemashita.

Note that the tense of the whole sentence is given by the verb at the end.

(*b*) This **ga** has already appeared in several **kaiwa**. It is different from **[noun] ga** which was introduced in Unit 3 Structures 2, and in meaning is similar to the English *but*:

Sumimasen ga, o-tearai wa dochira desu ka? *Excuse me, but which way is the toilet?*

Zenbu tabemashita ga, oishiku arimasen deshita. *I ate it all, but it didn't taste good.*

Note that the comma comes after **ga** rather than before. In speech as well, any pause will come after the **ga** rather than before.

Ga is also used where the first part of a sentence is setting the scene for the rest, and where *but* would not therefore be an appropriate English equivalent:

Kesa Ken-san ni aimashita ga, hansamu desu ne. *I met Ken this morning; isn't he handsome!*

Kore wa tako desu ga, tabeta koto ga arimasu ka? *This is octopus—have you ever eaten it?*

Note also how, as at the end of the **Kaiwa** in Unit 4, it is possible to stop talking after the **ga**, leaving your listener to work out what you were going to say. This can be a useful way of implying, rather than directly saying, something which might offend your listener:

Sore wa sō desu ga . . . *That is so, but (I don't totally agree . . .)*

You will sometimes find **ga** at the beginning of a sentence, where it has the meaning of *but*, *however*. **Demo** (Unit 2 **Kaiwa**) and the more formal **shikashi** (Unit 4 Structures 5) are more common in this position, though they cannot be used to join two sentences together as **ga** can.

5 *Past forms of adjectives*

In English, adjectives themselves do not change according to tense; tense is shown by *is*, *was*, etc. In Japanese, **na** adjectives work in a similar way. To indicate the past tense they therefore use **deshita**, the past form of **desu**:

Kono heya wa shizuka desu. *This room is quiet.*
Rōma no hoteru wa shizuka deshita. *The hotel in Rome was quiet.*

Similarly, the negative past uses **de wa/ja arimasen deshita**:

Ano inu wa amari kirei de wa arimasen. *That dog isn't very clean.*
Rondon no basu wa amari kirei de wa arimasen deshita. *The London buses weren't very clean.*

By contrast, **-i** adjectives actually change their form:

Ano resutoran wa oishi**i desu**. *That restaurant is good.*
Itaria no tabemono wa oishi**katta desu**. *The food in Italy was good.*

Michiko-san no uchi wa tō**i desu**. *Michiko's house is a long way away.*
Resutoran wa eki kara tō**katta desu**. *The restaurant was a long way from the station.*

As you can see, **-i desu** is replaced by **-katta desu**. Note that **ii desu** is again an exception, having the past form **yokatta desu**.

With the negative past form of **-i** adjectives there are two possibilities, as with the negative present form. **-ku arimasen** becomes

-ku arimasen deshita. Since **nai**, the plain form of **arimasen**, itself acts like an **-i** adjective, **-kunai desu** becomes **-kunakatta desu**:

Ano resutoran wa amari oishiku arimasen. Ano resutoran wa amari oishikunai desu.	*That restaurant is not very good.*
Igirisu no tabemono wa amari oishiku arimasen deshita. Igirisu no tabemono wa amari oishikunakatta desu.	*The food in Britain was not very good.*

The plain past forms of adjectives follow on logically from the above:

na *adjectives*:	kirei da kirei de wa/ja nai	kirei datta kirei de wa/ja nakatta
-i *adjectives*:	oishii oishikunai	oishikatta oishikunakatta

6 *Expressions of time in Japanese*

We have already been using various expressions of time. Most of them have been expressions of relative time, that is, words like **sengetsu** *last month*, which means last month relative to this month, and will refer to March in April, April in May, etc. Here are some common expressions of relative time:

	year	*month*	*week*	*day*
last	kyonen	sengetsu	senshū	kinō (*yesterday*)
this	kotoshi	kongetsu	konshū	kyō (*today*)
next	rainen	raigetsu	raishū	ashita (*tomorrow*)
every	mainen (*or* maitoshi)	maigetsu (*or* maitsuki)	maishū	mainichi

These words can be followed by certain particles, for example by **wa** if some contrast is implied:

Kinō wa samukatta desu. *Yesterday was cold.*
Kyō wa ii o-tenki desu ne. *Isn't it lovely weather today!*

Usually, however, they are not followed by any particles at all:

Ashita nani o shimasu ka?

It is also worth noting at this stage that these relative expressions can act like nouns and be joined to other time words through the use of **no**:

kinō no yoru *yesterday night*
rainen no natsu *next* (*year's*) *summer*

There will be more information about time expressions, including how to tell the time, in Units 6 and 8.

7 [Vehicle] de *with verbs of motion*

With such verbs, **de** can be used to indicate the means of transport. This is a natural extension of its use to indicate the instrument with which an action is performed:

Basu/densha de kaerimashō. *Let's go home by bus/train* (**densha**).

Note that where English would say *on foot*, Japanese uses the **-te** form of the verb **aruk.u** (*to walk*), **aruite**:

Aruite kaerimashita. *I went home on foot.*

Renshū

1 Supply the missing particles and put the verbs into the past (**-masu**) form, making them positive unless otherwise indicated:

Rei: Kinō resutoran (*a*) (**taberu**)→(*a*) de; tabemashita

(i) Tomu-san wa senshū basu (*a*) Narita (*b*) (**iku**).
(ii) Michiko-san wa kinō Ken-san (*c*) Kyōto no shashin (*d*) (**miseru**).
(iii) **A** Kesa shinbun (*e*) (**yomu**) ka?
B Iie, (**yomu** negative).
(iv) Kyonen (*f*) natsu doko (*g*) (**iru**) ka?

(vi) **A** Kinō uchi (*h*) nani (*i*) (**benkyō suru**) ka?
B (**Benkyō suru** negative); (**asobu**).

2 The Japanese like asking foreigners if they have had any authentic 'Japan experiences'. Use the **[verb (past plain form)] koto ga aru** construction to ask and answer about the following. (Do this with a partner if possible.)
Rei: Seeing Mt Fuji (**Fuji-san**)
Fuji-san o mita koto ga arimasu ka?
Hai, (mita koto ga) arimasu.
Iie, (mita koto ga) arimasen.

(*a*) Eating octopus/raw fish (**sashimi** or **sushi**).
(*b*) Drinking sake/Japanese tea (**o-cha**).
(*c*) Going to Kyōto/Nara.
(*d*) Seeing Noh/Kabuki drama.
(*e*) Staying at a Japanese-style inn (**ryokan ni tomar.u**).

3 Join the following sentences using either the **-te** form of the verb or the ordinary sentence final form and **ga**:
Rei: Yōroppa ni ikimashita. Shashin o takusan torimashita.
→Yōroppa ni itte, shashin o takusan torimashita.
Yōroppa ni ikimashita. Kenbutsu shimasen deshita.
→Yōroppa ni ikimashita ga, kenbutsu shimasen deshita.

(*a*) Tomodachi ni aimashita. Hanashimashita.
(*b*) Tomodachi o yobimashita. Kimasen deshita.
(*c*) Shashin o mimashita. Amari yoku arimasen deshita.
(*d*) Shashin o mimashita. Rondon o omoidashimashita.
(*e*) Jiru-san wa Nihongo de tegami o kakimashita. Tanaka-san ni misemashita.

4 Put the following into the past:
Rei: Rōma wa atsui desu.→Rōma wa atsukatta desu.

(*a*) Rondon wa amari atsukunai desu.
(*b*) Okkusufōdo wa shizuka desu.
(*c*) Itaria no resutoran wa oishii desu.
(*d*) Ano kissaten wa amari kirei de wa arimasen.
(*e*) Tenki wa amari yoku arimasen.

Language and Society

1 *Souvenirs* (o-miyage)

The Japanese love travelling and travel has inevitably become ritualised. Commemorative photographs (**kinen shashin**) must be taken, and **o-miyage** must be bought, for one's neighbours, relatives and colleagues at school or work. If you go to Japan, particularly if you are going to stay with Japanese friends, or if someone is going to be looking after you in some way, you should arm yourself with a choice selection of **o-miyage**: from appropriately emblazoned key-rings to bottles of brandy and scarves or ties with famous designer names.

When presenting a gift to someone, it is usually appropriate to say: **Kore wa tsumaranai mono desu ga . . .** (Lit.) *This is a trivial* (**tsumarana.i**) *thing but* . . . In the case of an **o-miyage**, however, you would probably say: (**Kore wa**) **Igirisu/Amerika no o-miyage desu. Tsumaranai mono desu ga, dōzo** . . . *This is a souvenir from Britain/America. It is a trivial thing, but please* (*accept it*). The happy recipient can respond in various ways, most simply of course with **Dōmo arigatō gozaimasu** (a polite *Thank you*).

2 *Inverted sentences*

You will come across these frequently in everyday spontaneous conversations. The speaker adds information as an afterthought to a sentence which is already complete, possibly to clarify the meaning or for emphasis:

Hansamu desu ne, Ken-san wa. *Handsome isn't he, Ken I mean.*
Hoteru kara ikimashita, basu de. *We went from the hotel, by bus.*
Rondon wa ame deshita, mainichi. *In London we had rain, every day.*

(For inverted questions, see Unit 22 Structures 1(*h*).)

3 *Special uses of the past tense of* wakaru *and* kuru

In certain situations, the past forms of these verbs take on a special meaning. When A, who is junior to B, has been listening to instructions or advice given by B, the reply **Hai, wakarimashita** will imply not only that A has understood, but also that he or she will carry out what B has said. (A more formal equivalent to **wakarimashita** in this context is **kashikomarimashita**.)

If you catch sight of the bus or train that you are waiting for, in English you say *It's coming!*. In Japanese, however, you say **Kimashita!** (Lit. *It has come*). You may feel that this is a natural reflection of the greater speed and efficiency of Japanese transport systems . . .

4 *The feminine sentence endings* wa *and* no

Differences between male and female speech are much more obvious in Japanese than in many other languages. In general, women tend to use polite endings more than men, and to use more honorific and humble forms, as we shall see. When women do use the plain form, with close friends, or when talking out loud to themselves, they will often soften it with a sentence ending. **Wa** is one of these, **no** another. (Note that they are unrelated to the **wa** and **no** which come after nouns and which we first met in Unit 1.) **No** is slightly more assertive than **wa**; in questions it replaces **ka**, which women otherwise omit in informal speech:

Ja, kaeru wa. *Well, I'm going home.*
Samuku nai no. *I'm not cold.*
Doko e iku no? *Where are you going?*

Note that in front of **no**, **da** becomes **na**:

Daijōbu desu ka?→Daijōbu na no? *Are you all right?*

You will hear men using **no**, mainly if they are asking a woman with whom they are on close terms a question, and **wa** as well, particularly if they are from the west of Japan.

6 Yūbe wa zuibun nonda deshō?
You had quite a lot last night, didn't you?

This unit introduces plain negative verb forms, and looks at a number of expressions (uncertainty, probability and reason) that are used with plain forms. You will also learn how to count, tell the time, and how to show off!

Kaiwa

Yūbe, Anzai-sensei wa Tomu-san o tsurete chikaku no nomiya ni itta. Futari wa gozen niji sugi ni issho ni kaette, sugu neta. Soshite, ima wa nichiyōbi no o-hiru chikaku da ga, futari wa yatto okita . . .

Okusan Osoi desu nē – yūbe wa zuibun nonda deshō?

Anzai to Tomu Ee . . . itete . . . (*atama o osaeru*)

Okusan O-furo ni hairanakatta deshō?

Anzai to Tomu Sumimasen.

Okusan Ha mo migakanakatta deshō?

Anzai to Tomu Gomen nasai.

Okusan Montō mo kesanakatta deshō?

Anzai to Tomu K-kesanakatta ka mo shiremasen . . .

Okusan Komatta hitotachi desu. Sa, nani o meshiagarimasu ka? Gohan? Pan?

Anzai to Tomu Nani mo iranai . . . o-cha dake kudasai. Sore kara, igusuri mo!

酒

sake

yūbe *last night*
tsure.ru *to take, accompany*
futari *two persons, the two*
gozen *a.m.* ● S6
niji *two o'clock* ● S6
[time] sugi *after* [*time*] ● S6

issho ni *together*
ne.ru *to lie down; sleep*
nichiyōbi *Sunday*
o-hiru *lunch, lunchtime*
o-hiru chikaku *nearly lunch time*
yatto *finally, at length*
oki.ru *to get up*
zuibun *a fair deal, a lot*
[sentence] darō (deshō) ● S2
[noun] to [noun] [*noun*] *and* [*noun*] ● Unit 8 S3
itete *ouch*
atama *head*
atama o osae.ru *to hold one's head* (**osae.ru** *to hold down*)
o-furo *bath*
o-furo ni hair.u *to take a bath*
hairanakatta plain negative past tense form of **hair.u** ● S1
sumimasen *excuse me/us; I/we am/are sorry* ● LS1
ha o migak.u *to brush one's teeth*
ha mo migakanakatta *didn't brush teeth, either*
gomen nasai *I/we am/are sorry* ● LS1
montō *outside light* (often attached to gate post)
kes.u *to switch off*
[sentence] ka mo shirenai (ka mo shiremasen) *may, perhaps* ● S3
komatta hito *a troublesome person, a nuisance*
sa = sā
meshiagar.u honorific equivalent of **tabe.ru** ● Unit 18 S1(*c*)
pan *bread*
nani mo [negative] *nothing* ● S6
ir.u *to need*
iranai plain negative present of **ir.u** ● S1
o-cha (*Japanese*) *tea*
[noun] dake *only* [*noun*] ● Unit 19 S2
igusuri *'stomach medicine', digestive pills*

True or false?

1 Futari wa amari nomanakatta.
2 Futari wa ha o migaita.

Sanji han goro, Jiru-san wa Tomu-san o mukae ni kuru.

Jiru Gomen kudasai!
Okusan A, Jiru-san! O-agari kudasai. O-cha wa ikaga?
Jiru Itadakimasu. Ano futari wa osokatta deshō kara, yūbe wa taihen datta deshō?
Okusan Ē, demo, watashi wa saki ni neta kara . . .
Jiru Sore wa yokatta desu. De, ano futari wa? Mata neta deshō ka?

Okusan Iie, achira no heya de mukaezake o . . .
Jiru (*isu kara ochiru*)

han *half past*
[time] goro *about [time]* ● S6
mukae ni kuru (*come to*) *meet, pick up* (**mukae** = **-masu** base of **mukae.ru** *to meet* ● Unit 7 S2)
itadakimasu *yes please* (when accepting offer of food or drink)
taihen datta deshō *you must have had a difficult time*
saki ni *ahead of someone else, first*
[sentence] kara *[sentence] and so* ●S4
(sore wa) yokatta desu *I* (*was*) *am glad* (*about that*) (Lit. *It was good.*)
de [sentence] *and so [sentence]*
mukaezake *a pick-me-up to combat a hangover*
achira no heya de mukaezake o . . . (**nonde imasu**, *are drinking*, is understood ● Unit 11 S2)
isu *chair*
ochi.ru *to fall, fall off*

True or false?

3 Anzai-sensei no okusan wa saki ni neta.
4 Jiru-san wa o-cha o nomanakatta.

Structures

1 *Plain negative forms of verbs*

The plain negative form of verbs is obtained in the following manner:

(*a*) With **-iru/-eru** verbs, substitute **-nai** for **-ru** to obtain the plain present negative, and to obtain the corresponding past tense form, change **-nai** to **-nakatta** (recall the past tense formation of **-i** adjectives):

oki.ru	oki nai	oki nakatta
tabe.ru	tabe nai	tabe nakatta
mi.ru	mi nai	mi nakatta

(*b*) With **-u** verbs, change the final **-u** to **-a-**, then attach **-nai** for present tense, **-nakatta** for past.

tor.u	tora¦nai	tora¦nakatta
hanas.u	hanasa¦nai	hanasa¦nakatta
nom.u	noma¦nai	noma¦nakatta
oyog.u	oyoga¦nai	oyoga¦nakatta

Notice that verbs ending in **-tsu** change to **-ta-**, and verbs with a vowel before the **-u**, to **-wa-** (although **awanai** and other such forms sound in fact more like **aanai** in normal rapid speech):

mats.u	ma¦ta¦nai	ma¦ta¦nakatta
a.u	a¦wa¦nai	a¦wa¦nakatta
ka.u	ka¦wa¦nai	ka¦wa¦nakatta

(*c*) The two irregular verbs **suru** and **kuru** work as follows:

suru	shi¦nai	shi¦nakatta
kuru	ko¦nai	ko¦nakatta

(*d*) Notice that **ar.u** does not have regular negative forms (**aranai** does not exist); instead, **nai/nakatta** are used:

O-kane ga nai. *There is/I have no money.*
Hon ga nakatta. *The book wasn't there.*

2 *Indicating probability with* darō

Darō (and its polite equivalent **deshō**) means something like *probably is/was* or *is/was likely to* (there is no fixed English equivalent).

Darō is attached to nouns, adjectives and verbs in their present and past affirmative and negative forms as seen in the table below:

Nouns				
Ano hito wa Nihonjin			deshō.	*That man probably is Japanese.*
		datta		*was*
		ja nai		*isn't*
		ja nakatta		*wasn't*
na *adjectives*				
Kono heya wa shizuka			deshō.	*I expect this room is quiet.*
		datta		*was*
		ja nai		*isn't*
		ja nakatta		*wasn't*
-i *adjectives*				
Natsu wa	atsu	i	deshō.	*Summer must be hot.*
	atsu-	katta		*have been hot*
	atsuku-	nai		*be cool (not hot)*
	atsuku-	nakatta		*have been cool (not hot)*
Verbs				
Kanojo wa	ik	u	deshō.	*She probably will go.*
	it-	ta		*went.*
	ika-	nai		*won't go.*
	ika-	nakatta		*didn't go.*

Note that **sō** behaves like a noun (**sō darō/deshō**).

In ***questions*** ending in **darō/deshō?**, the speaker signals to the listener to confirm the assumption presented in the question:

Yūbe wa zuibun nonda deshō? *You had quite a lot last night, didn't you?*

O-furo ni hairanakatta deshō? *You didn't take a bath, did you?*

Ha mo migakanakatta deshō? *You didn't brush your teeth either, did you?*

When the question is about something associated with the speaker, the implication is often one of showing off (in this use falling intonation is generally used):

(photo of boyfriend) Hansamu deshō? *Don't you think he's handsome?*
(home-baked cake) Watashi no kēki wa oishii deshō? *My cakes are not bad, eh?!*

If **ka?** is attached after **darō/deshō**, the meaning normally is *I wonder if*:

(Knock at the door) Dare darō ka? *Who might that be?*
Kono sukāto wa takai deshō ka? *Is this skirt* (**sukāto**) *expensive, I wonder?*
Ken-san mo iku deshō ka? *I wonder if Ken is going, too?*

When **deshō** is used instead of **desu** in a question (with normal question intonation), it results in a very polite question:

Ii desu ka? *Is it all right?*
Ii deshō ka? *Would it be all right?*

O-tearai wa doko desu ka? *Where is the cloak-room?*
O-tearai wa doko deshō ka? *Where would the cloak-room be, please?*

When said with a falling intonation, the speaker's doubt as to the validity of the assumption expressed in the question is expressed:

Ii deshō ka? *I wonder if it's all right?*
Kyō wa hontō ni nichiyōbi darō ka? *Is today really Sunday, I wonder?*

3 [sentence] ka mo shirenai *and* [sentence] kashira? *indicating uncertainty*

Ka mo shirenai/shiremasen literally means *there is no knowing whether*; it is used instead of **darō** where the speaker is less certain about the likelihood of an action or state occurring.

Ka mo shirenai is attached to the same forms as **darō**: note the differences in meaning when compared to the sentences given above under **darō/deshō**:

Ano hito wa Nihonjin	ka mo shiremasen.	*. . . might/may be a Japanese.*
Kono heya wa shizuka datta		*. . . may have been quiet.*
Natsu wa atsukunai		*. . . may not be hot.*
Kanojo wa ikanakatta		*. . . may not have gone.*

Kashira? came up in Unit 5; as mentioned there, it is restricted to female speech in standard Japanese (although men use it regularly in certain dialects, such as those spoken in the Kyoto/Osaka area). With a meaning similar to **deshō ka?** (and the more masculine **darō ka?**), **kashira?** is attached to the same forms as **ka mo shirenai**. Below, some more examples are given:

Dare kashira? *Who might that be?*
Kono sukāto wa takai kashira? *Is this skirt expensive, I wonder?*
Kono hoteru wa shizuka kashira? *I wonder if this hotel is quiet?*
Ken-san mo iku kashira? *I wonder if Ken will go, too?*
Kesa no shinbun wa konakatta kashira? *Am I right in thinking that the paper didn't come this morning?*

4 *Linking sentences with* kara *(because/and so)*

In Unit 5, we saw the use of the **-te** form and **ga** to link two sentences in the sense of *and* and *but*. In the sequence **S_1 kara S_2**, **kara** links two sentences in the sense of *because*. Note that in Japanese the reason is always given in the first (or subordinate) sentence, whereas in English the reason sentence can come second as well as first (recall the differences in basic word order between the languages):

Tenki ga ii kara ikimasu. *We will go because the weather is fine.*
Futari wa osokatta kara sugu nemashita. *The two went straight to bed because it was late.*
Heya ga shizuka datta kara, watashi wa yoku nemashita. *I slept well because the room was quiet.*
Jiru-san ga kimashita kara, issho ni o-cha o nomimashita. *Because Jill came, we drank tea together.*

In normal polite speech, **kara** is more likely to be attached to the plain forms of verbs and adjectives rather than to **desu/-masu** forms.

Note that the subject of the whole sentence (marked by **wa**) may come at the beginning of the sentence, or in the second half after **kara**. If the subordinate sentence has a different subject (***heya ga* shizuka datta**), it is generally marked by **ga** (see Unit 10). This applies equally to sentences where the overall subject is understood, such as the first example given above. In full this would read as follows:

Tenki ga ii kara **watashi-tachi** wa ikimasu.

In English it is possible to say *Because Michiko didn't* (*go*) in reply to a question such as *Why didn't you go?*. Similarly, sentences consisting only of the part indicating the reason are possible in Japanese, too:

Michiko-san ga ikanakatta kara.

5 *How to count*

Japanese has two sets of numerals, an indigenous set and one imported from China. The Japanese set is used only for numbers up to and including ten.

Number	*Japanese*	*Chinese* (*alternatives*)	
1	hito-tsu	ichi	
2	futa-tsu	ni	
3	mit-tsu	san	
4	yot-tsu	shi	(yon)
5	itsu-tsu	go	
6	mut-tsu	roku	
7	nana-tsu	shichi	(nana)
8	yat-tsu	hachi	
9	kokono-tsu	kyū/ku	
10	tō	jū	

The alternatives to the purely Chinese words, **yon** and **nana**, are derived from the Japanese set, and are more common than **shi** and **shichi**.

On their own, the Chinese numerals are used to count from one to ten, one to a hundred and so on, for example in doing arithmetic. For counting things, it is normal to combine them with specific counters. (See Structures 6 about counting hours and minutes, and Unit 9 for more information.) The Japanese set of numbers is also used to count things, but generally only in the case of objects which have no specific counter assigned to them. One could say that **-tsu** is the counter for such objects.

After ten, the tens are indicated by attaching **ni, san . . .** before **jū**, while the ones are made up by attaching **ichi, ni . . .** after **jū** (note the way that **yon** and **nana** are again used as common alternatives):

11	jū¦ichi	20	ni¦jū
12	jū¦ni	30	san¦jū
13	jū¦san	40	shi/yon¦ju
14	jū¦shi/yon	50	go¦jū
15	jū¦go	60	roku¦jū
16	jū¦roku	70	shichi/nana¦jū
17	jū¦shichi/nana	80	hachi¦jū
18	jū¦hachi	90	kyū/ku¦jū
19	jū¦kyū/ku		

The same principle applies with **hyaku** (*a hundred*) and **sen** (*a thousand*): thus 1984 would be **sen kyūhyaku hachijū yo-nen (-nen** = *year*; this is also the Japanese title of Orwell's *Nineteen Eighty-Four*), and *2001* **nisen ichi-nen**. Certain combinations undergo phonetic change, thus **sanbyaku** (not **sanhyaku**), **roppyaku** (not **rokuhyaku**), **happyaku** (not **hachihyaku**). Check Appendix 1 for a list of common phonetic changes.

The basic unit for large numbers is not 1,000 but 1,0000 (**ichi-man**); calculate by remembering that there are ***four*** noughts, not three, as with thousands:

20,000	ni¦man	(2,0000)
50,000	go¦man	(5,0000)
70,000	shichi/nana¦man	(7,0000)
100,000	jū¦man	(10,0000)
1,000,000	hyaku¦man	(100,0000)
10,000,000	is¦sen¦man (***not*** ichi-¦sen¦man)	(1000,0000)

6 *Telling the time*

The hours are indicated by adding **-ji** (meaning *o'clock/hours*) to the (mainly Chinese) numerals 1 to 12, or in formal announcements, 0 (**rei**) to 23:

ichi ji	*1 o'clock*	shichi ji	*7 o'clock*
ni ji	*2 o'clock*	hachi ji	*8 o'clock*
san ji	*3 o'clock*	ku ji	*9 o'clock*
yo ji	*4 o'clock*	jū ji	*10 o'clock*
go ji	*5 o'clock*	jūichi ji	*11 o'clock*
roku ji	*6 o'clock*	jūni ji	*12 o'clock*
rei ji	*0 hours (midnight)*	nijū ji	*20 hours*
jūku ji	*19 hours*	nijūsan ji	*23 hours*

Where necessary, the a.m./p.m. distinction can be indicated by putting **gozen** (*a.m.*) or **gogo** (*p.m.*) in front. Thus, **gozen ichiji** is *one a.m.*

Half-past is indicated by adding **han** (*half*): **sanji han** (*half past three*). Alternatively, you can say **sanji sanjuppun** (*three thirty*).

The minutes are expressed by combinations of the numerals 1–59 in combination with **-fun/-pun** (see Appendix 1 for combinations).

Hours and minutes are generally combined as follows:

Shichiji gofun	(7.05)	Hachiji yonjūgofun	(8.45)
Sanji jūgofun	(3.15)	Ichiji gojuppun	(1.50)
Kuji nijuppun	(9.20)	Yoji gojūgofun	(4.55)
Jūji sanjuppun/han	(10.30)	Jūichiji gojūhachifun	(11.58)

It is possible to attach **sugi** (*past/after*) to the minutes past the hour: **shichiji gofun sugi** *five past seven.*

After the half hour, it is also possible to give the minutes to the hour by adding **mae** (*before*):

Kuji jūgofun mae	*Fifteen minutes to nine.*
Goji gofun mae	*Five minutes to five.*
Niji juppun mae	*Ten minutes to two.*
Jūniji nifun mae	*Two minutes to twelve.*

For approximate times, **goro** (*about*), **chikaku** (*nearly*) and **sugi** (*past/after*) can be used, while **chōdo** (*just/exactly*) is attached before the hour:

時 -ji

Shichiji goro *Sevenish, about seven o'clock.*
Shichiji chikaku *Nearly seven.*
Shichiji sugi *After seven.*
Chōdo shichiji desu. *It's just on seven.*

For asking the time, **nanji** (*what time/hour*) is used.

7 Ni *with expressions of time*

In this use, **ni** indicates that you are doing something at a specific time. It is therefore attached to specific times such as the hour of the day, the day of the week or month, and the month, year, etc. (These expressions are similar in that they indicate a point on a scale/dial/calendar and so on – see Language and Society 2 and Appendix 1 for dates, the days of the week and the names of the months.)

Kesa rokuji han ni okimashita. *I got up at six this morning.*
Sanji ni ikimashō. *Let's go at three o'clock.*
Gozen niji sugi ni kaerimashita. *They came back after 2 a.m.*
Doyōbi ni kaimono shimashita. *I did some shopping on Saturday.*

On the other hand, it cannot be used with relative times (recall Unit 5 Structures 6):

Mainichi bīru o nomimasu. *I drink beer every day.*
Kinō eiga o mimashita. *I saw a film* (**eiga**) *yesterday.*

Other expressions of time are either specific or general in meaning; these can be used without **ni** in a general sense, or with **ni** to give them a more specific feel. This distinction does not exist in English – if in doubt use these expressions without **ni**.

Asa (*morning*)	(ni)	denwa shimashita.
Gogo	(ni)	kaerimashita.
Fuyu (*winter*)	(ni)	Rōma ni ikimasu.
Sanji goro	(ni)	ikimasu.

8 [question word] mo (dare mo, doko mo, nani mo) [+negative]

This combination is similar in meaning to *no-* or *not any-* in English, **dare mo** being *no one* or *not . . . anyone*, **doko mo** *nowhere* or *not . . . anywhere*, and **nani mo** *nothing/not . . . anything*. Particles **ga** and, usually, **o** are omitted; others such as **ni** combine with **mo** (***preceding*** it). With **iku**, however, **ni/e** can be left out.

> Dare mo kimasen deshita. *No one came.*
> Dare mo yobimasen. *I shall invite no one.*
> Dare ni mo aimasen deshita. *I didn't meet anyone.*
> Doko (ni) mo ikimasen deshita. *We didn't go anywhere.*
> Nani mo irimasen. *I don't want anything.*

Note that **itsu mo** cannot be used with negative forms; it is, however, commonly used with positive forms in the sense of *always* (Unit 7): **Itsu mo shichiji ni kaerimasu.** *I/he always return/s at seven.*

Renshū

1 Tell the time in Japanese as indicated (give two versions where possible):

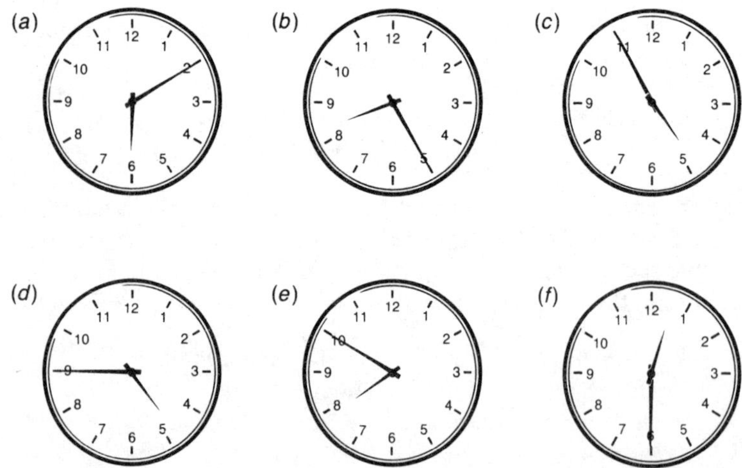

2 Answer the **[question word] ka** questions by **[question word] mo [+negative]** answers as shown in the model:
Rei: Dare ka kimashita ka?→Iie, dare mo kimasen deshita.

(*a*) Doko ka ni ikimashita ka?
(*b*) Nani ka tabemashita ka?
(*c*) Dare ka ni aimashita ka?
(*d*) Nani ka kaimasu ka?

3 Show off about the following:
Rei: (girlfriend; pretty)→Watashi no gārufurendo wa kirei deshō?

(*a*) (car; fast)
(*b*) (room; big)
(*c*) (blouse [**burausu**]; pretty)
(*d*) (jam; tasty)
(*e*) (dog; cute)

4 Put the following English sentences into Japanese:

(*a*) I bought it because I had the money.
(*b*) Because Ken went, I went too.
(*c*) I got up early this morning because I went to bed early last night.

Language and Society

1 *Saying 'sorry' in Japanese:* su(m)imasen, dōmo, *and* gomen nasai

Sumimasen (often shortened to **suimasen**) can be used (sometimes with **ga**) to attract people's attention in the sense of *excuse me*:

Suimasen! *Excuse me! (Calling the waiter, etc.)*
Sumimasen – toire wa doko desu ka? *Excuse me, where is the toilet?*
Suimasen ga, ima nanji deshō ka? *Excuse me, what is the time, please?*

In the sense of *I am sorry*, both (**dōmo**) **sumimasen** and **gomen nasai** (the latter tends to be used by females) are used in a wide range of situations: you may have trodden on someone's foot, caused a traffic accident or got caught by a policeman for not carrying your foreigner's registration card – in all these cases, **sumimasen** is the thing to say. More informally, **dōmo** is used by itself.

(Dōmo) sumimasen is also used to acknowledge people's kindness when receiving gifts or favours, and in its form **su(m)imasen deshita** it can refer to misdeeds or blunders committed in the past. **Shitsurei shimashita** can be used in the same situations.

Ii purezento o sumimasen. *Thanks for the lovely present.*
Yūbe wa sumimasen deshita. *Sorry about last night.*
Kinō wa dōmo shitsurei shimashita. *I do beg your pardon about yesterday.*

(The latter two do not necessarily imply some grave social blunder – it may be that you were late for an appointment, or simply visited someone out of the blue!)

2 *Giving the date*

7月31日
-gatsu -nichi

In Japanese, the order of time expressions is from the general to the specific (the larger unit to the lesser): **kesa rokuji**, **gozen niji**, **sanji gofun**, etc. The same order applies with dates (year, month, day rather than vice versa):

15th December 1980: 1980(sen kyūhyaku hachijū)-nen 12 (jūni)-gatsu 15(jūgo)-nichi

-nen is attached to the years, **-gatsu** (*month*) to the months, and **-nichi** (*day*) to the days. The months have no names, but are numbered from 1–12.

The year can also be indicated by the somewhat flowery name given to the era of an emperor's reign. If you ask someone when they were born, they will normally give you the relevant era year rather than the year according to Western reckoning. The first year in an era is known as **gannen**. The current era is called **Heisei** (*achieving peace*), while the previous era was **Shōwa** (*enlightened peace*). **Heisei gannen** corresponds to 1989, while **Shōwa gannen** is equivalent to 1926, **Shōwa ninen** to 1927, and so on. **Heisei** years can therefore be converted into Western calendar years by adding (19)88, and **Shōwa** years by adding (19)25. **Shōwa 55 (Shōwa gojūgo-nen)**, for example, being *1980*, and **Heisei 12 (Heisei jūni-nen)**, *2000*.

The days of the week are as follows:

Getsuyōbi	*Monday*	Kin'yōbi	*Friday*
Kayōbi	*Tuesday*	Doyōbi	*Saturday*
Suiyōbi	*Wednesday*	Nichiyobi	*Sunday*
Mokuyōbi	*Thursday*	Nan'yōbi?	*What day?*

You will hear people omitting the final **-bi**.

3 *Japanese drinking habits*

There is a great deal of drinking in Japan, unbridled by licensing hours. It forms an important part of the semi-official end of work or business negotiations (see Unit 4 **Kaiwa**), but is also rampant without any such excuse.

Entertainment of friends and customers generally takes place outside the home, and you will therefore find establishments of all descriptions (and prices!) from the humble **ippai nomiya** (small drinking places where locals have a drink at the counter) or **yakitoriya** (specialising in barbecued chicken and/or pork offal) through the more respectable **bā** (*bar*) to various types of restaurants, and establishments offering female companionship, such as **kyabarē** (*cabaret*).

The constant round of social drinking explains why there is such a wide range of tonics, digestive aids and hangover cures on offer. Some of the better known brands are Mamushi dor-inku, Seirogan and Panshiron, respectively.

7 Yakyū o mi ni ikimasen ka?
Won't you come and see the baseball?

In this unit you will become familiar with further uses of some particles which you already know, and learn how to make explanatory statements. You will also find information on public holidays.

Kaiwa

Michiko-san wa Ken-san to issho ni Shinjuku e asobi ni iku. Doyōbi wa itsu mo hokōsha-tengoku da. Sore de futari wa dōro no mannaka o aruku . . .

Michiko Ii o-tenki desu ne . . .

Ken Ē, totemo kimochi ga ii desu. Demo, sugoi hito desu ne!

Michiko Doyōbi wa itsu mo kō na n' desu yo.

Ken Hē . . . raishū wa gōruden uīku deshō? Sono toki wa motto sugoi deshō ne.

Michiko Demo, minna umi ya yama e dekakeru deshō.

Ken Sō ka . . . Michiko-san-tachi mo desu ka?

Michiko Ē, watashi-tachi wa umi e oyogi ni iku n' desu. Yokattara, issho ni ikimasen ka?

Ken Dōmo arigatō . . . demo, watashi-tachi mo dekakeru n' desu.

Michiko Ara, dochira e?

Ken Karuizawa desu. Yama o aruku n' desu.

[noun] to issho ni *with [noun]* ● Unit 8 S3
Shinjuku one of the downtown Tokyo centres
asobi, -masu base of **asob.u** *to play, engage in activities other than work* ● S2
itsu mo *always*
hokōsha-tengoku '*pedestrians' paradise*', road temporarily closed to vehicles, e.g. on holidays
sore de [sentence] *so, therefore [sentence]*
dōro *road*
mannaka *middle, centre*
[noun] o *along [noun]* ● S4
kimochi *feeling*
  kimochi ga ii '*feeling is good*', i.e. *one feels good*
sugo.i *terrible, formidable*
  sugoi hito *a formidable (number of) people, a huge crowd*
kō *like this* ● S6
[sentence] n' desu ● S5
hē exclamation indicating surprise
gōruden uīku '*Golden Week*', term used to refer to the string of public holidays which occurs between late April and early May ● LS
min(n)a *all, everyone*
yama *mountain, hill*
umi ya yama *the sea and the hills* (**ya** ● Unit 10 S1)
dekake.ru *to set/go out*
oyog.u *to swim*
yokattara *if it's all right with you, how about . . .* (phrase often used to introduce an invitation) ● Unit 19 S1
ara exclamation of surprise
Karuizawa famous summer resort in the mountains northeast of Tokyo

True or false?

1 Michiko-san-tachi wa yama ni iku.
2 Ken-san-tachi wa oyogi ni iku.

Michiko	Yūgata Tōkyō Dōmu e yakyū o mi ni ikimasen ka? Kippu ga aru n' desu.
Ken	Doko to doko desu ka?
Michiko	Kyojin to Hanshin desu yo.
Ken	Ii desu ne . . . Sono ato wa disuko ni odori ni ikimashō ne!
Michiko	Sekkaku desu ga . . . mongen ga jūji na n' desu!

yūgata *evening*
Tōkyō Dōmu *'Tokyo Dome'*, covered baseball stadium in Tokyo, home of the Kyojin team
yakyū *baseball*
mi, -masu base of **mi.ru** ● S2
kippu *ticket*
Kyojin, Hanshin famous rival professional baseball teams, based in Tokyo and Osaka respectively
disuko *disco*
odori, -masu base of **odor.u** *to dance* ● S2
sekkaku desu ga . . . *that's very kind of you but . . .* (phrase used to decline an invitation or offer)
mongen *'lock-up time', time one has to be home by*

True or false?

3 Michiko-san wa yakyū no kippu ga aru.
4 Futari wa disuko ni ikanai.

Structures

1 *The use of* iku *and* kuru

These two verbs are used in a somewhat different way from English *come* and *go*. In English, *come* and *go* are used loosely in expressions such as *I'll come with you* or *I can't come tomorrow* when we actually mean *I'll go with you/I can't go tomorrow*; Japanese makes a more rigorous distinction: **iku** refers only to movement away from the speaker/the domain of the speaker, and **kuru** to movement toward the speaker.

1 Ashita ikimasu. *I'll come/go (to your place) tomorrow.*
2 Ashita kimasu. *I'll come (to your place) tomorrow.*
3 Issho ni ikimasen ka? *How about coming/going with us?*
4 Issho ni kimasen ka? *How about coming with us?*

The first example may be said on the telephone, or written in a letter, i.e. when the speaker is away from the listener; by contrast, the second sentence is only possible if the speaker is at the listener's place. The distinction between the third and fourth sentences is less clear-cut, but the implication in **4** is that the speaker asks the listener to join him/her to go to a place that is perceived as his/her domain, either by virtue of ownership (e.g. the speaker's country cottage) or habit (*we always go there in the summer*).

2 [-masu base] ni iku/kuru

The **-masu** base of verbs is what remains when **-masu** is taken off:

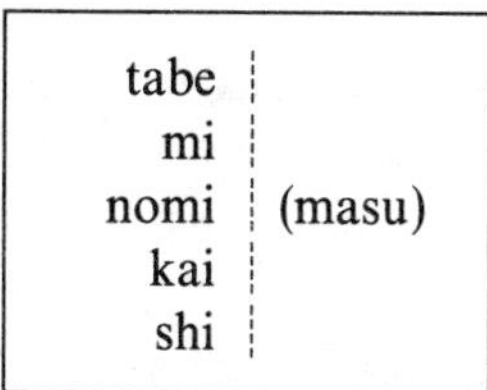

These forms may be understood as the noun-form of verbs, since the **-masu** base of some verbs can act as an independent noun, e.g. **oyogi** *swim(ming)*, **asobi** *play(ing)*, **odori** *dance/dancing*.

Ni can be attached to the **-masu** base of most verbs in combination with a following **iku** or **kuru**; the meaning is very similar to **ni** expressing the direction of an action, although by force of context the implication is often one of purpose. Compare the following pairs (note that **e** cannot be used to indicate purpose):

Shinjuku e/ni ikimasu. *I am going to Shinjuku.*
Oyogi ni ikimasu. *I am going swimming.*

Sensei ga uchi e/ni kimasu. *The teacher is coming to our house.*
Sensei ga nomi ni kimasu. *The teacher is coming to have a drink.*

This structure can also be used when verbs have an object:

Eiga o mimasu. *I am seeing a film.*
Eiga o mi ni ikimasu. *I am going to see a film.*

Where directional **e/ni** and **ni** indicating purpose are used together, direction always comes first (to avoid repetition, **e** is sometimes preferred to **ni**):

Shinjuku e asobi ni ikimasu. *I am going out to Shinjuku.*
Umi e oyogi ni ikimasu. *I am going to the ocean for a swim.*
Disuko ni odori ni ikimasu. *I am going dancing at a disco.*
Tomodachi no ie ni tomari ni ikimasu. *I am going to a friend's place to stay the night.*

3 Kara *and* made

These have come up already in the **Kaiwa** of Units 4 and 5, **kara** after a place word meaning *from*, and **made** with time words in the sense of *until*. In fact, both can be used after time ***or*** place words, just like *from/after* and *to/until* in English; like the English prepositions, they are often found in pairs:

Getsuyōbi kara kinyōbi made hatarakimasu. *I work from Monday to Friday.*
Asa kara ban made terebi o mimashita. *I watched TV from morning till evening.*
Kaisha kara Okkusufōdo Dōri made arukimashita. *I walked from the office to Oxford Street.*

4 O *with verbs of motion*

In Unit 4, we saw how **de** was used to indicate the place of action; with verbs indicating motion such as **aruku** or **oyogu, o** is often used instead of **de** to indicate the area over which the motion takes place:

Kono michi o aruita koto ga arimasu. *I have walked along this street* (**michi**).
Pūru o oyogimasu. *I will swim the length of the swimming pool.*

De will still be used, however, if the meaning of covering a distance is not implied, or if the action takes place aimlessly:

Pūru de oyogimashō. *Let's swim (around) in the pool.*

5 [sentence] n' da/desu

N' da/desu (and its more formal variant **no da/desu**) may be regarded as an emphatic equivalent of **da/desu**. Note the forms that nouns, adjectives and verbs take in front of **n' desu**:

Nouns			
Igirisujin	na	n' da/desu.	*He is British, you see.*
	datta		*was*
	ja nai		*isn't*
	ja nakatta		*wasn't*
na *adjectives*			
Shizuka	na	n' da/desu.	*It is quiet, you see.*
	datta		*was*
	ja nai		*isn't*
	ja nakatta		*wasn't*
-i *adjectives*			
Samu-	i	n' da/desu.	*It is cold, you see.*
	katta		*was*
	kunai		*isn't*
	kunakatta		*wasn't*
Verbs			
Ik-	u	n' da/desu.	*I am going!*
It-	ta		*did go!*
Ika-	nai		*am not going!*
Ika-	nakatta		*didn't go!*

Note that **sō** behaves like a noun (**sō na n' da/desu**).

The **n' desu** form has an explanatory/highlighting force (*it's a matter of*. . .) that is most typically seen in question-answer exchanges between two speakers. As you may gather from the English equivalent to the answer, the meaning is not as strong as *because* . . . (for that, **kara** is available); instead, it may conveniently be thought of as equivalent to *you see*, or perhaps an exclamation mark:

(Dōshite) ikanai n' desu ka? (*Why*) *aren't you going?*

O-kane ga nai n' desu. { *I haven't got any money (you see).* / *I haven't got the money!* }

Here, an explanation is called for in the question, and is given in the reply. Statements ending in **n' desu** are not necessarily answers to questions; explanatory statements occur in other contexts as well:

Ken Sugoi hito desu! *What a crowd!*
Michiko Doyōbi wa itsu mo kō na n' desu yo. *On Saturdays it's always like this!*

Michiko Yokattara, issho ni ikimasen ka? *How about coming with us?*
Ken Dōmo arigatō . . . demo, watashi-tachi mo dekakeru n' desu. *Thanks, but we are going away as well!*

Explanatory statements may also be attached by the same speaker to something he himself has said:

Michiko Ara, dochira e? *Oh, where to?*
Ken Karuizawa desu. Yama o aruku n' desu. *To Karuizawa. We are going hill-walking.*

6 Kō, sō, ā *indicating the way things are*

These words are parallel in meaning to **kore/sore/are**: **kō** means *this way*, while **sō** means *that way* (**ā** is rarely used).

Doyōbi wa itsu mo kō desu. *On Saturdays it's always like this.*
Kō shimashō. *Let's do it this way.* (*i.e. as follows*)
Sō shimashō. *Let's do that.* (**Sore o shimashō** is ***not*** idiomatic Japanese)
Sō desu ka? *Is that so?*

Renshū

1 Answer the questions using the **n' desu** form.
Rei: Dōshite konai n' desu ka?
(*I am busy*)→Isogashii n' desu.

(*a*) Dōshite eiga o minai n' desu ka?
(*I have work to do* Lit. *there is study*)
(*b*) Dōshite ikanai n' desu ka?
(*I have no time*)
(*c*) Dōshite disuko ni ikanai n' desu ka?
(*I have to be back by* 9.30—use **mongen**)
(*d*) Dōshite kakanakatta n' desu ka?
(*I didn't have a pen!*)
(*e*) Dōshite shashin o totta n' desu ka?
(*It was pretty*)
(*f*) Dōshite sētā (*sweater*) o kita n' desu ka?
(*It/I was cold*)

2 After a domestic discord, you are in an obstinate mood and threaten to go out by yourself (use either **[noun] ni iku** or (**[noun] o**) **-masu** base **ni iku**).
Rei: I'm going to see a baseball match!→Yakyū o mi ni iku!

(*a*) I'm going to the pub!
(*b*) I'm going to see a film!
(*c*) I'm going to a restaurant to eat!
(*d*) I'm going to stay overnight at a friend's place!

3 Tell a Japanese friend about what you did in Shinjuku yesterday, using **kara** or **made**, or both, as indicated by the arrows.
Rei: Ie ⟷ eki; aruku: Ie kara eki made arukimashita.

(*a*) Shinjuku-eki ⟷ depāto; takushī (*taxi*) de iku.
(*b*) Niji →; depāto no resutoran de gohan o taberu.
(*c*) →Tomodachi no ie; aruite iku.
(*d*) Yoji →: tomodachi no ie de asobu.
(*e*) Yoru no jūji ⟷ jūniji; disuko de odoru.

Language and Society

Public holidays (kyūjitsu)

In Japan, these are as follows:

January 1	New Year's Day (**Gantan**)
January 15	Coming-of-age Day (**Seijin no hi**)
February 11	National Foundation Day (**Kenkoku kinenbi**)
March 21	Vernal Equinox Day (**Shunbun no hi**)
April 29	Greenery Day (**Midori no hi**)
May 3	Constitution Day (**Kenpō kinenbi**)
May 5	Children's Day (**Kodomo no hi**)
September 15	Respect-for-the-aged Day (**Keirō no hi**)
September 23	Autumnal Equinox Day (**Shūbun no hi**)
October 10	Sports Day (**Taiiku no hi**)
November 3	Culture Day (**Bunka no hi**)
November 23	Labour Thanksgiving Day (**Kinrō kansha no hi**)
December 23	Emperor's Birthday (**Tennō tanjōbi**)

When any of the above falls on a Sunday, the following Monday is treated as a holiday (**furikae kyūjitsu** *transfer holiday*). During **gōruden uīku** (the week between April 29 and May 5), which contains three public holidays, most employers grant a week's holiday.

Offices, banks and shops are generally closed for a three to five day period over the New Year (**O-shōgatsu**), but shops and department stores are usually open all day on Saturdays and Sundays (they are normally closed on one weekday instead). Banks, post offices and government offices are now closed on Saturdays.

8 Jūsu ga hoshii *I want some juice*

In this unit, you will find out how to express wishes and requests, likes and dislikes, including liking some things more than others. There will also be some useful words and phrases to do with train journeys in Japan, and some information on informal speech and given names.

Kaiwa

Yatto gōruden uīku ni natta. Anzai-san-tachi wa eki ni iru. Kore kara, kisha ni notte umi e iku no da keredomo, noriokureru ka mo shirenai . . .

Tarō	Boku wa uchi de tomodachi to asobitai n' da. Umi e ikitakunai.
Michiko	Watashi mo sō yo. Ken-san to issho ni Karuizawa e ikitakatta wa.
Okusan	(*Tarō-kun to Michiko-san ni*) Ii kagen ni shi nasai yo! (*Anzai-sensei ni*) Kippu wa?
Anzai	Koko ni aru.
Okusan	Shimoda-yuki wa nanbansen kashira?
Michiko	Jūji-han-hatsu wa sanban yo. Otōsan, okāsan, hayaku, hayaku! Mō nijūgofun sugi da wa.

nar.u *to become* ● S2
kore kara *after this, now*
kisha *train* ● LS1
nor.u *to get on train, etc.* (Note: **[vehicle] ni noru**)
keredomo *but, however* (functions like **ga** ● Unit 5 S4)
[vehicle] ni nori-okure.ru *to be late for [vehicle]* ● LS2
[noun] to ● S3
[-masu base]-tai *to want to [verb]* ● S4
Watashi mo sō yo. Note omission of **da** ● LS3

Ii kagen ni shi nasai yo! *Behave yourselves!*
[-masu base] nasai ● S5
Shimoda seaside city on tip of Izu peninsula
[place]-yuki (*the train/bus*) *bound for/terminating at [place]*
nanbansen? *what platform?* ● Unit 9 S7 on counters
[time/place]-hatsu (*the train/bus*) *leaving at [time]/starting from [place]*
sanban(sen) *platform* 3
otō-san *father* (form used for addressing) ● Unit 16 LS1
hayaku *quickly* ● S1
mō *already* ● Unit 11 S5

True or false?

1 Anzai-san-tachi wa kore kara Karuizawa e iku.
2 Jūji-han-hatsu ni noriokureru ka mo shirenai.

Anzai-san-tachi wa kaisatsuguchi de kippu o misete, isoide hōmu ni iku.

Anaunsu	Mamonaku sanbansen ni densha ga mairimasu. Abunai desu kara, hakusen no uchigawa e o-sagari kudasai.
Michiko	Chōdo ma ni atta. Demo, hito ga ōi ne.
Okusan	Yahari, shiteiseki o katte yokatta wa. Sa, norimashō.

(*Seki o mitsukete, suwaru. Anzai-sensei wa nimotsu o tana ni noseru.*)

Tarō	Boku, nodo kawaita. Jūsu ga hoshii.
Okusan	Mō nomitaku natta no? Shimoda made sanjikan kakarimasu yo.
Tarō	Okāsan, jūsu dashite!
Okusan	Hai, hai. (*Ue kara fukuro o orosu.*) Orenji to remon to ringo to painappuru ga aru keredo, dore ga hoshii?
Tarō	Boku wa orenji ni suru. Remon to ringo ga kirai da kara.
Okusan	Michiko wa remon deshō?
Michiko	Iie, remon yori ringo no hō ga ii wa.
Okusan	(*Anzai-sensei ni*) Anata wa?
Anzai	Boku wa shizuka ni hon ga yomitai ne.

kaisatsuguchi *ticket barrier*
isoide *hurriedly* (**-te** form of **isog.u** *to hurry*)
hōmu *platform*
anaunsu *announcement*
Mamonaku sanbansen ni densha ga mairimasu. Abunai desu kara, hakusen no uchigawa e o-sagari kudasai. Stock station announcement: *A train will be arriving shortly at platform 3. It is dangerous, so please stand back from the white lines.*
o-[-masu base**] kudasai** *please [verb]* ● S5
ma ni au *be in time* (**[noun] ni ma ni au** *be in time for [noun]*)
ō.i *many* ● S6
yahari *after all/just as I thought*
shiteiseki *reserved seat*
seki *seat/one's place*
katte yokatta *I'm glad that we bought (them)* ● Unit 13 S4
mitsuke.ru *to find*
suwar.u *to sit*
nimotsu *luggage*
tana *shelf*
nose.ru *to place on/load*
Boku, nodo kawaita. Note omission of **wa** and **ga** ● LS3
nodo ga kawaku *to become thirsty* (Lit. *throat gets dry*)
jūsu *juice*
[noun] ga hoshi.i *(I) want [noun]* ● S6
sanjikan *(for) three hours* ● S8
kakar.u *to last (of time)*
dashite! **-te** form for informal requests ● S5
fukuro *bag*
oros.u *to take off/unload*
orenji *orange*
[noun] to [noun] *[noun] and [noun]* ● S3
remon *lemon*
ringo *apple*
painappuru *pineapple*
keredo colloquial abbreviation of **keredomo**
dore? *which?* (out of three or more things)
[noun] ga kirai da *(I) hate [noun]* ● S6
[Y] yori [A] no hō ga ii *(I) prefer [A] to/rather than [Y]* ● S7 (Note that **ii** (here) indicates choice/preference ● Unit 9 S4)
shizuka ni *quietly* ● S1

りんご
ri n go

True or false?

3 Michiko-san wa remon-jūsu ga kirai ka mo shirenai.
4 Anzai-sensei wa ringo-jūsu o nonda.

Structures

1 *Adverbial forms of adjectives*

Many Japanese adverbs, such as **sugu** and **takusan**, are fixed in their form. As in English, however, it is possible to turn adjectives into adverbs. With **na** adjectives, **na** becomes **ni**; with **-i** adjectives, **-i** is replaced by **-ku**, producing the form which you have already met in turning **-i** adjectives into the negative:

Jiru-san wa taihen shinsetsu ni Eigo o oshiemasu. *Jill teaches English very kindly.*
Ken-san wa hayaku arukimashita. *Ken walked fast.*

Note that the adverbial form of **ii** is **yoku**:

Yoku benkyō shimashita! *You studied well!*
Asoko e yoku ikimasu ka? *Do you go there a lot/often?*

Note that the adverbial forms of some **-i** adjectives can act like nouns and join together with particles. **Chikaku** (Unit 2 Structures 5) and **ōku** are found in both the **A** and the **B** position in **A no B** patterns:

chikaku no nomiya *a nearby bar*
nomiya no chikaku *near the bar*
ōku no Nihonjin *most/many Japanese*
Nihonjin no ōku *the majority of Japanese*

The others (**furuku, hayaku, osoku**, and **tōku**) can be found in the following common phrases:

furuku kara *from olden times*
osoku made *until late*
hayaku kara *from early on*
tōku kara *from far away*

2 *Nouns and adjectives with* naru/suru

If you want to link a noun or an adjective to **naru** or **suru** in order, for example, to talk about something becoming cold, or about making something hot, you must do the following:

noun	*noun*	+	**ni**	**naru/suru**
na *adjective*	**na**	→	**ni**	
-i *adjective*	**-i**	→	**-ku**	

Jiru-san wa sensei ni narimashita. *Jill became a teacher.*
Uisukī ni shimashō ka? *Shall we have whisky* (**uisukī**)?
Tomu-san wa sugu genki ni naru deshō. *I expect Tom will become well/recover very soon.*
Heya o kirei ni shimashō. *Let's make the room clean/tidy the room.*
Samuku narimashita ne. *Hasn't it got cold.*
O-furo o atsuku shimashō ka? *Shall I make the bath hot?*

Note that time words are often found with **ni naru** where English would probably use *come*:

Yatto haru ni narimashita *Spring* (**haru**) *has come at last.*
Niji ni narimashita. Ikimashō ka? *Two o'clock has come/It's two o'clock. Shall we go?*

There are some further 'idiomatic' uses of **naru** in Unit 9 **Kaiwa**.

3 [noun] to: *for joining nouns*

To is used to join nouns (but not verbs or adjectives) in the same way as *and* in English. Note, however, that even when joining more than two nouns, **to** must be used between each word, and you will sometimes even find it after the last noun as well:

sake to bīru; Igirisu to Nihon to Ōsutoraria; jamu to chīzu to aisukurīmu (to)

See how **to** works with the noun **issho**, used both with **desu**, and adverbially with **ni**:

Watashi wa tomodachi to issho desu. *I am with a friend.*
Tanaka-san to issho ni ikimashita. *I went with Tanaka-san.*

In sentences like the last one, it is in fact possible to leave out **issho ni**:

Tanaka-san to ikimashita. *I went with Tanaka-san.*

Note the similar use of **to** with some verbs, such as **asobu** and **hanasu**, in the same way as *with* in English:

Tarō-kun to asobimashō. *Let's play with Tarō.*
Suzuki-san to hanashimashita ka? *Did you talk with Suzuki-san?*

(Compare the latter with:

Suzuki-san **ni** hanashimashita ka? *Did you talk **to** Suzuki-san?*)

4 *Expressing wishes:* [noun] ga hoshi.i [-masu base]-ta.i

(*a*) The **-i** adjective **hoshii** is used in expressing wishes for concrete things. Note that the basic pattern is **A wa X ga hoshii**, **A** being the person with the wish, and **X** the thing which they wish for:

Watashi wa kōhī ga hoshii desu. *I want some coffee.*
Jiru-san, nani ga hoshii desu ka? *Jill, what do you want?*
Nani mo hoshikunai desu. *I don't want anything.*
Tomu-san wa bīru ga hoshii deshō. *I expect Tom wants beer.*

(*b*) In order to express the wish to do something, rather than the wish for a concrete thing, you add the **-tai** ending to the **-masu** base (Unit 7 Structures 2) of the appropriate verb. The **-tai** ending has negative and past forms just like other **-i** adjectives:

Watashi wa hayaku kaeri¦ta¦i desu. *I want to get back early.*
Michiko-san ni ai¦ta¦kunai desu ka? *Don't you want to meet Michiko?*
Ken-san wa Shimoda e iki¦ta¦katta deshō. *I expect Ken wanted to go to Shimoda.*

Note that **A wa X o suru** can become either **A wa X o shitai**, or **A wa X ga shitai** (compare **A wa X ga hoshii**):

Watashi wa Nihon de kamera ga/o kaitai desu. *I want to buy a camera in Japan.*
Jiru-san wa tako ga/o tabetakunai deshō. *I expect Jill doesn't want to eat octopus.*

In spoken Japanese, **hoshii** and the **-tai** ending are normally used to express the feelings of the speaker or, in questions, to ask about the feelings of the person being spoken to. They are not normally used to describe the wishes of third persons, unless in reported speech, or in sentences with endings equivalent to *it seems* or *apparently* (Unit 15 Structures 2, 4; Unit 17 Structures 6; also see Unit 14 Structures 4).

5 *Expressing requests using* kudasai *and* nasai

We have already met the structure **[noun] o kudasai** as a method of asking for concrete things (Unit 4 Structures 3). Verbs can be linked to **kudasai** in two ways in order to ask people to do things:

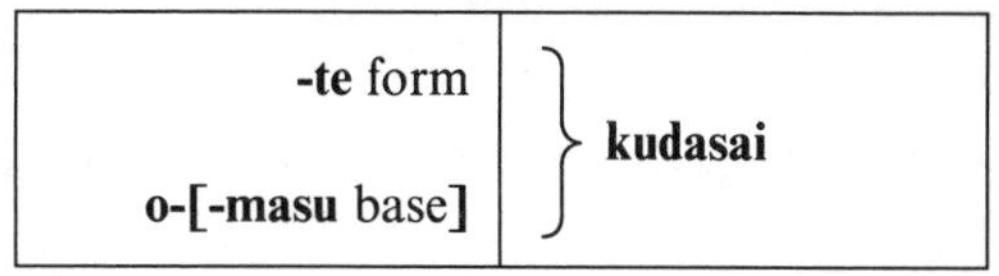

-te form o-[**-masu** base]	} **kudasai**

Motto yukkuri hanashite kudasai. *Please speak more slowly* (**yukkuri**).
Soko ni go-jūsho o o-kaki kudasai. *Please write your address there.*

The second way is the more formal. Also note the following, even more polite, alternatives:

Shōshō o-machi kudasaimase. *Perhaps Sir/Madam would wait a little* (**shōshō**).
O-namae o kaite kudasaimasen ka? *Would you be kind enough to write your name?*

Kudasaimase is a more formal version of **kudasai**. **Kudasaimasen ka?** is polite because the request is framed indirectly, as a negative question (Lit. *Wouldn't you please . . . ?*).

The structure using the **[-masu** base**] nasai** is more abrupt; you will be most likely to hear mothers using it to their children:

Hayaku tabe nasai! *Eat it up quickly!*

However, note that the phrase **O-yasumi nasai**, which literally means *Rest!* is the Japanese equivalent of *Good night* and not at all abrupt.

The most straightforward way of forming negative requests, that is, of asking people not to do things, is as follows:

[present plain negative]-de kudasai
Karuizawa e ika¦nai¦de kudasai. *Please don't go to Karuizawa.*
Mi¦nai¦de kudasai. *Please don't look.*

The verb form in front of **kudasai** is really a negative equivalent of the **-te** form (Unit 17 Structures 5).

Note that between friends and within families you will hear the positive and negative **-te** forms being used alone, without **kudasai**, as informal, friendly, requests.

> Chotto matte! *Wait a bit!*
> Shinaide yo! *Don't do it!* (feminine)

6 *Likes and dislikes: more on* wa – ga *patterns*

The adjective **suki na** (used for likes) and its opposites **kirai na** and **iya na** (which is more specific and forceful) work in a way similar to **hoshii**:

> Watashi wa Nihon no bīru ga suki desu. *I like Japanese beer.*
> Ano sensei ga iya desu! *I hate that teacher!*
> Tako ga amari suki de wa nai n' desu ka? *Don't you like octopus very much?*

So also do **jōzu na/heta na**, which deal with being good/bad at particular skills such as a language or sport, and the slightly overlapping **tokui na/nigate na**, which deal with having/lacking confidence in one's ability in general areas, such as academic subjects as well as sports, etc. Note that you would never use **jōzu** to refer to your own prowess at something, while **tokui** would be perfectly acceptable.

> Michiko-san wa Eigo ga jōzu desu. *Michiko is good at English.*
> Nihongo ga o-jōzu desu ne! *Aren't you good at Japanese!* (note the honorific **o-**; see **o-genki desu ka?** Unit 2 Language and Society 1)
> Ken-san wa tenisu ga heta desu. *Ken is bad at tennis.*
> Watashi wa sūgaku ga nigate desu. *I am hopeless at maths* (**sūgaku**).

A similar structure is used as a basic way of giving more information about any noun **A**, particularly in describing people. This is really an extension of our very first pattern, **A wa B desu**, to **A wa B ga [adjective] desu**:

> Michiko-san wa me ga kirei desu. *Michiko has pretty eyes.* (**me** *eyes*)
> Rondon wa tenki ga warui desu. *The weather in London is bad.*

Note also the following set phrases, which fall nicely into this pattern:

se ga takai/hikui *tall/short* (**se** *stature*)
atama ga ii/warui *clever/stupid*

Tomu-san wa se ga takai desu.
Jiru-san wa atama ga ii desu.

Note also the behaviour of the **-i** adjectives **ō.i**, *many*, and **sukuna.i**, *few*:

Igirisu wa ame ga ōi desu. *Britain has a lot of rain.*
Tōkyō wa kōen ga sukunai desu. *Tokyo has few parks.* (**kōen** *park*)

It might help you to grow used to this kind of **wa – ga** pattern if you think of it as meaning literally *As for A, B is . . . (wanted, liked, disliked, pretty, many, few, etc.).* More information on such patterns will be given in Unit 10 Structures 3.

7 *Comparisons*

Since adjectives in Japanese have no special comparative forms, comparison is indicated through the use of sentence structures based on the following:

(*a*) ***Comparing two things, A and Y***
(i) **A wa Y yori [adjective] desu** *A is [adjective]-er than Y*

In this pattern, **A** is described through comparison with **Y**. **Yori** is a particle equivalent to *than* in English:

Jiru-san wa Tomu-san yori shinsetsu desu. *Jill is kinder than Tom.*
Rondon wa Rōma yori samukatta desu. *London was colder than Rome.*

(ii) **Y yori A no hō ga [adjective] desu** *A is [adjective]-er than Y*
This gives us exactly the same information as the first pattern, but we are comparing **A** to **Y** rather than describing **A** by means of **Y**. **Hō** is a noun meaning *side/direction*, and is therefore joined to **A** by using **no**:

Tomu-san yori Jiru-san no hō ga shinsetsu desu.
Rōma yori Rondon no hō ga samukatta desu.

The factual content is the same, but rather than describing Jill's personality, or the weather in London, we have been talking about the relative qualities of Tom and Jill, Rome and London.

Note that although these are the basic structures, a wide number of variations are possible. For example:

Jiru-san wa Ken-san yori hayaku okimasu. *Jill gets up earlier than Ken.*

[Adjective] hō works out as equivalent to *the* [*adjective*]*-er one* in English:

Yasui hō o kaimashō. *Let's buy the cheaper* (**yasu.i**) *one.*

Motto, equivalent to *more*, is used to reinforce comparisons, and to make a comparison clear when **Y** is not stated:

Tōkyō wa Shidonī yori motto ōkii desu. *Tokyo is bigger than Sydney.*
Motto shizuka ni hanashite kudasai. *Please speak more quietly.*

(*b*) ***Comparing three or more things***
(A to B to . . . Z no naka de) A ga ichiban [adjective] desu (*Out of A*, *B*, *. . . and Z*) *A is the* [*adjective*]*-est*

Ichiban is equivalent to English *most*.

Rondon to Pari to Rōma no naka de Rōma ga ichiban furui desu. *Out of London*, *Paris and Rome*, *Rome is the oldest.*

If you are singling something out from a general category **Q** rather than from among specific alternatives, **Q no naka de** is sufficient:

Ginza no naka de koko ga ichiban takai desu. *This is the most expensive* (**taka.i**) *place in the Ginza area.*

With this structure too, many variations are possible:

Hādo-san-tachi no naka de Jiru-san ga asa ichiban hayaku okimasu. *Jill is the first of the Herds to get up in the morning.*

8 *Expressing length of time*

In Unit 5 Structures 6 and Unit 6 Structures 6, 7 and 8, you encountered various expressions concerned with the time at which things are done, that is with points of time. Here we are looking at expressions to do with how long things take. For instance, **-ji** is used to denote the hour at which something is done, while **-jikan** denotes the number of hours which something takes:

Ken-san wa yūbe ichijikan denwa de hanashimashita. *Ken talked on the phone for an hour yesterday evening.*

No particle is needed with expressions of length of time, but **gurai/kurai** can be attached to give the idea of *about*, just as **goro/koro** is used with expressions of point of time:

Nijikan gurai machimashita. *I waited for about two hours.*

Note also that to ask about length of time you should use **dono gurai/kurai**:

Dono gurai kakarimasu ka? *How long does it/will it last?*

See Appendix 1 for more expressions of length of time, and details of how they combine with numbers.

時間

-ji kan

Renshū

1 You are busy getting ready for an outdoor party and your rather nosy next-door neighbour, hoping to be invited, offers to help. With a partner if possible, supply both parts of the conversation, first accepting, then refusing.
Rei: o-sake o akeru (ake.ru *to open*)
Neighbour: O-sake o akemashō ka? **You:** Hai, akete kudasai.
Iie, akenaide kudasai.

(*a*) tēburu o dasu
(*b*) kyabetsu o kiru (**kyabetsu** *cabbage*)
(*c*) chīzu o kai ni iku
(*d*) koppu o arau (**koppu** *glass*) (**ara.u** *to wash*)

2 Here is a list giving the likes and dislikes and other pieces of information about some of our characters.

	suki	kirai	tokui	nigate	tokuchō (*special characteristics*)
Jiru	kōhī	tako	tenisu	Furansu-go	nagai kami*
Tomu	bīru	jūsu	gitā*	ryōri	se ga takai
Ken	Michiko	benkyō	yakyū	ragubī*	ōkii karada*
Michiko	Ken	niku	Eigo	piano	kirei na me

***kami** *hair* ***gitā** *guitar* ***ragubī** *rugby* ***karada** *body*

Use the **A wa X ga [adjective] desu** construction to make five sentences about each of them, and then make similar sentences about yourself:
Rei: Jiru-san wa kōhī ga suki desu; tako ga kirai desu; tenisu ga tokui desu; Furansugo ga nigate desu; sore kara kami ga nagai desu.

3 Using the same list, work out their respective responses to the question **Nani o shimashō ka?** (Note: (here) **tenisu** (etc.) ***o* suru** *play tennis* (and other sports); **gitā/piano o hiku** *play the guitar/piano*):
Rei: (Jill) Watashi wa kōhī ga/o nomitai desu *or* Watashi wa tenisu ga/o shitai desu.

4 Again using the list, work out the probable response to each question of the person specified in brackets:
Rei: Bīru ga suki desu ka? (Jill)
Iie, bīru yori kōhī no hō ga suki desu.

(*a*) Kōhī ga suki desu ka? (Tom)
(*b*) Ragubī ga tokui desu ka? (Ken)
(*c*) Furansu e ikitai desu ka? (Michiko)
(*d*) Yakyū ga mitai desu ka? (Jill)

5 Put the following dialogues into polite style Japanese:

(a) **A** How long do you study every day? **B** Three hours.

(*b*) **A** At what time are you meeting Michiko? **B** At 5 o'clock.
(*c*) **A** Apples are the fruit (**kudamono**) I like the best. **B** I like oranges rather than apples.
(*d*) **A** Hasn't it become warm! **B** I expect you're glad we came to Shimoda.

Language and Society

tok kyū

1 *Train journeys*

The train is a vital form of transport in Japan, not only for commuting but also for going on holiday. If you are planning to go by train during the peak seasons (at New Year, during Golden Week, and in August), it is advisable to book seats well in advance. These reserved seats are called **shiteiseki**; there are always carriages containing unreserved seats, **jiyūseki**, but you would have no chance of getting one of these unless you arrived very early at the station from which the train starts.

Kisha is a term used for long-distance trains as opposed to commuter trains, which are known as **densha**; the underground, or subway, is **chikatetsu**. **Kyūkō** denotes an express train, and **tokkyū** a super-express. In 'Japanese English' the latter is confusingly known as a 'limited express'; this is short for 'limited-stopping express'. And, of course, we must not forget the **shinkansen**, Japan's famous 'bullet train'.

Tickets for normal journeys (**kippu** or **jōshaken**) can be purchased from automatic machines. If there is no romanised price chart, ask someone how much your ticket will cost: **X made ikura desu ka?** *How much is it as far as X*? Tickets for long distances, and the special tickets for travelling by express, etc. (**kyūkōken**, **tokkyūken**) which you need in addition to your **jōshaken**, must be purchased over the counter. You might find the following phrases of use. (Note that tickets are counted using **-mai**):

Kyōto made ichimai. *One to Kyōto.*
Shinkansen de Morioka made sanmai kudasai. *Three to Morioka by shinkansen please.*

Ōfuku desu da? *Is that a return* (**ōfuku**)?
Iie, katamichi desu. *No, it's one way* (**katamichi**) *only.*

jiyūseki tokkyūken to Narita

No train journey in Japan would be complete without the purchase of a packed lunch (**o-bentō**) at the station or on the train. In the summer, you might try the packs of frozen mandarin oranges (**mikan**).

2 *Verb combinations such as* noriokureru

Noriokureru, *to be late for a train*, is formed by adding the **-masu** base

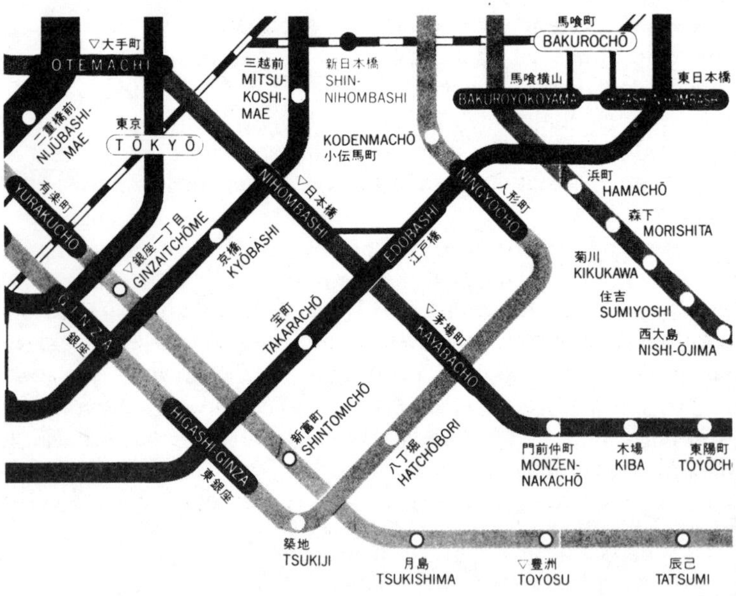

Tokyo underground system

of **nor.u**, *to get on a train*, to **okure.ru**, *to be late*. Many similar such combinations exist. Some examples include:

hanashi-au *to talk together, discuss* (**a.u** meaning *to match/harmonise*, not *to meet*)
tori-dasu *to take out, produce*
omoi-dasu *to remember* (in the sense of *take something out of your memory* – **omo.u** *to think, feel*)

3 Some notes on informal speech

As a foreigner, you may not have much opportunity to use informal speech yourself, but you will hear it all around you, and may develop friendships with people of your own age and status, with whom its use would often be appropriate. Within the family, of course, the Anzais speak informally to each other. This involves using the plain forms of verbs and adjectives at the ends of sentences, although, like Mrs Anzai, the women in particular will use ***polite*** forms as well, and certainly say **deshō** rather than **darō**. **Da** at the end of sentences will be avoided by women, even before **yo**, or softened by adding **wa** (Unit 5 Language and Society 3). In informal speech, both males and females will sometimes omit the particles **wa**, **ga** and **o**:

Kore wa kirei deshō!→Kore kirei deshō!
Nodo ga kawakimashita.→Nodo kawaita.
Gohan o tabemashita ka?→Gohan tabeta?

(For more information on informal speech, see Unit 22.)

4 *Given names in Japanese*

As we saw in Unit 1 Language and Society 1, in Japanese adults are addressed and referred to by their surnames rather than by their given names. When addressing or referring to a child, however, the given name is normally used. Common endings for girls' given names are **-ko**, **-e** and **-mi** (Yukiko, Kazue, Mayumi); for boys' names **-rō**, **-o**, **-ya**, and **-hiko** (Jirō, Kazuo, Shinya, Haruhiko). Note that in Japanese it is customary for the surname to precede the given name: Anzai Michiko rather than Michiko Anzai.

9 Kono chairo no enpitsu wa ippon ikura desu ka? *How much is one of these brown pencils?*

In this unit you will learn how to ask prices and costs per unit, count items, and use colour terms. You will also get acquainted with stock phrases used between sales personnel and customers in shopping.

Kaiwa

Ken-san wa Michiko-san to issho ni kaimono ni iku. Futari wa Ginza de chikatetsu o orite, chikaku no depāto made aruite iku. Depāto ni haitte, sōdan suru.

Michiko Ken-san, donna mono ga kaitai desu ka?
Ken Sō desu ne . . . Iroiro arimasu ga, mazu sukoshi mitai desu.
Michiko Sō desu ka? Ja, ikkai kara mimasu ka?

kaimono *shopping*
Ginza famous shopping area in Tokyo; station on the Ginza and Marunouchi underground lines
ori.ru *to climb down; get off* ● S1
depāto *department store*
sōdan (suru) *to consult* (*each other*)
sō desu ne . . . *let me see . . .*
mazu *first of all*
ikkai *ground floor* ● LS1

(*Tokei-uriba de*)

Ken Ii tokei ga arimasu ne . . . Bando dake aru ka na?
Michiko Arimasu yo, kitto . . . Hora, koko ni takusan arimasu yo.
Ken Kono akai no wa totemo ii desu ne . . .

Sumimasen, kono aka no bando wa ikura desu ka?

Ten'in Hai. Kore desu ka? Nisen happyaku-en desu ga . . .

Ken A, kore ga ii. Kore o kudasai.

Ten'in Kashikomarimashita. O-tsuke shimashō ka?

Ken Ē, o-negai shimasu.

Ken Ja, ichiman-en de o-tsuri o kudasai.

Ten'in Komakai no wa gozaimasen ka?

Ken Ē, chotto . . .

Ten'in Ichiman-en o-azukari shimasu. Shōshō o-machi kudasai.

Ten'in O-matase itashimashita. Nanasen nihyaku-en no o-tsuri desu. Arigatō gozaimashita.

tokei *watch, clock*
uriba *sales counter, section*
bando *strap, belt*
[sentence] ka na? *I wonder if [sentence]* (informal male equivalent of **kashira**)
kitto *no doubt, surely; definitely*
aka.i *red* ● S2
kono akai no *this red one* ● S3
aka noun-form of **aka.i** ● S2
ten'in *salesperson, shop assistant*
hai *at your service, sir/madam* ● LS5
en *yen*
kore ga ii *this is the right one* ● S4
kashikomarimashita *very well, sir/madam* ● LS2
o-tsuke shimashō ka? *would you like me to attach it (to your watch)?* ● S5
ichiman-en de o-tsuri o kudasai *please give me change from ¥10,000* ● S6
komakai no *'small one'* (=**komakai o-kane** *small change*)
gozaimasu formal equivalent of **aru** ● Unit 18 S2
ē, chotto . . . *I am afraid not* ● LS4
o-azukari shimasu ● LS6
o-matase shimashita *sorry to have kept you waiting* (● Unit 20 S1 on causative verb forms)
nanasen nihyaku-en no o-tsuri desu *here is your change of ¥7,200*

True or false?

1 Ken-san wa aka no bando o kaimashita.
2 Bando wa ichiman-en deshita.

(*Bunbōgu-uriba de*)

Ken	Sumimasen . . . kono chairo no enpitsu wa ippon ikura desu ka?
Ten'in	Hyaku-en desu.
Ken	Kono gurīn no wa?
Ten'in	Sore wa hyaku hachijū-en desu. Doitsu-sei de gozaimasu.
Ken	Chairo no de ii na. Sore de wa, chairoi no o sanbon kudasai. Sore kara, kōkū-binsen to fūtō ga arimasu ka?
Ten'in	Hai, gozaimasu. Kochira ni narimasu ga . . .
Ken	Fūtō wa ichimai ikura desu ka?
Ten'in	Yonjū-en desu.
Ken	Jā, kono pinku no binsen o hitotsu to, kono fūtō o jūmai kudasai. Zenbu de ikura desu ka?
Ten'in	Chōdo sen-en ni narimasu.
Ken	Hai, sen-en.
Ten'in	Chōdo itadakimasu. Maido arigatō gozaimasu.

Ken-san-tachi wa hoka ni tīshatsu o nimai to jisho o issatsu kaimashita.

bunbōgu *stationery*
chairo *brown*
ip-pon ikura desu ka? *how much is each?* (Lit. *how much for one?*) ● S7 and 8
gurīn *green*
[noun]-sei *made in/of* [*noun*]
chairo no de ii *the brown one*(*s*) *will do* ● S9
de gozaimasu formal equivalent of **desu** ● LS2 (see also Unit 18 S2)
kōkū-binsen *air* (*mail*) *letter-paper/pad*
fūtō *envelope*
kochira ni narimasu *this is it, this is the type*(*s*) *we have*
ichi-mai *one* (*flat object*) ● S7
pinku *pink*
zenbu de *altogether, in all*
sen-en ni narimasu *it comes to ¥1,000*

chōdo itadakimasu *thank you, sir/madam* (Lit. *I have received the exact amount*)
hai, sen-en *here is ¥1,000* (Lit. *here you are, ¥1,000*)
maido arigatō gozaimasu *thank you, sir/madam* (Lit. *thank you each time*)
tīshatsu *T-shirt*
jisho *dictionary*
is-satsu *one bound object, one volume* ● S7

True or false?

3 Gurīn no enpitsu wa ippon hyaku-en desu.
4 Ken-san-tachi wa tīshatsu o nimai kaimashita.

Structures

1 *Verbs with a choice between* o *and* kara

Verbs like **ori.ru** and **de.ru** (*to come/go out, leave*) commonly take **o** to mark their object, i.e. the place one alights from, or comes/goes out of:

Kyōto de kisha o orimashita. *We got off the train at Kyoto.*
Futari wa Michiko-san no ie o demashita. *The two left Michiko's house.*

Instead of **o**, **kara** also can be used in these sentences; the difference being that the idea of *out of* is emphasised with **kara**, so if you tell someone to get out of your room, **kara** is the one to use for maximum effect!

Watashi no heya kara dete yo! *Get out of my room!*

2 *Colour terms*

Words indicating colour may be **-i** adjectives (**aka.i, kiiro.i**) or nouns (**chairo**, **gurīn**). All colour adjectives have alternative noun forms (lacking the final **-i**), while not all nouns indicating colour have adjective forms. Thus the adjective **aka.i** has the noun form **aka**, whereas no adjective form is available for **midori** (the final **i** here is ***not*** an adjective ending) or **bēju** (see list). Some noun colour terms have two forms because **iro** (*colour*) can optionally be attached to them, e.g. both **midori** and **midori-iro** are used.

Below is a list of some common colour terms and any alternative forms they have.

Adjective	*Noun*	*English equivalent*
aka.i	aka	red
ao.i	ao	blue/green
kuro.i	kuro	black
shiro.i	shiro	white
kiiro.i	ki(iro)	yellow
chairo.i	cha(iro)	brown
	kon(iro)	navy blue
	midori(iro)	green
	murasaki(iro)	purple
	orenji(iro)	orange
	bēju(iro)	beige
	burū	blue
	gurē	grey
	gurīn	green

Aoi/ao is a notoriously vague term, being used for colours such as that of the sky, the sea, the green of traffic lights, the pale green of young leaves, and even the paleness of a face. **Midori** is also used for colours normally observed in nature such as fully-grown leaves and evergreens, while **gurīn** and **burū** (and most other English-derived terms) are mainly used for the colour of dresses or shoes.

When ***describing*** the colour of some object, the adjective form is used where available; when a ***choice*** of colours is made (Ken's **aka no bando**), or something is described which has two colours or more, the noun form is used.

Kono shatsu (*shirt*) wa akai desu. *This shirt is red.*
Kono shatsu no iro wa aka desu. *The colour of this shirt is red.*
Kanojo wa itsumo shiro o kimasu. *She always wears white.*

Shingō (*traffic lights*) wa aka deshita. *The traffic lights were at red.*
Kon to aka no nekutai (*tie*) ga kaitai desu. *I want to buy a red and blue tie.*

3 *Use of* no *standing in for other nouns*

In expressions such as **akai no**, **no** stands for **bando**, functioning in much the same way as *one* in English (e.g. *the red one*). Ken is able to avoid repeating **bando** as it is obvious what he is referring to.

When the salesgirl later on says **komakai no**, it is clear from the context that **no** refers to **o-kane**, even though **o-kane** has not actually been mentioned. Adjectives preceding **no** in this sense take the same form as when preceding nouns.

Salesman Kono nekutai wa ikaga desu ka? *How about this tie?*
Customer Motto kirei na no wa arimasen ka? *Haven't you got anything nicer?*
or Motto yasui no wa arimasen ka? *Aren't there any cheaper ones?*

4 Wa *and* ga *with* ii

Besides meaning *it is good*, **ii** can also mean *it's all right/I don't want it*. (Thus **ii desu** is often used to refuse an offer of something: **Kōhī o nomimasen ka? – Iie, ii desu**.)

Compare the meaning of the following pair of sentences, identical except for **wa** and **ga**:

Kore wa ii desu.
Kore ga ii desu.

Said by a customer to a salesperson, these two sentences will have a rather different effect: while the **wa** sentence means *I don't want this one*, the **ga** sentence means *This is what I want* (i.e. *I'll take it*; recall that **ii** can indicate choice or preference, Unit 8). The difference in meaning is largely due to the distinctive focus (see Unit 3 Structures 2 and Unit 10 Structures 3) provided by **wa** (as far as this one is concerned, it's ***OK***) and **ga** (***this is the one*** that's good).

5 *'Humble' offers and statements with* o-[masu *base*] suru

In Unit 8 we saw that **kudasai (mase)** can be used after **o-[-masu** base] to make a (very) polite request.

Making 'humble' offers or statements is another way of being polite to people, as in effect you raise the listener's position by lowering your own. Such offers or statements are formed by attaching **shimashō ka** or **shimasu** instead of **kudasai** to **o-[-masu** base]. The implication is that the action is to be performed for the benefit of the listener:

O-tsuke	shimashō ka? *Shall I/would you like me to attach it?*
O-mochi	shimashō ka? *Shall I hold* (**mots.u**) *it for you?*
O-yomi	shimasu. *I shall read it for you.*
O-machi	shimasu. *I shall wait for you.*

See Unit 18 for more information on humble expressions; see also Language and Society 1 and 6 in the present unit.

6 De *with amounts of money*

Here, **de** really indicates the instrument by means of which an action is performed (see Unit 4 Structures 3), in the sense of the action of buying (or selling) something for an amount of money:

Ichiman gosen-en de kaimashita. *I bought it for 15,000 Yen.*

Note that you can have two instances of **de** in a sentence, with the other one indicating the location of the action of buying:

Kono shatsu wa depāto de sanzen-en de kaimashita. *I bought this shirt at a department store for 3,000 Yen.*

De is also used in giving the total sum of money for which one wants change:

Gosen-en de o-tsuri ga arimasu ka? *Do you have change from 5,000 Yen?*

7 *Counters*

In Japanese, most nouns are counted with the use of specific 'counters'; English only does this with some nouns, for instance bread, which is counted in either *loaves* or *slices*: *one loaf/slice of bread*.

Counters are normally attached to the Chinese set of numerals, although alternative forms using Japanese numerals are commonly used for the numbers *four* and *seven*. In some combinations, numerals and counters will assume slightly different forms due to phonetic change: thus **-hon** becomes **-pon** or **-bon**. See Appendix 1 for a list of common combinations. (Counters which begin with the same consonant almost always undergo similar phonetic changes.)

Many counters are not restricted to use with one particular noun, but combine with a variety of nouns referring to things of common shape or type. Thus, **-hon** is used for long, thin, and often cylindrical, objects such as pencils, cigarettes, bottles, trees, legs and bananas. Belts, ties, and even wrinkles are also counted with **-hon**.

Flat things like sheets of paper, records, paper money, stamps, tickets and some items of apparel (flat in their folded state), like shirts and kimonos, are counted with **-mai**. For bound matter, like books, magazines and notebooks, **-satsu** is used.

Other useful counters include **-hai** for cup-, glass- and spoonfuls and such like; **-dai** for machines and appliances such as typewriters, computers, cars, and TV sets; **-wa** for birds and fowl; **-hiki** for animals and insects, and, last but not least, **-nin** for the human species (note the irregular forms **hito-ri** and **futa-ri** for one and two persons respectively).

Some more abstract nouns (plans, problems, lectures and the like) lack specific counters; for these, **-tsu** (see Unit 6) is used with the Japanese numerals 1–9. Thus, nine lectures would be counted as **kokono-tsu**, ten as **tō**, and eleven onwards with Chinese numerals (**jūichi**, **jūni** . . .). **-tsu** (or alternatively **-ko**) can also be used with some concrete objects like apples, pears, oranges, boxes and other things of varying shape. If you can't recall any specific counter for a noun, it is always worth trying **-tsu**!

Things like cigarettes and pencils can also be counted in packet- or boxfuls (**-hako**), and bottles in casefuls (**-kēsu**).

Weights, measures and currency units are also used like counters: **kiro** (kilogram/kilometre), **guramu** (gram), **en** (yen), **doru** (dollar), **pondo** (pound of weight/sterling).

Counters are most commonly used in basic structures such as **(A ni)**

B ga aru/iru and **(A wa) B o suru**; in either structure the combination **numeral + counter** occupies the same position that adverbs of quantity like **takusan** would occupy; they are also similar in that no particles are attached.

Uchi ni	neko (*cat*)	ga takusan	imasu.
Uchi ni	neko	ga san-biki	imasu.
	Nihonjin no tomodachi	ga shichi-nin	imasu.
	Wain	ga ni-hon	arimasu.
	Kami (*paper*)	ga nan-mai	arimasu ka?
	Kōgi (*lecture*)	ga iku-tsu	arimasu ka?

The first two sentences mean: *There are many cats at home*; *There are three cats at home*.

Watashi wa	jīnzu (*jeans*)	o ni-hon	kaimashita.
	Ringo	o mit-tsu/san-ko	kudasai.
	Kōhī	o nihyaku-guramu	kudasai.
	Bīru	o nan-bon	kaimashō ka?

The first sentence means: *I bought two pairs of jeans.*

Counters are also commonly added to enumerations; note that **o** and **ga** are normally added to all items but the last.

Tīshatsu to jisho o kaimashita.
→Tīshatsu o nimai to jisho o issatsu kaimashita.
Banana to remon to orenji ga arimasu.
→Banana ga sanbon to remon ga ikko/hitotsu to orenji ga sanko/mittsu arimasu.

Apart from being used after the nouns they count, counters are also found before nouns, with **no** attached. This is especially common in titles of books or films, and other situations where a scene is being set:

Shichinin no samurai. *The Seven Samurai.*
Futari no Amerikajin ga chikatetsu o orimashita. *Two Americans got off the underground.*

If understood from the context, the noun (and any attached particle) preceding the counter is omitted, leaving the combination **numeral + counter** on its own (again without particle):

> Kyō rekōdo o kaimashita. – Watashi mo sanmai kaimashita yo. *I bought some records today. – I bought three, too.*

Note that **hitori**, **futari** . . . are also used as nouns, with particles attached:

> Futari wa takusan nonda. *The two/both drank a lot.*

8 *Cost per unit*

In combination with the numeral ***one*** only, counters are used to indicate cost per unit in the following way.

Kono meron (*melon*)	wa	hito-tsu/ik-ko	sanzen-en	desu.
Banana	wa	ichi-kiro	happyaku-en	desu.
Kōhī	wa	ip-pai	ikura	desu ka?

(The meanings of the above sentences are as follows: *These melons are ¥3,000 each. Bananas are ¥800 a kilo. How much is a cup of coffee?* (Lit. *How much is coffee per cupful?*).)

9 De *with* ii

With **ii** (here used in its basic meaning *is good*), **de** indicates sufficiency:

> Yasui no de ii desu. *A/the cheap one will suffice.*
> Ashita de ii desu. *Tomorrow will do.*
> Sen-en de ii desu. *1,000 Yen will be fine.*

Renshū

1 Describe the contents of the picture on p. 118, using the pattern: **B ga [numeral + counter] arimasu/imasu**

Rei: Isu ga mittsu arimasu.

(*a*) Kodomo (*child*)
(*b*) Neko
(*c*) Hon
(*d*) Tori (*bird*)
(*e*) Pen

Then, in the same order, and preferably with a partner, practise asking questions about the contents of the picture, using the pattern:
B ga [question word + counter] arimasu ka?/imasu ka?
Rei: Isu ga ikutsu arimasu ka?

2 Ask how much ***one*** of each of the following items is:

(*a*) Shinbun
(*b*) Kan-bīru (*can of beer*)
(*c*) Kōhī
(*d*) Kodomo no shatsu
(*e*) Fuji-san no e-hagaki (*picture postcard*)
(*f*) Aka no enpitsu
(*g*) Neko
(*h*) Kono manshon ('*mansion*' *luxury apartment*)

Rei: Orenji wa hitotsu ikura desu ka?

This time, ask the question as before and then reply as indicated, using **no**. (Preferably do this with a partner.)
Rei: orenji (ōkii, ¥100)
Q Orenji wa hitotsu ikura desu ka?
A Ōkii no wa hitotsu hyaku-en desu.

(*i*) Shinbun (Furansugo, ¥1,000)
(*j*) Kan-bīru (tsumetai, ¥600)
(*k*) Kodomo no shatsu (Itaria-sei, ¥20,000)
(*l*) Fuji-san no e-hagaki (chiisai, ¥120)
(*m*) Neko (sono genki na, ¥10,000).

3 Complete by supplying the appropriate counter:
Rei: Ringo o (4) kudasai: Ringo o yottsu kudasai.

(*a*) Supōtsukā (*sports car*) o (5) kaimashita.
(*b*) Kitte o (10) kaimashita.
(*c*) Kinō hon o (3) yomimashita.
(*d*) Maiasa tōsuto (*toast*) o (2) to yude-tamago (*boiled egg*) o (2) tabemasu.
(*e*) Sore kara, kōhī o (1) nomimasu.

4 How would you say the following in Japanese? (If in difficulty, search the text for clues.)

(*a*) Excuse me, but where is the camera sales counter?
(*b*) Do you have lenses (**renzu**) by themselves?
(*c*) How much is this small one? – This one? It's ¥35,000.
(*d*) How much are the apples? – ¥50 each.
(*e*) In that case, I'd like five please. – That will be ¥250.
(*f*) Yesterday, Tarō ate four hamburgers (**hanbāgā**) and six ice creams. Last night he fell ill (**byōki ni naru**).

Language and Society

1 *Counting floors*

Ik-kai (ground floor) literally means *first floor*, as Japanese follows American usage. When converting British English floor numbering into Japanese, it is therefore necessary to add one number: e.g. *second floor* becomes **san-gai**.

2 *Speech levels*

In Japanese, levels of speech play an important role in differentiating people's status in society. Customers, for instance, are treated as superiors by sales personnel, who will use very polite language towards them. Conversely, some customers, in particular rural males, will speak down to the persons serving them.

Such a customer might use (not necessary consistently) **ikura**? without the ending **desu ka** that is used between equals in normal polite conversation, whereas salespeople will often employ the very polite ending **de gozaimasu** instead of **desu**. Another example is the assistant's use of **kashikomarimashita**; this form would never be used by a customer.

The difference in status is also obvious in that sales personnel will thank customers very politely for any purchase, while customers will not normally say 'thank you' at all; if they do, they are likely to use a less polite expression such as **dōmo** or **arigatō**, or perhaps the combination **dōmo arigatō**.

3 *Negative questions and their answers*

Komakai no wa arimasen ka? (*Haven't you anything smaller?*) is a question containing a negative (**arimasen**). In English, if the answer to such a question uses a positive verb, it will begin with *Yes*; if the answer uses a negative verb, it will begin with *No*. In Japanese, however, the use of *Yes* or *No* depends on whether the reply agrees, or disagrees, with the assumption behind the question:

Question	Komakai no wa gozaimasen ka? *Haven't you any change?*
Answer	Hai/ē, arimasen. *Yes, you're right, I haven't* (=*No, I haven't*).
Answer	Iie, arimasu. *No, you're wrong, I have* (=*Yes, I have*).

Thus, if the answer also contains a negative (**arimasen**, etc.), it is introduced by **hai** (or the less formal **ē**) in the sense of *Yes, you are correct in what you suggest*; if, on the other hand, the answer diverges from what has been suggested in the question, it is introduced by **iie** (*No, what you are suggesting is not correct*). Such answers are normally accompanied (or replaced) by nodding (**hai**, **ē**) or shaking (**iie**) of the head.

Invitations/offers that are made in the form of a negative question are answered differently:

A Eiga ni ikimasen ka? *How about going to see a film?*
B Arigatō gozaimasu. *Thank you (for inviting me).*

To decline the offer, one normally gives some excuse (**isogashii**, etc.), but it is also very common just to intimate vaguely that you cannot go by using an unfinished sentence like: **Sumimasen ga, kyō wa chotto . . .** (on **chotto**, see below).

4 Ē, chotto . . .

This is an unfinished answer: Ken's answer to the salesgirl's negative question would in full be:

A Ē, chotto arimasen.

Chotto (*a bit; somehow*) is commonly used in this way to turn down requests, invitations, etc. without being too abrupt.

5 *Uses of* hai *and* naruhodo

Apart from its meaning of (formal) *yes*, **hai** is also used to indicate that one understands a question or follows what is being said. It does not necessarily signal agreement, so beware, particularly in business negotiations! This use is especially common on the telephone, where it is not possible to rely on other signals of being 'with it', such as nodding. In informal conversation, **ē** and **(u)n** are widely used instead of **hai**, again accompanied by frequent nods.

Another way of chiming in with others' remarks is by saying **naruhodo** (*I see, indeed*, see Unit 14 **Kaiwa**). It can be used instead of **hai** for the sake of variety.

Hai (dōzo) is also used informally in the sense of *here you are* when handing over things.

6 O-azukari shimasu

This is a formal expression used to acknowledge that you take custody of some object or person. In particular it is used by sales personnel as a verbal confirmation that you have paid and that some change is due. Compare this to **chōdo itadakimasu**, which is used to acknowledge that you have paid the exact amount.

10 Bīru mo wain mo reizōko ni ireta? *Did you put both the beer and the wine in the fridge?*

This unit reviews the various uses of the particles **wa**, **ga** and **mo** that are so important in the language, including some new uses such as how to say *both . . . and* and *neither . . . nor*. You will also become familiar with a way of linking nouns in the sense of *among others*, and find some information about the way Japanese entertain their guests.

Kaiwa

Doyōbi no gogo, Anzai-sensei no kazoku wa Hādo-san-tachi o shokuji ni shōtai shita. Sore de, Anzai-sensei no okusan to Michiko-san wa ima yūhan no yōi ni isogashii.

Okusan	Bīru mo wain mo reizōko ni ireta?
Michiko	Un, ireta wa yo.
Okusan	Hādo-san-tachi wa o-sashimi ya o-sakana no shioyaki nado wa daijōbu kashira?
Michiko	Daijōbu yo, okāsan.
Okusan	A, dezāto ga nai deshō!
Michiko	Kēki ga chanto aru ja nai desu ka! Iyā ne, okāsan, wasureta no?
Okusan	A, sō datta wa ne. Yokatta . . .
Michiko	Okāsan hitoyasumi shite, o-cha demo nomanai?
Okusan	Sore ga ii wa ne.

kazoku *family*
shokuji (suru) *a meal*
shōtai (suru) *to invite*
yūhan *dinner, supper*
yōi (suru) *preparation*
[noun] ni/de isogashi.i *to be busy with [noun]*
reizōko *refrigerator*

[noun] mo [noun] mo *both [noun] and [noun]* ● S2
ire.ru *to put in, insert*
sashimi *sliced uncooked seafood*
[noun] ya [noun] *[noun] and [noun]* ● S1
shioyaki dish of whole broiled fish with a coat of salt
[noun] nado *[noun] and the like, etcetera* ● S1
dezāto *dessert*
chanto *properly*
aru ja nai desu ka! *Come on, there is!* ● LS2
iyā ne *oh no/dear me* (fem.)
wasure.ru *to forget*
hitoyasumi (suru) *to take a little rest*
[noun] demo *[noun] or such like* ● S3

True or false?

1 Michiko-san wa bīru mo wain mo reizōko ni irenakatta.
2 Dezāto ga aru.

Yoru ni natta ga, Hādo-san-tachi wa nakanaka konai . . .

Okusan Hādo-san-tachi wa osoi desu ne. Dō shita n' deshō . . .
Anzai-sensei Michi ni mayotta no ka na?
Michiko Tomu-san wa kita koto ga aru kara, daijōbu yo.
Okusan Sore ni shite mo osoi wa yo. Ne, anata, denwa shimashō yo.
Anzai-sensei Wakatta yo, suru yo.
(*denwa de*) Moshi-moshi. A, Hādo-san desu ne. Anzai desu ga, mada irasshaimasen ka? E? Iyā, kore wa shitsurei shimashita. Dōmo, uchi no kāsan wa kioku ga warukute ne. Sore ja, raishū no doyōbi ni o-machi shite imasu. Sayōnara.
Minna Okāsan!!

nakanaka [negative verb] *to be slow/late [in doing something]; [do something] with difficulty*
dō shita n' deshō *I wonder what's happened*
michi ni mayo.u *to lose one's way, get lost*
sore ni shite mo *even so, despite that*
denwa (suru) *telephone*

moshi-moshi *hello* (telephone, etc.)
mada (*not*) *yet* ● Unit 11 S6
irassharu honorific for **kuru** (● Unit 18 S1)
kore wa shitsurei shimashita *I am so sorry about this*
uchi no kāsan *my wife* (Lit. *our mother*), less formal than **kanai**
kioku (*memory*) **ga warui** *to have a bad memory, be forgetful* ● S4
warukute conjunctive form of **warui**, here giving a reason ● Unit 11 S5
o-machi shite imasu *we will be waiting for you* (● Unit 11 S2 for the **-te imasu** form)

True or false?

3 Tomu-san wa kita koto ga nai.
4 Anzai-san wa Hādo-san ni denwa shita.

Structures

1 [noun] ya [noun] (nado)

In Unit 8, we saw that **to** implies that every relevant item has been mentioned. **Ya** also links nouns in the meaning of *and*, but the implication is that not all relevant items have been mentioned. **Ya** does not come after the last item, which can, however, be followed by **nado** (*and others*), which serves to reinforce the meaning of **ya**:

Bīru ya wain (nado) o kaimashita. *I bought beer, wine and such like.*
Orenji ya ichigo (nado) ga arimasu. *There are oranges, strawberries and other fruit.*
Tōkyō ya Kyōto (nado) ni/e ikimashita. *We went to Tokyo and Kyoto, among other places.*

Nado can also be used on its own:

Bīru nado o kaimashita. *I bought beer, among other things.*
Orenji nado ga arimasu. *There are oranges and such like.*

2 *More on* mo *(including summary of its uses)*

Unlike **to**, which can be attached to the last noun in a sequence, and **ya**, which cannot, **mo** ***must*** be repeated after each noun.

When **mo** is used after one noun only, it is equivalent to English *also*, *too* in positive sentences (see Unit 1), whereas in negative sentences it means (*not*) *either*. Recall the following example from the Unit 6 **Kaiwa**:

Ha mo migakanakatta deshō? *You didn't brush your teeth either, did you?*

When **mo** is used with more than one noun, the meaning is *both . . . and* in a positive sentence, and *neither . . . nor* in a negative one:

Tarō-kun mo	Michiko-san mo	kimashita.	*Both Tarō and Michiko came.*
		kimasen deshita.	*Neither Tarō nor Michiko came.*
Orenji mo	ichigo mo	kaimashita.	*We bought oranges as well as strawberries.*
		kaimasen deshita.	*We bought neither oranges nor strawberries.*

Mo replaces **wa** and **ga** and, usually, **o**:

Watashi	wa	ikimashita→	Jiru-san	mo	ikimashita.
Tomu-san	ga	kita. →	Michiko-san	mo	kita.
Bīru	o	katta. →	Wain	(o) mo	katta.

De, **ni**, etc. combine with **mo** as **de mo**, **ni mo**, etc. Below are some examples:

Rajio (*radio*)	de	mo	kikimashita.	*I heard it on the radio, too.*
Michiko-san	ni	mo	aimashita.	*I met Michiko, too.*
Yokohama	e	mo	ikitai desu.	
Tomu-san	kara	mo	denwa ga arimashita.	

Resutoran	de	mo	bā	de	mo	bīru o nomimashita.
Doyōbi	ni	mo	nichiyōbi	ni	mo	uchi ni imasu.

Recall also the use of **mo** after question words in negative sentences (Unit 6 Structures 6).

3 [noun] demo

Demo is distinct from the combination **de mo** and can therefore be attached to other particles, such as **ni** (although it replaces **wa**, **ga** and **o**).

Demo has a similar effect to English expressions like *or something*, making an invitation or suggestion less direct:

O-cha demo nomanai? *How about a cup of tea or something?*
Doyōbi ni demo ikimashō. *Let's go on, say, Saturday.*

4 *Uses of* wa *and* ga

Let us briefly review the uses of **wa** and **ga** that we have encountered thus far:

(*a*) In the pattern **A wa B desu**, **wa** signals that **B desu** is a statement about **A**.

Kore	wa shinbun	desu.
Kono shinbun	wa Nihon no	desu.
Watashi no shinbun	wa Nihon no	de wa arimasen.

As we have noted in Unit 3, **A** is already known or understood; the focus is therefore on **B desu**. The pattern **A ga B desu**, on the other hand, focuses on **A**. Question-words like **nani**, **dare** cannot take **wa**, as this would contradict their role of asking about focal information, for example when talking about photos:

Kore ga Michiko-san desu. ***This*** *is Michiko.*
Dore ga Tomu-san desu ka? *Which one is Tom?*

(*b*) In Unit 3, we saw that **wa** can also signal a contrast; this distinction depends on the context, in other words, ***another*** noun C, which contrasts with A, must be either present or implied. In this use, **wa** replaces **ga** or **o**, while it combines with other particles as **ni wa**, **de wa**, etc.:

Wain wa aru ga, bīru wa arimasen. *We have* ***wine*** *but no* ***beer***. (replacing **ga**)
Wain wa katta ga, bīru wa kaimasen deshita. *I bought* ***wine***, *but not any* ***beer***. (replacing **o**)
Tōkyō ni wa itta ga, Kyōto ni wa ikimasen deshita. *I went to* ***Tokyo***, *but not* ***Kyoto***.

Tōkyō de wa mita ga, Rondon de wa mimasen deshita. *I saw (some) in **Tokyo**, but not in **London**.*
Kyōto ni wa ikimashita. *I **did** go to **Kyoto**.* (implying that there are places where you ***didn't*** go)

Wa is often found in negative sentences (negatives express some kind of contrast in Japanese – perhaps there is an implicit contrast to positive situations):

Kinō wa ikimasen deshita. *I didn't go **yesterday**.*
Tako wa suki ja arimasen. *I don't like **octopus**.*
Komakai no wa arimasen ka? (Unit 9) *Don't you have anything **smaller**?*

(*c*) We also met **wa** and **ga** in the patterns **B (ni) wa A ga aru** (Unit 3) and **A wa X ga hoshii** (Unit 8), which indicate possession and desire, respectively. In either case the object of possession/desire is marked by **ga**, whereas the person possessing or desiring is marked by **wa**.

Similar to these is the pattern **A (ni) wa B ga wakar.u/ir.u** *A understands/needs B*; the object of understanding/need is marked by **ga**, and the person understanding/needing by **wa**:

Ken-san wa Nihongo ga wakarimasu. *Ken understands Japanese.*
Watashi ni wa ano hito ga wakarimasen. *I don't understand that person.*
Watashi wa o-kane ga iru. *I need money.*

See also Unit 14 Structures 5 (**A (ni) wa B ga dekiru**).

Whenever you have both **wa** and **ga**, **wa** will always come first.

(*d*) Another **wa – ga** pattern that came up in Unit 8 is **A wa B ga [adjective]/A wa B ga [noun] desu**; below are some further examples:

Uchi no kāsan	wa	kioku	ga	warui desu. *Mother has a bad memory.*
Michiko	wa	me	ga	ōkii desu. *Michiko has large eyes.*
Kono sētā	wa	iro	ga	kirei desu. *This sweater is a pretty colour.*
Kanojo	wa	otōsan	ga	sensei desu. *Her father is a teacher.*

These sentences are an extension of the basic **A wa B desu** pattern with **B desu** becoming **B ga [adjective]/[noun] desu**. In this pattern, **B** is something that belongs to **A**, and you might therefore expect **no** instead of **wa**:

Uchi no kāsan	no	kioku	wa	warui desu.
Kanojo	no	otōsan	wa	sensei desu.

In fact, these sentences are acceptable, but the **wa** – **ga** way of putting this is more natural, idiomatic Japanese (see also Unit 8, Structures 6).

(*e*) As we saw above, **A wa** signals that a considered statement/comment is about to be made (about **A**). If, for instance, you make a well-considered comment about Tarō, having long been aware of his good looks, you would say:

Tarō-kun wa hansamu desu.

When some situation is, however, perceived spontaneously (by the five senses), **ga** is normally used; imagine, for instance, that it suddenly occurs to you that Tarō (because of the light, the way he is dressed, etc.) is really quite handsome. If you pass this observation straight on to your friend, you would say:

Tarō-kun ga hansamu desu ne!

Recall also the following sentences, both spontaneous expressions:

Kimochi ga ii desu. (Unit 7)
Hito ga ōi ne. (Unit 8)

Adjectives like **suki na**, **kirai na** and **iya na**, too, are generally concerned with the spontaneous expression of like/dislike, and therefore mostly take **ga** rather than **wa**. Below are some more examples:

A, densha ga kita. *Oh, the train is coming.*
Mizu ga tsumetai! *The water is cold!*
Ano hito ga kirai desu. *I hate that person.*

(*f*) **Ga** and **wa** in subordinate sentences. Recall that **ga** is normally used in subordinate sentences if they have a different subject from the main sentence:

Tenki ga ii kara, oyogi ni ikimashō. *Let's go for a swim because the weather is nice.*

Rōrusu–roisu ga takai kara, watashi wa kaimasen. *The Rolls Royce is expensive, so I am not going to buy it.*

When there is a sense of contrast, however, **wa** is used:

Rōrusu–roisu wa takai kara, watashi wa kaimasen. *Rolls Royces (unlike some other cars I can think of) are expensive, so I shan't buy one.*

See also Unit 14 Structures 1 about the use of **ga** in relative clauses.

Renshū

1 It's Sunday, but you don't feel like doing anything (including staying at home!). Make unenthusiastic suggestions to your girlfriend based on the cues:

Rei: Disuko ni ikimashō ka?→Disuko ni demo ikimashō ka?

(*a*) Terebi o mimashō ka?
(*b*) Ginza e ikimashō ka?
(*c*) O-sake o nomimashō ka?
(*d*) Yakyū o mi ni ikimashō ka?

2 You have been out shopping; tell your friend what you bought by using **mo**, **ya (nado)** or **to** as indicated in the cues to join the listed items.

Rei: binsen, fūtō, pen (mo)→Binsen mo fūtō mo pen mo kaimashita.

(*a*) Remon, orenji, painappuru, ichigo (to)
(*b*) Zasshi, shinbun (ya)
(*c*) Bīru, wain, uisukī, igusuri (mo)
(*d*) Tako, sakana (ya, nado)

3 Fill in the blanks, choosing between **wa** and **ga**.

(*a*) Kinō . . . . . kaisha ni ikimasen deshita.
(*b*) Okāsan, tomodachi . . . . . kimashita.
(*c*) Rondon . . . . . kōen . . . . . ōi desu.
(*d*) Orenji . . . . . katta ga, painappuru . . . . . kaimasen deshita.
(*e*) Ken-san . . . . . se . . . . . takai desu.
(*f*) Kyō . . . . . totemo kimochi . . . . . ii desu.

Language and Society

1 *Entertaining guests in Japan*

The Japanese go to great lengths in entertaining guests. Partly because of the restricted space at home and the difficulties of preparing a proper banquet in the kitchen, most entertaining takes place outside in specialist establishments (**sushiya**, **tenpuraya**, etc.) or in Japanese, Chinese or Western restaurants.

Occasionally, however, one receives the honour of being invited to a Japanese home. There one is likely to be plied with a great variety and quantity of food and drink, all prepared by the lady of the house, although it is also quite common to supplement the home fare by home-deliveries (**demae**) of delicacies like **sushi** or **unagi** (broiled eel).

When invited to a meal by someone, at home or in a restaurant, it is normal to say **itadakimasu** before starting to eat, and **gochisōsama deshita** as an expression of thanks directly afterwards, but also again when leaving. When meeting your host next time, it is customary to acknowledge the favour again by saying **Yūbe [senjitsu] wa gochisōsama deshita** (*thank you for last night's [the other day's] meal*), something that is easily forgotten by us Westerners as we do not have such a custom!

broiled eel

2 *Negative questions used as emphatic statements*

Imagine that your wife tries to stop your child from watching a film on TV, whereas you think that it's perfectly OK. The Japanese equivalent of reactions like *come on, don't be so fussy/surely it's all right* will often take the form of a negative question:

Ii ja nai ka! (Lit. *It's all right, isn't it!*)

Or you might try and stop your wife from buying a new dress; her reply may well be a defiant:

Yasui ja nai! *Oh really, it's not expensive!*

The same pattern is often used when someone has failed to notice the obvious, as when Mrs Anzai forgets that the dessert has already been taken care of; it would also be used when someone is looking for his spectacles, although they are in a very obvious place:

Tēburu no ue ni aru ja nai! *Really, they're on the table, right in front of you!*

11 Yamada-san ga matte iru
Yamada-san is waiting

In this unit you will learn how to express the idea of continuous action, and other uses of the **-te** form of the verb; you will also encounter the conjunctive form of adjectives. In addition, there will be some information on working in Japanese companies.

Kaiwa

Yūbe Tomu-san wa shigoto no kankei de osoku made nondari, uta o utattari shite ita. Sore de kesa nebō shita. Kōhī o ippai nonde kara isoide dekaketa ga, sore de mo sanjippun chikoku shita. Hisho no Yamada-san ga jimusho de matte iru.

Tomu	Ohayō.
Yamada	Shachō – daijōbu desu ka? Shinpai shite orimashita.
Tomu	Osoku natte warukatta ne. Kesa iroiro taihen datta kara.
Yamada	Sō desu ka? Asa-gohan wa mada deshō?
Tomu	O-naka ga itakute, nani mo tabete inai. (*Techō o miru*) Ēto, kyō wa Yamanaka Māketingu no Suzuki-san ga kuru darō?
Yamada	Mō miete imasu. Ōsetsu-shitsu de o-cha o nonde irasshaimasu.
Tomu	Taihen da!

kankei *relation, connection*
[noun] no kankei de *in connection/relation with [noun]*
nondari, -tari form of **nom.u** *drink (and do other things)* ● S1
uta o uta.u *to sing (a song)*

shite ita past form of **-te iru** *was (do)-ing* ● S2
nebō (suru) *to oversleep, get up late*
[verb]-te kara *after doing [verb]* ● S3
sore de mo *even so*
chikoku (suru) *to be late* (**kaisha ni chikoku suru** *to be late for the office*)
hisho no Yamada-san *Yamada-san, his secretary* ● S4
hisho *(personal) secretary*
jimusho *one's place of work, office*
shachō *head of a firm* (here used as a form of address)
shinpai (suru) *worry* (**[noun] o shinpai suru** *to worry about [noun]*)
orimashita humble equivalent of **imashita** ● Unit 18 S1
Osoku natte warukatta *It was bad of me to be late* ● Unit 13 S4
asa-gohan *breakfast* (Lit. *morning-meal*)
o-naka *stomach*
itakute conjunctive form of **ita.i** *painful* ● S5
mada *(not) yet* ● S6
techō *pocket diary/notebook*
Yamanaka Māketingu *Yamanaka Marketing* (name of imaginary firm)
mō miete imasu *(he) has already come* ● S6
mie.ru (here) honorific equivalent of **kuru** ● Unit 18 S1
ōsetsu-shitsu *reception room*
irasshaimasu honorific equivalent of **imasu** ● Unit 18 S1

True or false?

1 Yūbe Tomu-san wa uchi de Nihongo o benkyō shita.
2 Suzuki-san wa ōsetsu-shitsu de matte iru.

Tomu-san wa shorui o matomete kara ōsetsu-shitsu ni hairu. Suzuki-san wa o-cha o nomi-nagara shorui o yonde iru.

Tomu Suzuki-san—taihen o-matase shimashita. Dōmo . . .

Suzuki Ie, ie, dō itashimashite. Repōto o mada yonde inakatta kara kaette yokatta desu.

Tomu Sō desu ka? Ano repōto wa nagai desu ne. Boku mo mada zenbu yonde imasen.

Suzuki Shikashi, Hādo-san, kao-iro ga warui desu ne. Hataraki-sugi ja nai desu ka?

shorui *documents, papers*
matome.ru *to collect together, put in order*
[-masu base**]-nagara** *while doing* [*verb*] ● S7
dō itashimashite *don't mention it*
repōto *report*
kaette *on the contrary, in fact*
kao-iro ga warui (*you*) *look unwell*
kao-iro *facial colour/complexion*
hataraki-sugi noun form of **hataraki-sugiru**
[-masu base**]-sugi.ru** *to over-*[*verb*]

True or false?

3 Suzuki-san wa o-cha o nomanakatta.
4 Suzuki-san wa yūbe repōto o zenbu yonda.

Structures

1 *The* -tari *form*

The **-tari** form of a verb is made by adding **ri** to the plain past form of the verb(s) in question. It is possible to have only one verb in the **-tari** form, or a whole series, but the sequence must finish with **suru**, or less often **da**, in the appropriate tense and level of politeness:

Terebi o mitari, hon o yondari shimashita/deshita. *I watched television, read a book . . .*

There is no straight English equivalent for **-tari**; it implies that the verb to which it is attached represents merely one activity out of several that actually took place. (**Nado** performs a similar function with nouns, see Unit 10 Structures 1.) Thus, in the sentence above, the two verbs in the **-tari** form are examples of what I did; they represent the sort of activities in which I was involved, but are not an accurate and exhaustive list. It is possible to string more than two verbs together in this way, and it is also possible to give just one verb:

Doyōbi wa tomodachi ni attari shimasu. *On Saturdays, I meet friends (and so on).*

The **-tari** form can also be used for two actions taking place alternatively. In this case, the two verbs in question are

(*a*) opposites:

ittari kitari (suru) *to go and come*, i.e. *to go to and fro*
naitari warattari (suru) *to laugh and cry* (**nak.u** *to cry;* **wara.u** *to laugh* – note that in this phrase the verbs combine in the opposite order from English)

or (*b*) sets of positive and negative pairs:

ittari ikanakattari (suru) *to sometimes go and sometimes not go*
benkyō shitari shinakattari (suru) *to sometimes study and sometimes not* (note that it is not necessary to repeat **benkyō**)

Tarō-kun wa tattari suwattari shimashita. *Tarō kept on standing up and then sitting down.* (**tats.u** *to stand*)
Michiko-san wa Ken-san ni attari awanakattari shimasu. *Michiko goes through phases of meeting Ken, and then not meeting him.*

2 [verb]-te i.ru

This combination of the **-te** form of verbs and the verb **iru** is used in three ways. Note that it can have inanimate as well as animate subjects despite the presence of **iru**, and that **da**, **aru**, and **iru** itself, have no **-te iru** form.

(*a*) ***Habitual actions***
This overlaps with the use of the present form to describe habitual action (Unit 4 Structures 1), but puts more stress on the repetition of the action. It will often occur when describing what someone does for a living, or with words like **itsu mo** or **mainichi**:

Watashi wa Nihon de Eigo o oshiete imasu. *I teach English in Japan.*
Suzuki-san wa maiban o-sake o nonde imasu. *Suzuki-san drinks every evening.*

(*b*) ***Continuous actions***

Here **-te iru** is equivalent to *is -ing* in English, describing actions which are actually going on in the present, or which were going on at some time in the past:

Nani o shite imasu ka? *What are you doing?*
A Dōshite konakatta n' desu ka? *Why didn't you come?*
B Terebi o mite ita kara. *Because I was watching television.*

It can also refer to what you will be doing in the future. For example, you arrange to wait until a friend has finished clearing up at work:

Asoko de matte imasu. *I'll be waiting over there.*

(See also the humble equivalent **O-machi shite imasu** in Unit 10 **Kaiwa**.) As would seem logical, only actions which do in fact occur continuously take the **-te iru** form in this sense. As we shall see in (*c*), however, some actions which English thinks of as occurring continuously are thought of in Japanese as involving an immediate change of state.

(*c*) ***States resulting from actions***

This sense of **-te iru** has no one English equivalent, but it is probably nearest to the 'present in the past' tense formed with *have*. It conveys the idea that while the action of the verb has already taken place, the state which it has brought about is still in existence. It is often used in conjunction with the adverbs **mō** and **mada** (Structures 6).

-te iru in this sense often occurs with a group of verbs which in Japanese, as mentioned above, are thought of as involving an immediate change of state rather than happening over time. Take, for example, the verb **kekkon suru**, to get married:

Honda-san wa ashita kekkon shimasu. *Honda-san is getting married tomorrow.*
Miura-san wa kyonen kekkon shimashita. *Miura-san got married last year.*

In the **-te iru** form, however, it refers to the state that Miura-san is in now, as a result of getting married:

Miura-san wa kekkon shite imasu. *Miura-san is married.*

We can use this form in the negative too, as follows:

Honda-san wa kekkon shite imasen. *Honda-san is not married.*

Here are some other verbs of this type. Many of them are intransitive (Unit 12 Structures 1), i.e. they do not take objects. **Ak.u**, for example, means *to open* in the sense of a door opening of its own accord, not *to open* in the sense of someone opening a door.

ak.u (intrans.) *to open, become vacant*	**aite iru** *to be open, vacant*
shimar.u (intrans.) *to close, shut*	**shimatte iru** *to be closed, shut*
hajimar.u (intrans.) *to begin*	**hajimatte iru** *to have begun, be under way*
owar.u (trans. & intrans.) *to end*	**owatte iru** *to be ended, over*
futor.u (intrans.) *to become fat*	**futotte iru** *to be fat*
yase.ru (intrans.) *to become thin*	**yasete iru** *to be thin*
deki.ru (intrans.) *to be made, prepared*	**dekite iru** *to be ready, completed*
ki.ru (trans.) *to put on, wear* (for items worn from the shoulders, e.g. shirts, dresses)	**kite iru** *to have on, be wearing*
hak.u (trans.) *to put on, wear* (for items worn from the waist downwards, e.g. skirts, shoes)	**haite iru** *to have on, be wearing*
oboe.ru (trans) *to learn, memorise* (rather than study)	**oboete iru** *to remember* (i.e. *not forget*, as opposed to **omoidasu** *to remember something forgotten*)
shin.u (intrans.) *to die*	**shinde iru** *to be dead*
tsukare.ru (intrans.) *to get tired*	**tsukarete iru** *to be tired*

Asa-gohan ga dekite imasu yo. *Breakfast is ready.*

A Ano nomiya o oboete imasu ka? *Do you remember that bar?*

B O-sake o takusan nonda kara, nani mo oboete imasen. *I drank so much, I don't remember anything.*

Also note the following expressions:

nodo ga kawak.u *to get thirsty* | **nodo ga kawaite iru** *to be thirsty*

o-naka ga suk.u *to get hungry* (Lit. (*my*) *stomach gets empty*) | **o-naka ga suite iru** *to be hungry*

With these verbs which involve an immediate change of state, there is very often little difference in actual meaning between the past tense and the **-te iru** form:

Ā, tsukaremashita! *I'm tired!* (Lit. *I got tired*)
Ā, tsukarete imasu! *I'm tired!* (Lit. *I am in the state which results from getting tired.*)

In the case of the former, you have just finished doing something which has made you tired – perhaps you have just been carrying something heavy. In the case of the latter, you are in a general state of tiredness – you are having a busy week at the office.

The verbs of motion **iku**, **kuru**, **hairu**, **deru**, **dekakeru**, **ochiru**, but not **aruku** and **oyogu**, belong to this group. In the **-te iru** form they therefore refer to where you are after moving. For example, Honda-san was in the same room as you, but has just gone to the bank (**ginkō**). If someones comes in and asks:

Honda-san wa doko ni imasu ka?

you can, of course, just reply:

Ginkō ni ikimashita.

However, you will also hear:

Ginkō ni itte imasu.

in the sense of *He/she is in the state which results from going to the bank*; i.e. *He/she has gone to the bank/is at the bank*. Similarly, note:

Tomodachi ga kite imasu yo. *A friend of yours has come/is here.*
Sumisu-san wa Igirisu ni kaette imasu. *Mr/Ms Smith has gone back to/is back in England.*
Handobaggu ni nani ga haitte imasu ka? *What is in your handbag?*
Nani ka ochite imasu yo. *Something has fallen./There's something on the floor./You've dropped something.*

Naru behaves in a similar way:

Shizuka ni natte imasu ne. *Hasn't it got quiet?*

The **-te iru** form of these verbs cannot be used in the (*b*) sense introduced above, but in fact, in English, the *is -ing* form of many of them does not refer to continuous action, but to the future. The Japanese equivalent of *He's coming in a second* is therefore **Sugu kimasu**. Similarly:

Ginkō wa nanji ni akimasu ka. *When is the bank opening?*
Doa ga shimarimasu. *The doors* (**doa**) *are closing*. (station warning)

Finally, note some verbs which are more likely to be used in the **-te iru** form than in the present form:

mots.u *to hold, take* — **motte iru** *to be holding, possess, have*

Mochimashō ka? *Shall I carry it (for you)?*
Nani o motte imasu ka? *What are you holding/have you got there?*
Watashi wa kamera o motte imasen. *I haven't got/don't own a camera.*

([place] ni) sum.u *to take up residence* — **sunde iru** *to be settled, live (in a place)*

Itaria ni sumitai desu. *I want to live in Italy.*
Anzai-san wa Yokohama ni sunde imasu. *Anzai-san lives in Yokohama.*

shir.u *to get to know* — **shitte iru** *to know (things, people)*

Ken-san o doko de shirimashita ka? *Where did you get to know Ken?*

Suzuki-san wa Furansu o shitte imasu. *Suzuki-san knows France.*

I don't know does not usually occur in the **-te iru** form, but is simply **shirimasen**:

Michiko-san no denwa bangō o shitte imasu ka?
Iie, shirimasen.

The verb **([company] ni) tsutome.ru**, *to work (for a firm)*, is also normally found only in the **-te iru** form.

Suzuki-san wa Yamanaka Māketingu ni tsutomete imasu. *Suzuki-san works for Yamanaka Marketing.*

In informal situations, the **i** of the **iru/imasu** in **-te iru** constructions is often lost:

Nani o nonde 'ru no?
Yasete 'masu ne.

3 [verb]-te kara *after/since doing [verb]*

We have already met **[noun] kara** meaning *from/after/since* in a temporal sense (Unit 7 Structures 3). If you want to use *after* with a verb rather than with a noun, you put the verb into the **-te** form:

Sore	kara	doko e ikimashita ka? *Where did you go after that?*
Gohan o tabete	kara	dekakemashō. *Let's set out after having our meal.*

If the subject of the **-te kara** part of the sentence is different from that of the main sentence, it will take **ga** (Unit 10 Structures 3):

Eiga ga owatte kara kissaten ni hairimashita. *After the film was over we went into a coffee shop.*

Honda-san ga kekkon shite kara rokunen ni narimasu. *It's six years since Honda-san got married.*

Notice that, as with many European languages, if the situation in the main sentence after **-te kara** is still going on in the present (in other words, where *since* rather than *after* would be used in English) Japanese will use the present tense of adjectives, of **da**, **iru**, and **aru**, and the **-te iru** form of other verbs, where English uses the past tense with *have*:

Gakki ga hajimatte kara mainichi isogashii desu. *Since the term* (**gakki**) *started, I have been busy every day.*
Nihon ni kite kara jikan ga amari arimasen. *Since coming to Japan I haven't had much time.*
Kesa eki de soba o tabete kara nani mo tabete imasen. *I haven't eaten anything since having some noodles* (**soba**) *at the station this morning.*

This use of the **-te** form with **kara** must not be confused with **kara** meaning *because* following the final forms of verbs (Unit 6 Structures 4).

4 *The appositional* no

In this variation of the **X no B** pattern (Unit 1 Structures 6), **X**, a general noun, tells us who or what, **B**, a proper noun, is:

tomodachi no Jon *my friend John*
ha-isha no Anzai-sensei *Anzai-sensei, the dentist*
shūten no Ueno-eki *Ueno station, the terminus* (**shūten**)

5 *The conjunctive form of adjectives*

The conjunctive form of **na** adjectives is made by turning **na** to **de**; in the case of **-i** adjectives, **-kute** is substituted for **-i**. Note that **ii** becomes **yokute**. In the case of adjectives in the negative, **nai** becomes **nakute** (**wa** is sometimes omitted from the negatives of **na** adjectives):

shizuka na taka.i	shizuka de takakute	shizuka de (wa)/ja nakute takakunakute

This form has functions similar to the **-te** form of verbs. One use, for example, is in joining two adjectives together, or in joining a sentence which ends in an adjective to one which ends in a verb:

Kore wa shizuka de kirei na resutoran desu. *This is a quiet, clean restaurant.*
Ken-san wa se ga takakute hansamu desu. *Ken is tall and handsome.*
Rondon wa samukunakute, honto ni yokatta desu. *London wasn't cold, and I really liked it/It was really good as London wasn't cold.*
Suzuki-san wa o-sake ga suki de takusan nomimasu. *Suzuki-san likes sake and drinks a lot.*

Often, as in the last two or three sentences, the conjunctive form contains the implication that the first half of the sentence is the reason for the second half (Unit 13 Structures 3):

Kono kasa wa benri de ii desu. *This umbrella is wonderfully convenient.*
O-naka ga itakute, nani mo tabemasen deshita. *I didn't eat anything because I had a stomach-ache.*
Hādo-san wa amari genki ja nakute, zannen desu ne. *Isn't it a shame that Hādo-san isn't very well.*

(Also see Unit 10 **Kaiwa**.)

6 Mō *and* mada: *already/not any more and still/not yet*

Mō and **mada** are both adverbs. **Mō** conveys the idea of completion, or near completion, and **mada**, its opposite, the idea of non-completion. This is so regardless of whether they are in positive or negative sentences, although their English equivalents will differ accordingly.

(*a*) **mō** in positive sentences: *already/yet*
In this sense, **mō** is usually found in the past:

Mō owarimashita. *I have already finished.*
Mō tabemashita ka? *Have you eaten yet?*

It will also be found with the **-te iru** form of verbs in the (*c*) sense, mainly with verbs involving an immediate change of state:

Mō o-furo kara dete imasu. *I am already out of the bath.*
Suzuki-san wa mō dekakete imasu. *Suzuki-san has already set out.*

With such verbs in the ***present*** form and with **darō**, **mō** (often joined to **sugu**) will refer to something which is nearly completed, or just about to happen:

Mō sugu owarimasu. *I'm nearly finished.*
Tanaka-san wa mō kuru deshō. *Tanaka-san should be coming any minute.*

In addition, as one would expect, **mō** is found with positive adjectives, and with nouns:

Mō osoi desu. *It's too late now.*
Mō iya desu. *I can't stand any more.*
Mō jikan desu. *It's time.*
Mō aki no o-tenki desu ne. *The weather is already autumnal, isn't it* (**aki** *autumn*).

(*b*) **mō** in negative sentences: *not any more/no longer*
In the negative, **mō** still conveys its basic idea of completion: the situation or event is over, and will not occur any more. When the speaker is the subject, there is often the idea of negative intention:

Mō ano nomiya e wa ikimasen. *I'm not going/will not go to that bar any more.*
Konban mō benkyō shitakunai desu. *I don't want to study any more this evening.*
Watashi wa mō sonna ni wakaku arimasen. *I'm not that young any more.*
O-kane ga mō nai deshō *I don't suppose you have any money left.*
Jiru-san wa mō asoko de wa Eigo o oshiete imasen. *Jill isn't teaching English there any more.*

(*c*) **mada** in positive sentences: *still*
In the positive, **mada** is used with situations or events which are

uncompleted and therefore still going on (for **mada da** by itself, however, see (*d*)):

> Tarō-kun wa mada chiisai kodomo desu. *Tarō is still a small child.*
> Kēki ga mada arimasu. *There is still some cake./There is some cake left.*
> Mada tabete iru n' desu ka? *Are you still eating?*
> Mada nani ka tabemasu ka? *Will you eat something more?*

(*d*) **mada** in negative sentences*: not yet*
In the negative, **mada** is used with situations or events which are not yet completed; it is often found with **-te iru** in the (*c*) sense, here referring to the state you are in as a result of not doing something!

> Kore wa mada kirei ni natte imasen! *This isn't clean yet!*
> Michiko-san wa mada kimasen ka? *Hasn't Michiko come yet?*
> Tomu-san wa mada dekakete imasen. *Tom has not left yet.*
> Watashi wa mada nani mo yonde imasen. *I haven't read anything yet.*

Note that when **mada** is followed directly by **da** or a form of **da** it has the meaning of *not yet*:

> **A** Tabemashita ka? **B** Iie, mada desu.

Notice what happens in the following exchanges, remembering that **mō** and **mada** are opposites:

A	Mō shashin o torimashita ka?	**A**	*Have you taken the photo yet?*
B	Iie, mada totte imasen.	**B**	*No, I haven't yet.*
A	Mada Michiko-san to dēto shite imasu ka?	**A**	*Are you still dating* (**dēto surū**) *Michiko?*
B	Iie, mō shite imasen.	**B**	*No, not any more.*

7 [**-masu** base]**-nagara** *while doing [verb]*

This is used when the ***same*** person is simultaneously doing two different actions over the ***same*** length of time. The less important action goes before **-nagara** and is in the **-masu** base form whatever the tense at the end of the sentence:

Tomu-san wa maiasa uta o utai-nagara shawā o abimasu.
Every morning Tom showers (**shawā o abi.ru**) *while singing.*
Anzai-san wa Tarō-kun to asobi-nagara terebi o mimashita.
Anzai-san watched television while playing with Tarō.

Renshū

1 Here is a list of the favourite activities of some of our characters:

Jill:	shashin o toru; hirune o suru (**hirune** *afternoon nap*)
Tomu:	gitā o hiku; uta o utau
Michiko:	tomodachi to asobu; Tarō to kenka suru (**kenka** *quarrel*)
Tarō:	terebi o miru; chokorēto o taberu (**chokorēto** *chocolate*)
Anzai:	uisukī o nomu; tabako o suu (**tabako** *tobacco, cigarette;* **su.u** *to breathe in, smoke*)

(*a*) It is Sunday. Our characters have gathered in the Herds' minute garden and are all engaged in the first of their favourite activities. Use the **-te iru** form to describe the scene:
Rei: Jiru-san wa shashin o totte imasu.

(*b*) By the end of the day, they have been able to engage in both their favourite activities, and fit in other things as well. Use **-tari -tari suru** to describe what they each did:
Rei: Jiru-san wa shashin o tottari, hirune o shitari shimashita.

2 Join the following sentences, using the conjunctive forms of adjectives:
Rei: Kono kamera wa chiisai desu. Benri desu.
Kono kamera wa chiisakute benri desu.

(*a*) Kono bīru wa tsumetai desu. Oishii desu.
(*b*) Koko wa karē (*curry*) ga yūmei desu. Yoku tabe ni kimasu.
(*c*) Rondon wa ame ga ōkatta desu. Iya deshita.
(*d*) Michiko-san wa atama ga ii desu. Kirei desu.
(*e*) Atsukunakatta desu. Kimochi ga yokatta desu.

3 A stranger comes up, clearly out of breath. Reply to his/her questions in the affirmative or the negative as indicated, using **mō** or **mada** as appropriate.

Rei: Eiga wa mō hajimarimashita ka? Hai, mō hajimatte imasu.
Iie, mada desu/hajimarimasen.

(*a*) Ginkō wa mō shimarimashita ka? (Hai)
(*b*) Depāto wa mō akimashita ka? (Iie)
(*c*) Tokkyū wa mō kimashita ka? (Hai)
(*d*) Tokkyū wa mō demashita ka? (Iie)

4 Compare the comparatively relaxed daily schedule of Tom Herd, the typical Western businessman, with the frenzied schedule of Suzuki-san, the typical (?) Japanese businessman by combining the pairs of activities first with **-te kara**, then with **-nagara**:

Rei: ha o migaku; shawā o abiru
Hādo-san wa ha o migaite kara shawā o abimasu.
Suzuki-san wa ha o migaki-nagara shawā o abimasu.

(*a*) shinbun o yomu; shatsu o kiru
(*b*) hisho to hanasu; memo o kaku
(*c*) keiyaku o musubu; o-sake o nomu (**keiyaku** *contract;* **musub.u** *tie, sign* [*a contract*])
(*d*) terebi o miru; neru

5 Put the following conversations into **-masu** form Japanese:

(*a*) **A** Do you know Ms Miura?
B Yes, I know (her). She lives in the flats (**manshon**) next to the bank.
(*b*) **C** You don't look well.
D I was writing a report until late last night. I'm still tired.
(*c*) **E** Kimura-san is clever and pretty, but she isn't married.
F Perhaps she doesn't want to get married.

Language and Society

Working in Japanese companies

Japanese companies are setting up more and more branches and factories abroad, and employing more and more foreign nationals, both in their countries of origin and in Japan. Japanese companies are known for their system of lifetime employment (**shūshin koyō**) and promotion of people according to age rather than ability (**nenkō joretsu**), although only the most able actually get right to the top. Change is occurring in these areas, however. If you work in a Japanese company you need to be prepared to do a lot of overtime (**zangyō**), and give the company an important place in your life, but holidays (**kyūka** or **yasumi**) are becoming more acceptable. Salaries may seem low, but remember that you will get a commuting allowance (**tsūkin teate**) to cover your travel expenses and a bonus (**bōnasu**) twice a year which in the good times may amount to as much as five or six times your normal monthly salary (**kyūryō**).

Advert for jobs with Goodyear

The following additional words and phrases might prove useful:

kaisha ni shūshoku suru *to join a company*
kaisha kara/o taishoku suru *to retire from a company*
sararīman *white-collar worker*
shain *company employee*
buchō *department head*
kachō *section head*
shōsha *a trading firm*
shōken-gaisha *a securities firm*
yushutsu (suru) *export*
yunyū (suru) *import*
tsūkin (suru) *commuting to work*
kyūryō ga takai *to have a good salary*
kyūryō ga hikui/yasui *to have a bad salary*
suto o suru *to strike*

12 Wareta n' ja nakute, watta n' deshō? *It didn't get broken, you broke it, didn't you?*

In this unit we shall take a look at ways of evading responsibility for a blunder with intransitive verbs and taking credit for a positive action by means of transitive verbs. We shall also see how to form impersonal sentences with **-te aru**, how to describe openly displayed emotions, and encounter examples of Japanese sound symbolism.

Kaiwa

Michiko-san wa Hādo-san-tachi to o-hiru o tabeta ga, sono ato de sara-arai o tetsudatte iru. Michiko-san wa sara o aratte, Ken-san wa fuite iru.

Ken	Kitchin-taoru wa?
Michiko	Hora, soko ni kakete aru deshō.
Ken	A, hontō da. Ēpuron wa?
Michiko	Ushiro no tēburu ni oite aru ja nai no . . . koko wa Ken-san no uchi no daidokoro deshō?
Ken	Demo, itsu mo no tokoro ni oite nai kara.

sono ato de *after that*
sara-arai *dish-washing, washing up*
[activity] o tetsudau *to help with [activity]*; **[person] o tetsuda.u** *to help [person]*
sara *dish, plate*
fuk.u *to wipe*
kitchin-taoru *wiping-up cloth*
kake.ru (transitive) *to hang up*
kakete aru *to be hung up* ● S1
ēpuron *apron*
ok.u *to put, place*
daidokoro *kitchen*
oite nai negative of **oite aru**

True or false?

1 Ken-san wa Michiko-san no uchi de o-hiru o tabeta.
2 Ēpuron wa itsu mo no tokoro ni oite nai.

Michiko Igirisujin no shufu wa shiawase desu ne, otoko no ko ga kōshite daidokoro no shigoto o tetsudattari suru kara. Nihon ja kangaerarenai wa.

Ken Mukashi kara narete iru kara ne. Sore ni, kozukai mo fueru shi ne. (*Te ga subette, sara ga ichimai yuka ni ochite wareru*) Ara . . . okāsan, sara ga wareta yo!

(*Jiru-san ga tonari no heya kara kuru*)

Jiru Ara, ichiban ii o-sara ja nai no. Dōshita no, Ken?

Ken Ochita n' da yo.

Jiru Ochita n' ja nai deshō?! Otoshita n' deshō!

Ken Ē, mā . . .

Jiru Sore kara, wareta n' ja nakute, watta n' deshō? Motto ki o tsuke nasai yo! Kongetsu wa o-kozukai nashi! (*Daidokoro o deru*)

Ken (*Unzari shite*) Da kara Nihon no otoko wa sara-arai o iyagaru n' darō . . .

shufu *housewife*
shiawase na *lucky*
otoko no ko *boy, young man*
kōshite *in this way*
ja = de wa
kangaerarenai *unthinkable*
mukashi *long ago; before, formerly*
nare. ru *to get used to*
kozukai *pocket money*
fue.ru (intransitive) *to increase*
shi *and besides* ● S3
te *hand*
suber.u *to slip*
yuka *floor*
ware.ru (intransitive) *to break*
are = ara
otos.u (transitive) *to drop*
ja nakute conjunctive form of **ja nai** ● Unit 17 S5
war.u (transitive) *to break*
ki o tsuke. ru *to be careful, pay attention*
nashi (= **nai**) *there isn't, there won't be*
unzari shite *disgustedly, in disgust* ● LS
da kara [sentence] *that's why/so [sentence]*
iyagar.u *to show dislike* ● S4

True or false?

3 Nihon no otoko no ko wa amari daidokoro no shigoto o tetsudawanai.
4 Sara ga nimai wareta.

Structures

1 *Intransitive and transitive verbs*

We have already seen some examples of intransitive verbs in Unit 11, noting that they differ from transitive verbs in that they do not take objects. This is a distinction that exists with many English verbs, too:

(*a*) John broke the cup.
(*b*) The cup broke.

(*a*) The stage-hand raised the curtain.
(*b*) The curtain rose.

The (*a*) sentences have an object, and the (*b*) sentences do not, but a more important difference is that in the (*a*) sentences the person responsible for the action of the verb is stated, whereas in the (*b*) sentences the same action is presented as a natural occurrence. This applies to Japanese, too.

Like English *break/break* or *rise/raise*, Japanese verbs often come in pairs of intransitive/transitive, distinguished by regular correspondences in their endings:

Intransitive		*Transitive*	
-iru		**-osu**	
oki.ru	*to rise, get up*	okos.u	*to rouse*
ori.ru	*to get off/down*	oros.u	*to take (something) down*
ochi.ru	*to fall, be dropped*	otos.u	*to drop (something)*

Intransitive		*Transitive*	
-eru		**-u**	
ware.ru	*to break, get broken*	war.u	*to break (something)*
nuke.ru	*to come/fall out*	nuk.u	*to pull out*
-eru		**-yasu**	
fue.ru	*to increase*	fuyas.u	*to increase (something)*
hie.ru	*to become cool*	hiyas.u	*to cool (something)*
-reru		**-su**	
koware.ru	*to break, get broken*	kowas.u	*to break (something)*
kakure.ru	*to hide*	kakus.u	*to hide (something)*
taore.ru	*to collapse*	taos.u	*to knock down*
-aru		**-eru**	
hajimar.u	*to begin*	hajime.ru	*to begin (something)*
kakar.u	*to hang*	kake.ru	*to hang (something) up*
shimar.u	*to close*	shime.ru	*to close (something)*
tomar.u	*to stop*	tome.ru	*to stop, turn off*
-u		**-eru**	
ak.u	*to open*	ake.ru	*to open (something)*
tsuk.u	*to be switched on; to be attached*	tsuke.ru	*to switch (something) on; to attach (something)*

Intransitive		*Transitive*	
-ru		**-su**	
naor.u	*to get fixed, heal*	naos.u	*to fix, heal (something)*
tōr.u	*to pass through*	tōs.u	*to pass (something) through*
-u		**-asu**	
ugok.u	*to move*	ugokas.u	*to move (something)*
kawak.u	*to get dry*	kawakas.u	*to dry (something)*

Since there are many other pairs of verbs which conform to these patterns it is useful to become familiar with them. There are also some irregular pairs:

hair.u	*to enter*	ire.ru	*to insert*
kawar.u	*to change*	kae.ru	*to change (something)*
kie.ru	*go out (fire etc.)*	kes.u	*to put out, extinguish*
mie.ru	*to be seen*	mi.ru	*to see*
nor.u	*to ride*	nose.ru	*to load, place (something) on*

Unlike English (*break/break* etc.), Japanese has hardly any identical pairs of intransitive/transitive verbs. One exception is **owar.u** (*to end*), which is used both ways, although a 'specialised' transitive verb **oe.ru (***to end something*) does exist:

Shigoto ga owarimashita. *The job is finished.*
Shigoto o owarimashita/oemashita. *I/we (etc.) finished the job.*

Below are some examples of sentences with intransitive/transitive verbs:

Ken-san wa mō okimashita ka? Iie, mada okite imasen. *Is Ken up yet? No, not yet.*
Ja, okoshite kudasai ne. *Well, please wake him, won't you.*

Kono bīru wa amari hiete imasen ne. Reizōko de hiyashimashō. *This beer isn't very cold, is it. Let's cool it in the fridge.*

Doa ga aite imasu yo. *The door's open, you know.*
Ē, atsui kara, mado mo akete kudasai. *Yes, please open the window too, as it's hot.*

Ara, tokei ga naorimashita ne. *Hey, the clock's been mended, I see.*
Watashi ga naoshimashita yo! ***I** mended it, you know!*

Tokei ga kowaremashita ka? *Is the clock broken?*
Tarō ga kowashita n' desu yo! ***Tarō** broke it, you know!*

It should be obvious from the last example above, and from some of the **Kaiwa** sentences, that transitive verbs can conveniently be used to make someone responsible for accidental or wilful damage, while intransitive verbs may be used to evade such responsibility by pretending that things came about naturally. Transitives can of course also be employed to take credit for a positive occurrence, as in the second from last example.

2 *Impersonal sentences with* -te ar.u

In Unit 11, we saw the use of **-te iru** after both intransitive and transitive verbs; **-te aru** is used after transitive verbs only.

Transitive verbs on their own indicate that someone is responsible for the action of the verb, even if that person is not mentioned (thus **kowashita** means *I/you/we/he/she/they broke it*); when **-te aru** is used with a transitive verb, the implication is that someone ***unspecified*** has performed the action, i.e. the sentence is 'impersonal'. In fact the person responsible for the action of the verb ***cannot*** be mentioned in a **-te aru** sentence.

Doa ga akete arimasu. *The door has been opened.*
Bīru ga hiyashite arimasu. *The beer has been cooled.*

Sentences such as these indicate the state brought about by some unspecified person in opening the door/cooling the beer etc. Compare the above examples with the following sentences, which use intransitive verbs:

Doa ga akimashita. *The door opened.*
Bīru ga hiemashita. *The beer became cold.*

Doa ga aite imasu. *The door is open.*
Bīru ga hiete imasu. *The beer is cold.*

In the past tense, the intransitive sentences merely say that an action occurred naturally, while the **-te iru** sentences indicate the state of affairs resulting from that happening. The **-te aru** sentences, on the other hand, imply that someone is responsible for the situation, without, however, telling us who that someone is.

In the negative, **-te aru** becomes **-te nai** (plain) or **-te arimasen** (polite):

Bīru ga hiyashite nai.
Kono tegami ni wa kaite arimasen.

3 *Signalling an addition with* shi

As we saw in Unit 5 Structures 4 and Unit 11 Structures 4, the basic use of both the **-te** form and the conjunctive form of adjectives is to connect sections of a sentence that could themselves be independent sentences, where English would use *and*:

Anzai-sensei wa tabako o sutte, o-sake mo nomimasu. *Anzai-sensei smokes, and drinks, too.*
Kore wa takakute, amari suki ja nai n' desu. *This is expensive, and I don't fancy it that much.*
Sono resutoran wa yasukute, oishii desu. *That restaurant is cheap and good.*
Kanojo wa kirei de, atama mo ii desu. *She is pretty and intelligent, too.*

Shi also connects sentences, in the sense of *for one thing . . . and besides, and moreover*. In this use, **shi** is normally attached to the plain form of verbs and adjectives:

Anzai-sensei wa tabako o suu shi, o-sake mo nomimasu. *Anzai-sensei smokes, and what's more, he drinks.*
Kore wa takai shi, amari suki ja nai n' desu. *For one thing this is expensive, and besides I don't fancy it that much.*
Sono resutoran wa yasui shi, oishii desu. *That restaurant is cheap, and good too.*
Kanojo wa kirei da shi, atama mo ii desu. *For one thing she is pretty, and besides she is intelligent, too.*

Compare the following examples, which all express the idea that Kyoto has hot summers and cold winters, making it a disagreeable place in the view of the speaker:

Kyōto wa natsu wa atsukute, fuyu wa samukute, suki ja nai desu.
Kyōto wa natsu wa atsukute, fuyu wa samui kara, suki ja nai desu.
Kyōto wa natsu wa atsui shi, fuyu wa samui shi, suki ja nai desu.
Kyōto wa natsu wa atsui shi, fuyu wa samui kara, suki ja nai desu.
Kyōto wa natsu mo atsui shi, fuyu mo samui kara, suki ja nai desu.

Note the use of contrasting **wa** with **natsu** and **fuyu**, and that while you can have more than one conjunctive form or **shi** in a sentence, **kara** can occur only once, at the end of the part expressing the reason.

Shi can also be used to add a further reason as an afterthought, as a separate sentence:

Kyōto wa natsu ga atsui kara, |
Kyōto wa natsu ga atsukute, | suki ja nai desu. Fuyu mo samui shi.
I don't like Kyoto because the summers are hot. What's more, the winters are cold, too.

Shi can be reinforced by introducing the afterthought with **sore ni**.

4 [adjective]-gar.u

This suffix (which itself works like an **-u** verb) is attached to certain adjectives which are concerned with the expression of emotion. In the case of **-i** adjectives, **-garu** replaces the final **-i**; with **na** adjectives, it replaces **na**:

samu	-i	samu garu	*to feel/look cold*
hoshi	-i	hoshi garu	*to show signs of wanting something*
ita	-i	ita garu	*to feel/look in pain*
isogashi	-i	isogashi garu	*to feel/look busy*
iya	na	iya garu	*to feel/show disgust*
fushigi (*mysterious*)	na	fushigi garu	*to feel mystified/find something mystifying*

-garu indicates that the feeling is being openly displayed or acted out, normally by someone other than the speaker. If a child, for example, is making a big fuss about some little scratch, its mother may say:

Sonna ni itagaranaide kudasai!

Here are some more examples. (Note that the **-garu** forms take **o**, just like any other verb.)

Michiko-san wa yūbe zuibun samugatte imashita yo. *Michiko was (showing signs of) feeling the cold last night.*
Tarō-kun wa itsumo aisukurīmu o hoshigatte imasu. *Taro is always clamouring for ice cream.*
Ken-san wa amari sara-arai o iyagarimasen ne. *Ken doesn't show much aversion to washing up.*

The number of adjectives to which **-garu** can be attached is limited, but it can also be attached to **-ta.i** (Unit 8); like **-tai**, **-tagaru** (*to show signs of wanting to do*) can be attached freely to any verb, and is one way of referring to the wishes of someone other than the speaker:

Tarō-kun wa gakkō ni ikitagaranai n' desu. *Tarō doesn't show any inclination to go to school* (**gakkō**).
Dōshite sonna ni ha o migakitagaranai n' desu ka? *Why are you so averse to brushing your teeth?*

In some cases, the noun form **-gari** (with the optional addition of **-ya** (Unit 2 Language and Society)) can be used to characterise a person who habitually engages in the sort of conduct indicated by the adjective:

Michiko-san wa samugari desu ne. *You are sensitive to the cold, aren't you, Michiko.*
Boku wa atsugariya da kara ne. *I feel the heat, you see.*

Renshū

1 Ingratiate yourself with your mum/dad by taking credit for the positive domestic occurrences, while blaming your younger sister An (*Anne*) for the negative ones in accordance with the cues:
Rei: Ringo ga ochite imasu. (An)→An ga otoshita n' desu.

(*a*) Yatto otōsan ga okimashita ne. (Watashi)
(*b*) Mado ga aite imasu ne! (An)
(*c*) Bīru ga yoku hiete iru ne. (Watashi)
(*d*) Terebi ga kowarete imasu ne! (An)
(*e*) Reizōko ga tomatte imasu ne! (An)

2 Put the following into Japanese, using **-te aru**.
Rei: The report is placed on the table.→Repōto wa tēburu ni oite aru.

(*a*) It was written in this morning's paper.
(*b*) The luggage is unloaded.
(*c*) The beer is in the fridge.
(*d*) The outside light has been turned off.
(*e*) Everything has been eaten.

3 Join the sentences, using **shi**.
Rei: Sono resutoran wa yasui desu. Oishii desu.→Sono resutoran wa yasui shi, oishii desu.

(*a*) Bīru mo arimasu. Wain mo arimasu.
(*b*) O-sushi mo tabetai desu. Sutēki (*steak*) mo tabetai desu.
(*c*) Kono kodomo wa genki desu. Atama mo ii desu.
(*d*) Michiko-san wa ikimasen. Ken-san mo ikimasen.
(*e*) Kono bīru wa yoku hiete imasu. Oishii desu.

4 You are trying to do some work in the same room with people

who keep voicing their complaints and desires; tell them to shut up according to the example.
Rei: Ā, isogashii isogashii!→Sonna ni isogashigaranaide kudasai.

(*a*) Ā, shigoto ga iya da iya da iya da!
(*b*) Ā, aisukurīmu ga hoshii. Ā, aisukurīmu ga hoshii . . .
(*c*) Ā, atsui nā, atsui nā . . .
(*d*) Ā, bīru ga nomitai, bīru ga nomitai!
(*e*) Ā, kaeritai nā! Ā, kaeritai nā!

Language and Society

Unzari suru *and some similar expressions*

Japanese has a large stock of words that characterise an action or a state by imitating a sound or a motion. These words tend to contain sound combinations such as double consonants or syllabic **n**, and/or endings like **to** (often doubled) or **ri**:

kitto, chotto (Unit 9)
chanto (Unit 10), unto (*a lot*)
hakkiri (*clearly*), yukkuri (Unit 8)
unzari, don'yori (*dull* [of the sky, etc.])

Many are used as adverbs, but some are used with **suru** (or occasionally, **da**) as predicates:

Unto tabeta. *I ate lots.*
Yukkuri itte kudasai. *Please say it slowly.*
Hakkiri mimashita. *I saw it clearly.*

Kore de hakkiri shimashita. *It has become clear now.*
Yukkuri shite kudasai. *Please take your time/make yourself at home.*
Unzari shimashita/desu. *I am fed up.*
Kyō mo don'yori shite imasu ne. *It's another gloomy day today, isn't it?*

Some of these expressions are created by repeating a sound:

noro-noro (*slowly, loiteringly*): Noro-noro arukanaide kudasai.
zun-zun (*walk briskly*): Zun-zun ikimashō.

13 Jiru-san wa dō omoimasu ka?
What do you think, Jill?

In this unit you will learn how to report what people say, how to give your own opinion, and a way of asking how to say something in Japanese. You will meet a form of the verb for trying to do things and thinking of doing them, and more on the **-te** form of verbs and the conjunctive forms of adjectives. There will also be some notes on marriages in Japan, and on how to congratulate people.

Kaiwa

kek **kon**

Kinō Tanaka-san ga yoru osoku Jiru-san ni denwa o kakete, tsugi no hi Jiru-san ni atte, iroiro hanashitai to itta. Sore de Merushī to iu kissaten de issho ni hiru-gohan o taberu koto ni shita.

(*Kissaten de*)

Tanaka Totsuzen yoru osoku denwa o kakete, dōmo shitsurei shimashita.

Jiru Ie, ie, dō itashimashite. Dō shimashita ka?

Tanaka (*kao ga sukoshi akaku naru*) Watashi, kekkon suru koto ni narimashita. Sugiura-san to. Atta koto ga aru deshō.

Jiru E, Sugiura-san! O-medetō!

[person/place] ni denwa o kakeru/suru *to telephone* [*person/place*]

[sentence] to itta (*Tanaka-san*) *said* [*sentence*] ● S1 (**i.u** *to say*)

Merushī to iu kissaten *a coffee-shop called 'Merci'* ● S2

hiru-gohan *lunch*

[verb (present plain form)] koto ni suru *decide to* [*verb*] ● S3

totsuzen *suddenly, without warning*

[verb]-te shitsurei shimashita *I'm sorry for doing* [*verb*] ● S4

kao ga akaku naru *to go red in the face, blush*
kao *face*
[verb (present plain form)] koto ni naru *to be decided to [verb]* ● S3
Sugiura-san to ([person] to kekkon suru) *to get married to [person]*
e! *oh!*
o-medetō! *congratulations* ● LS2

True or false?

1 Tanaka-san wa mō kekkon shite iru.
2 Jiru-san wa Sugiura-san o shiranai.

Uētā ga kite, Jiru-san to Tanaka-san wa sorezore supagetti to tsuna-sarada o chūmon suru. Sore kara, hanashi ga tsuzuku.

Tanaka	Sore de, kekkon suru kara, ima no shigoto o yameyō to omotte imashita ga . . .
Jiru	Hontō ni yameru no?
Tanaka	Sō desu ne . . . Kare wa shigoto o yamete, uchi de ryōri toka o-sōji nado shi nasai to itte imasu. Demo, watashi wa mō sukoshi hatarakitai to omoimasu.
Jiru	Sore wa komarimashita ne. Sugiura-san ni wa mō sukoshi hatarakitai to iimashita ka?
Tanaka	Iimashita ga . . .
Jiru	Dame deshita ka?
Tanaka	Kare wa 'Sore wa jōdan deshō' to itte, kīkō to shimasen deshita. Sore de, shigoto de wa nakute, kekkon o yameyō ka to kangaete imasu. Jiru-san wa dō omoimasu ka?
Jiru	Ara, komarimashita ne.

uētā *waiter*
sorezore *respectively*
supagetti *spaghetti*
tsuna-sarada *tuna salad*
[thing] o chūmon (suru) *order [thing]*
tsuzuk.u (intransitive) *to continue*
yameyō to omotte imasu *I'm thinking of giving up* ● S6, 7
yame.ru *to give up, cease*
kare *he*

sōji (suru) *cleaning (sweeping etc.)*
[verb]-tai to omoimasu *I would like to [verb]* ● S5
Sore wa komarimashita ne. *That's a problem./That's too bad.*
dame na *no good, useless*
jōdan *joke* (**jōdan o iu** *to tell a joke*)
[verb] -(y)ō to suru *to try to [verb]* ● S8
A de wa nakute B *not A but B* ● Unit 17 S5
kangae.ru *to think, consider*
dō omoimasu ka? *what do you think?*

True or false?

3 Tanaka-san wa ima no shigoto o yametai to itta.
4 Tanaka-san wa Sugiura-san ni jōdan o iwanakatta.

Structures

1 [Sentence] to [verb of saying] *reporting what people say*

In Japanese you report what someone says by adding the quoting particle **to** and the appropriate verb of saying at the end of the sentence. This **to** is equivalent to English *that*, and different from the **to** which joins nouns (Unit 8 Structures 3). **Iu** is the most common verb of saying, but you will also find, for example, **kik.u** (*to ask*, *hear*), **kotae.ru** (*to reply*), **kotowar.u** (*to refuse*), **okor.u** (*to get angry*), **sakeb.u** (*to shout*), **yorokob.u** (*to rejoice*), and, in the case of letters etc., **kaku** (*to write*).

As in English, it is possible to quote people's words directly. While English here omits *that*, however, Japanese must use **to**:

Doitsujin wa asa 'Gūten Morugen' to iimasu. *In the morning the Germans say 'Guten Morgen'.*
Jiru-san wa 'Hayaku tabe nasai' to Ken-san ni iimashita. *Jill said to Ken, 'Eat it up quickly'.*

'Issho ni Dizunīrando e ikimasen ka?' to Yamada-san ga kikimashita. *'Won't you come to Disneyland with me?', asked Yamada-san.*

'Shigoto o yametakunai desu' to Tanaka-san ga kotaemashita. *'I don't want to give up my job', replied Tanaka-san.*

When reporting people's words indirectly, Japanese is more straightforward than English, since the tense of the original statement is unchanged. All that happens is that any verbs or adjectives in the polite form go into the plain form. Note that even though English can omit *that* here as well, Japanese must always use **to**:

'Mada kekkon shitaku arimasen.' ***'I don't want to marry yet.'***

Watashi wa itsu mo **mada kekkon shitakunai** to iimasu. *I always say that I don't want to get married yet.*

Watashi wa **mada kekkon shitakunai** to Sugiura-san ni iimashita. *I told Sugiura-san that I didn't want to get married yet.*

'Ikimasen deshita.' ***'I didn't go.'***

Ken-san ni wa **ikanakatta** to iimasu. *I will tell Ken that I didn't go.*

Michiko-san wa **ikanakatta** to Ken-san ni kotaemashita. *Michiko replied to Ken that she hadn't gone.*

Indirect reporting of questions and commands will be dealt with in Unit 17 Structures 4.

The person doing the quoting will be followed by **wa** or **ga** as appropriate, but note that **[person] wa** will normally come at the beginning of the sentence, while **[person] ga** will come just after the quoting **to**:

Tomu-san wa mō tabeta to iimashita. *Tom said that he had already eaten.*

Gaijin da to chiisa na kodomo ga sakebimashita. *A small child shouted that there was a foreigner.*

When it is clear from the context who is speaking, the speaker will usually be omitted:

Tomu-san ga jūichiji sugi ni kaetta. 'Tsukareta,' to itta. *Tom came home after* 11 *o'clock. 'I'm tired', he said.*

Note the following:

(*a*) When quoting the words of a specific third person in the present, it is usual to put the verb of saying into the **-te iru** form:

Tarō-kun wa o-naka ga suita to itte imasu. *Tarō says he's hungry.*

Doitsu no bīru wa oishii to Suzuki-san ga Kerun kara kaite imasu. *Suzuki-san writes from Köln that German beer tastes good.*

(*b*) *What did he/she say?* is **Nan to iimashita ka?** Also notice:

Michiko-san wa nani mo iimasen deshita. *Michiko didn't say anything.*

Watashi wa sō iimashita. *I said so/that.*

Kō itte kudasai. *Please say this.*

2 [noun] to iimasu/[noun] to iu [noun]: *labelling things*

If you want to ask the Japanese for a word, or explain how to say something in English, you should use sentences based on the pattern **A o X to iu**, which literally means *We call A 'X'*:

Eigo de Rondon o London to iimasu. *In English we call 'Rondon' 'London'.*

Kore wa Nihongo de nan to iimasu ka? *What do you call this in Japanese?*

As we saw in Unit 1 (**Kaiwa**; Language and Society 1), with the humble form of **iu**, **mōs.u**, this is also a common way of introducing yourself to someone:

Hādo to mōshimasu.

Japanese often uses this pattern in front of general nouns, as a way of explaining what, or who, X, a proper noun (e.g. the name of a restaurant) is:

Kiku to iu Nihon ryōriya *a Japanese restaurant called Kiku*

Jill to iu Amerikajin *an American named Jill*

Taimuzu to iu Igirisu no shinbun *the British newspaper, **The Times***

Suzuki-san wa Yamanaka Māketingu to iu kaisha ni tsutomete imasu. *Suzuki-san works for a company called Yamanaka Marketing.*

3 [verb (present plain form)] koto ni suru/naru: *deciding to do things*

We have already met a construction involving **[verb (past plain form)] koto** (Unit 5 Structures 3), and the pattern **[noun] ni suru/naru** (Unit 8 Structures 2). The new structure has points in common with both. Note, however, that in this case the verb before **koto** is in the present plain form, either positive or negative.

(*a*) **koto ni suru**
This refers to conscious decisions, either positive or negative:

Kaeru koto ni shimashō ka. *Shall we decide to go home?*
Kekkon shinai koto ni shimashita. *I decided not to get married.*

With **suru** in the **-te iru** form, it refers to something which you consciously make a habit of doing:

Watashi wa maiasa goji ni okiru koto ni shite imasu. *I am in the habit of getting up at five every morning.*

(*b*) **koto ni naru**
This, on the other hand, conveys the idea of an impersonal decision which is not under the control of the speaker. It might not be clear who took the decision, or it might just be more polite not to say who did, particularly in situations where the speaker is clearly being honoured in some way. The nuance is not always easy to convey in English:

Kanai wa Nihon no kaisha ni tsutomeru koto ni narimashita. (*It has been decided that*) *my wife is to work for a Japanese company.*
Ōsutoraria e ikanai koto ni narimashita. *I am not to go to Australia.*

With **naru** in the **-te iru** form, it refers to an impersonal state of affairs, to the way things are:

> Josei wa koko kara hairu koto ni natte imasu. *Women* (**josei**) *are meant to enter from here/use this entrance.*

4 *Using the* -te *form to imply a reason*

Like the conjunctive form of adjectives (Unit 11 Structures 4), the **-te** form of verbs can be used to imply a reason:

> Nodo ga kawaite, jūsu o takusan nomimashita. *Becoming thirsty, I drank lots of juice.*
> Tomodachi to hanashite, Tanaka-san wa densha ni noriokuremashita. *Talking to a friend, Tanaka-san was late for the train.*

The same guidelines for the use of **wa** and **ga** apply as with **kara** (Unit 6 Structures 4).

Together with the conjunctive form of adjectives, the **-te** form is particularly common when giving reasons for an apology, and in front of certain verbs and adjectives, such as **komar.u** (*to get into difficulties*), and **yokatta** (*I'm glad*):

> Osoku natte dōmo sumimasen. *I'm sorry for being* (Lit. *becoming*) *late.*
> Shigoto ga ōkute komatte imasu. *There is a lot of work and so I'm in difficulties.* i.e. *There's so much work I don't know what to do.*
> Nihon e kite honto ni yokatta desu. *I'm really glad* (*because*) *I came to Japan.*

5 [sentence] to [verb of thinking]: *reporting what you think*

Virtually the same principles apply here as in indirect reporting of what people say (Structures 1), but note the following:

(*a*) In the ordinary present tense, you can report your own thoughts or opinions and ask about those of the person you are talking to, but not make statements about what a third person thinks:

> Omoshiroi eiga datta to omoimasu. *I think it was an interesting* (**omoshiro.i**) *film.*

Nihon no ringo wa oishii to omoimasu ka? *Do you find Japanese apples tasty?*

In the following sentence, it is therefore clear that we are talking about the likelihood of Michiko's coming, not about what Michiko thinks:

Michiko-san wa kuru darō to omoimasu. *I think that Michiko will probably come.*

As with reported speech, to relate what Michiko is thinking in the present, you should use the **-te iru** form:

Michiko-san wa omoshirokunai to omotte imasu. *Michiko finds it uninteresting.*

This is not necessary, however, when talking about what someone else thought in the past:

Ken-san wa Michiko-san ga konai darō to omoimashita. *Ken thought that Michiko probably wouldn't come.*

(*b*) Where English says '*I don't think . . .*', Japanese will usually say **-nai to omoimasu**:

Hādo-san wa amari genki de wa nai to omoimasu. *I don't think Mr Herd is very well.*

Suzuki-san wa oboete inakatta to omoimasu. *I don't think Suzuki-san remembered.*

If you want to give the sense of a strong denial, however, **to (wa) omoimasen** can be used:

Watashi wa Tanaka-san ga kekkon suru to wa omoimasen. *I don't think in the slightest that Tanaka-san will get married.*

(*c*) **To omoimasu** is often added to verbs in the **-tai** form as a polite, more adult way of expressing one's wishes, and asking about the wishes of the person you are talking to:

Ken-san no tomodachi ni naritai to omoimasu. *I would like to become Ken's friend.*

Watashi wa rainen Yōroppa o ryokō shitai to omotte imasu. *I would like to travel in Europe next year.*

Eiga o mi ni ikitai to omoimasen ka? *Wouldn't you like to go and see a film?*

(*d*) To ask someone's opinion, you should use **dō**:

Suzuki-san wa dō omoimasu ka? *What do you think, Suzuki-san?*

Also note:

Watashi wa kō omoimasu: *This is what I think:*
Tanaka-san mo sō omoimasen ka? *Don't you think so too, Tanaka-san?*

(*e*) When deeper thought, consideration rather than feeling, is involved, **kangaeru** may be used in place of **omou**:

Ima no Nihon wa dame da to omotte/kangaete imasu. *I think that present-day Japan is no good.*

To ask what someone is thinking, rather than what their opinion is, you should say:

Nani o kangaete imasu ka? *What are you thinking?*
Nani mo kangaete imasen. *I'm not thinking of anything.*

6 *The plain form of* [verb]-mashō

As with other plain forms, this is used in written-style Japanese, and when speaking in informal situations, to children, or to oneself. (For the **-mashō** form itself, see Unit 4 Structures 2.) With **-iru/-eru** verbs, you just add **-yō** to the **-masu** base:

mimashō	mi.ru	mi¦yō
tabemashō	tabe.ru	tabe¦yō
okimashō	oki.ru	oki¦yō

With **-u** verbs, the final **-u** of the present plain form is changed to **-ō**:

ikimashō	ik.u	ik¦ō
kaerimashō	kaer.u	kaer¦ō
nomimashō	nom.u	nom¦ō
asobimashō	asob.u	asob¦ō
hanashimashō	hanas.u	hanas¦ō
aimashō	a.u	a¦ō

Note what happens to verbs like **matsu** and the two irregular verbs:

machimashō	mats.u	mat¦ō
shimashō	suru	shi¦yō
kimashō	kuru	ko¦yō

Sā, sukoshi benkyō shiyō ka? (*to oneself*) *Well, perhaps I should get down to a little studying.*
Eiga o mi ni ikō. *Let's go and see a film.*
Takushī ni norō. *Let's take a taxi.*

In the next sections, you will find two patterns which use the plain **-mashō** form.

7 [verb]-(y)ō to omou/omotte iru: *contemplating an action*

This pattern is used when you are thinking of doing something but not sure that you will actually do it, or to refer to something which you thought of doing in the past but did not do. It is normally only used when the speaker is the subject:

Konban oishii tokoro de tabeyō to omoimasu ga, issho ni ikimasen ka? *I feel like eating at a good restaurant* (*place*) *tonight – won't you come too?*
Mada hayai desu kara, mō sukoshi matō to omoimasu. *It's still early, so I think I'll wait a little longer.*
Shashin o torō to omoimashita ga, kamera ga arimasen deshita. *I thought of taking a photograph, but I didn't have a camera.*

When **omotte iru** is used, the implication is that you have been thinking of doing whatever it is for some time:

Rainen Tai e ikō to omotte imasu. *I am thinking of going to Thailand* (**Tai**) *next year.*
Eigo no sensei ni narō to omotte imasu. *I am thinking of becoming an English teacher.*

Note the following:

(*a*) Inserting the question particle **ka** before **to** makes the idea even more tentative:

Atarashii kuruma o kaō ka to omotte imasu. *I am wondering whether to buy a new car.*

(*b*) If you are thinking of doing something which requires weighty consideration, **kangaeru** can be used in place of **omou**:

Yamanaka Māketingu o yamete jibun no kaisha o tsukurō to kangaete imasu. *I'm thinking of leaving Yamanaka Marketing and building my own* (**jibun no**) *company.*

(*c*) **[verb]-(y)ō to (wa) omowanai** is similar to English *I have no intention of*:

Anna tokoro e ikō to wa omoimasen. *I have no intention of going to a place like that.*

8 [verb]-(y)ō to suru: *attempting an action*

This is used:

(*a*) for actions which you try to do but in which you may fail or, in the past tense, for actions which actually failed:

Ima tegami o kakō to shite iru kara, ato de ikimasu. *I'm just trying to write a letter, so I'll come later* (**ato de**).

Hairō to shimashita ga, doa ga shimatte imashita. *I tried to go in, but the door was shut.*

(*b*) for actions which are about to take place:

Sakura wa mō sakō to shite imasu. *The cherry blossom* (**sakura**) *is already on the point of blooming* (**sak.u**).

Chōdo o-furo ni hairō to shite imasu. *I'm just about to have a bath.*

Renshū

1 Here is a list of original statements:

A 'Rondon wa samukatta desu.'

B 'Shushō (*Prime Minister*) ga shinimashita.'
C 'Koko no tako wa totemo oishii desu.'
D 'Ken-san wa kyō kimasen.'
E 'Anzai-sensei wa shinsetsu na ha-isha-san desu.'

Put them into indirect speech and fit them into the following sentences as in the example:
Rei: **A** + Tanaka-san ga kakimashita.
Rondon wa samukatta to Tanaka-san ga kakimashita.

(*a*) **B** + nyūsu de iimashita.
(*b*) **C** + Itariajin ga yorokobimashita.
(*c*) **D** + Michiko-san ga denwa de iimashita.
(*d*) **E** + Tomu-san ga kotaemashita.

2 Select one word from each of the colums to make meaningful sentences according to the same pattern as the following. It should be possible to use each word once only. Make sure you use the right particles!
Rei: Sakura to iu resutoran de tabeta koto ga arimasu ka?

Maria	machi (*town*)	au
Okkusufōdo	depāto	yunyū suru
Mango	Itariajin	taberu
Sakura	kudamono	tomaru
Mitsukoshi*	resutoran	iku

(*Mitsukoshi = Japanese equivalent of Harrods)

3 Use the same patterns to express decisions which (*a*) you have made consciously, and (*b*) have been made for you:
Rei: (*a*) Sakura to iu resutoran de taberu koto ni shimashita.
(*b*) Sakura to iu resutoran de taberu koto ni narimashita.

4 Tom is looking at his diary and going over his plans for next week with Yamada-san. Using **[verb]-(y)ō to omou**, work out what he actually says:
Rei: (getsuyōbi) repōto o kaku
Getsuyōbi ni repōto o kakō to omoimasu.

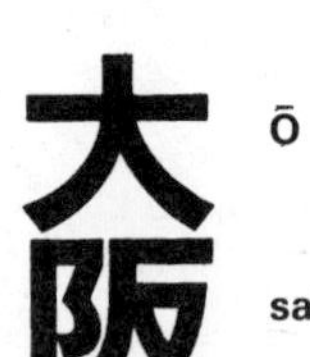

(*a*) (kayōbi) Ōsaka ni iku
(*b*) (suiyōbi) keiyaku o musubu
(*c*) (mokuyōbi) Ōsaka kara kaeru
(*d*) (kinyōbi) osoku made neru

5 Put the following conversations into **-masu** form Japanese:

(*a*) **A** I'm sorry I forgot the salad.
B It's all right (**ii**). I don't like salad very much.
(*b*) **C** I think Ken is ill.
D Why?
C It's because he says he doesn't want to eat anything.
(*c*) **E** This telephone is no good.
F Did you put in (**ire.ru**) (any) money?
E I tried to, but it didn't go in (**hair.u**).

Language and Society

1 *Getting married in Japan*

Vast amounts of money are spent on getting married in Japan, as the lavish advertising by hotels and specialised wedding establishments in trains and other public places indicates. **Ren'ai kekkon** (*love matches*) are increasingly common, but **miai kekkon** (*arranged marriages*) are still frequent. In the case of the latter, the families first exchange photographs and **rirekisho** (*curricula vitae*), which give information about the family as a whole as well as about the actual candidate. Even in the case of an arranged marriage, the couple will be given an opportunity to get to know each other, and to say no, before any final arrangements are made. Their first formal meeting is known as the **o-miai** (**o-miai o suru** being the verb), and they will be accompanied by the person who is arranging the marriage, the **nakōdo** (*go-between*). Since the **nakōdo** is an important figure during the wedding festivities, even couples who have met without the aid of a go-between will ask someone (e.g. the bridegroom's professor at university) to act in an honorary capacity.

2 *Congratulating people*

The stock phrase used in congratulating people is **o-medetō gozaimasu**:

Tanjōbi o-medetō gozaimasu *Happy birthday* (**tanjōbi**)

Go-shussan o-medetō gozaimasu *Congratulations on the birth* (**shussan**) *of your baby*

Nyūgaku o-medetō gozaimasu (**nyūgaku (suru)** *to enter school/university*)

Sotsugyō o-medetō gozaimasu (**sotsugyō (suru)** *to graduate from school/university*)

Nyūsha o-medetō gozaimasu (**nyūsha (suru)** *to enter a company*)

The Japanese celebrate New Year rather than Christmas. The customary greeting when meeting an acquaintance for the first time in the new year is **(Akemashite) o-medetō gozaimasu**. In informal situations, **gozaimasu** is usually omitted from all these greetings.

Japanese wedding photos

14 Watashi wa sorosoro kekkon shita hō ga ii desu *I ought to be getting married soon*

In this unit you will learn how to form the equivalent of English relative clauses in Japanese, how to allow or recommend a course of action, and how to say what you are able or unable to do.

Kaiwa

Nishūkan shite kara, Tanaka-san ga mata kekkon no koto de sōdan ga aru to itte, Jiru-san o resutoran e yobidashita.

Jiru	Sono go, kekkon no hanashi wa dō narimashita?
Tanaka	Kekkyoku Sugiura-san o kotowarimashita.
Jiru	Ara, shigoto o yamenasai to itta kara?
Tanaka	Ē, shigoto o shite mo ii to iu hito no hō ga ii wa.
Jiru	Naruhodo ne. Kekkon no koto de sōdan ga aru to iimashita ga, donna koto desu ka?
Tanaka	Jitsu wa nakōdo no kata kara hanashi ga mittsu kita n' desu ga, sono koto de . . .
Jiru	Ara, mittsu mo kita n' desu ka? Ii no ga arimasu ka?
Tanaka	Sō desu ne . . . mina-san shigoto mo yoku dekite, ii kata desu ga, amari hansamu ja nai no ga tama ni kizu.
Jiru	Tanaka-san wa zuibun menkui na n' desu nē!

[time] suru (here) [*time*] *passes*
[noun] no koto de *about* [*noun*]
yobidasu *to call, summon*
sono go *since, in the meantime*
hanashi (*here*) *proposal*

kekkyoku *eventually, finally*
[verb]-te mo ii *it is all right to, you may [verb]* ● S3
shigoto o shite mo ii to iu hito *A man who says it is all right (for me) to work* ● S1
jitsu wa *actually, in fact*
kata honorific equivalent of **hito**
nakōdo no kata *the go-between person*
[number] mo *as many as [number]*
mina-san *all of them, all of you*
A wa B ga yoku dekiru *A is good at, excels at B* ● S5
amari hansamu ja nai no *not being very handsome* ● S2
tama ni kizu *a fly in the ointment* (Lit. *a flaw on a precious stone*)
menkui *someone who attaches importance to good looks* (usually used of men)

True or false?

1 Tanaka-san wa Sugiura-san to kekkon suru koto ni narimashita.
2 Tanaka-san wa shigoto o shite wa ikenai to iu hito ga ii.

Jiru Shashin wa arimasu ka?
Tanaka Ē, kore na n' desu kedo.
Jiru Dore, dore. Ara, kono hito, nakanaka hansamu ja nai, Tomu Kurūzu no kanji de.
Tanaka Ē, demo, watashi wa megane o kaketa hito wa iya na no.
Jiru Hē . . . ja, kono hito wa?
Tanaka Tōdai-de de yūshū da keredo . . . zannennagara se ga hikukute ne. Watashi wa se no takai otoko ga ii wa.
Jiru Ara ara, zuibun urusai no ne. Kono hito mo waruku nai deshō?
Tanaka Demo, hana ga hikui deshō? Watashi wa hana no hikui otoko wa dame yo.
Jiru Komarimashita ne. De, sono sōdan to iu no wa?
Tanaka Ē, anō . . . Watashi wa sorosoro kekkon shita hō ga ii shi, nan to ka shitai to omou n' desu. Sore de kangaemashita ga, se no hikui no ya, hana no hikui no wa naoranai keredo, megane no hō wa kontakuto ni kaerareru deshō?

Jiru Sō yo, soshite tokidoki hazusu koto mo dekiru kara ne.

Tanaka Ē, dakara yahari kono hansamu na hito to o-miai o shiyō ka to omou keredo, dō deshō ka?

Jiru Ii n' ja nai? Hayai tokoro kimete, watashi o kekkon-shiki ni yonde kudasai ne!

kedo informal variant of **keredomo**
dore, dore! *let's see!*
Tomu Kurūzu *Tom Cruise* (*the film star*)
[noun] no kanji da *to have a feeling about/be like [noun]*
megane o kake.ru *to put on/wear glasses*
kake.ru *to put on*
Tōdai (Tōkyō daigaku) *Tokyo University* (one of Japan's top universities)
Tōdai-de *a Tōdai graduate*
yūshū na *brilliant*
keredo variant of **keredomo**
zannennagara *unfortunately, as a matter of regret*
se no takai otoko *a tall man, tall men* ● S1
urusa.i (here) *choosy*
hana *nose*
hana ga hikui *to have a flat nose*
dame na (here) *have an aversion to*
sono sōdan to iu no wa (nan desu ka)? *what was it that you wanted to talk about?* ● S1
sorosoro [verb] *it's about time to [verb]*
[sentence]-ta hō ga ii *it would be better if you/you'd better [sentence]* ● S4
nan to ka suru *to make an effort, do something about*
se no hikui no *being short* ● S2
kontakuto (renzu) *contact lenses*
A o B ni kae.ru *change A to B*
kaerare.ru *to be able to change to* ● S5
tokidoki *sometimes*
hazus.u *to take off* (*glasses*); *unfasten* (*buttons*)
hazusu koto mo/ga dekiru *to be able to take (them) off* ● S5
hayai tokoro = hayaku
kime.ru *to decide*
kekkon-shiki *wedding* (*ceremony*)

True or false?

3 Se no hikui otoko wa megane o kakete iru.
4 Tanaka-san wa mada kekkon shitakunai.

Structures

1 *Modifying a noun with a sentence-like sequence*

As we have seen in Unit 2, it is possible to give further information on a noun by modifying it with an adjective:

> Hon desu; takai desu.→**Takai** hon desu.
> Kore wa inu desu; genki desu.→Kore wa **genki na** inu desu.

This is also possible with sentence-like elements:

> Kinō hon o kaimashita; omoshiroi desu.→**Kinō katta** hon wa omoshiroi desu. *The book I bought yesterday is interesting.*
> Kinō watashi wa hon o kaimashita; mimashita ka?→ **Kinō watashi ga katta** hon o mimashita ka? *Did you see the book that I bought yesterday?*

The highlighted parts in the above sentences have the same meanings as English relative clauses; to form them, the order of the modifying section needs to be changed so that the verb comes before the noun and is put into the plain form (which is the usual form for verbs in front of nouns). Where **wa** is present, it needs to be converted to **ga**, as subordinate clauses use **ga** rather than **wa** (recall Unit 10).

The differences that exist between *who*, *whom*, *to whom*, *with whom*, etc. in English relative clauses are expressed by the context in Japanese (although in the last example below, *with* is expressed by **issho ni**):

1 Kinō hito ga kimashita. Hansamu deshita.→Kinō kita hito wa hansamu deshita. *The man **who** came yesterday was handsome.*

2 Kinō hito o mimashita. Hansamu deshita.→Kinō mita hito wa hansamu deshita. *The man **whom** I saw yesterday was handsome.*

3 Kinō hito to hanashimashita. Hansamu deshita.→Kinō hanashita hito wa hansamu deshita. *The man **to whom** I talked yesterday was handsome.*

4 Kinō hito to issho ni ikimashita. Hansamu deshita.→Kinō issho ni itta hito wa hansamu deshita. *The man **with whom** I went yesterday was handsome.*

Depending on the context, the second sentence could also mean *The man who saw* (*something not mentioned*) . . ., the third one, *The man who talked* . . ., and the last one *The man who went with me* . . .; however, the sentences they are based on would be different: **2** Kinō hito ga (watashi-tachi o *etc.*) mimashita; **3** Kinō hito ga hanashimashita (*gave a talk*); **4** Kinō hito ga issho ni ikimashita.

Where **ga** occurs inside the relative clause, it is normally changed to **no**:

Sode no nagai shatsu ga kaitai desu. *I want to buy a shirt with long sleeves* (**sode**).
(*But*: [Kono] shatsu wa sode ga nagai desu.)
Nihongo no wakaru hito wa imasu ka? *Is there anyone here who understands Japanese?*
(*But*: [Kono] hito wa Nihongo ga wakarimasu – recall Unit 10 Structures 3(*c*).)

Relative clauses can also modify nouns of a general meaning such as **mono**, **koto** and **no**:

Kinō katta **mono** wa kore desu. *This is what* (*the thing which*) *I bought yesterday.*
Kinō itta **koto** o wasuremashita. *I forgot what* (*the thing which*) *I said yesterday.*
Kinō katta **no** wa doko desu ka? *Where is the one I bought yesterday?*

Here, **mono/koto/no** are used instead of a more specific noun; in this use, **mono** and **no** refer to actual objects (or sometimes persons), whereas **koto** means *matter*, referring to more abstract deeds or happenings.

2 *Converting sentences into nouns with* koto *and* no

In the following examples, **koto** and **no** serve to convert whole sentences into nouns, so that they can be the subject, object etc. of a new sentence. (Note that here they can not be replaced by other, specific nouns);

Kono eiga o mita **koto** o wasurete imashita. *I had forgotten* (*the fact*) *that I had seen this film.*
Eiga o miru **no** o wasuremashita. *I forgot to watch the film.*

Ano hito no atama no warui **koto/no** o shitte imasu. *I know that that person is stupid.*

Koto and **no** differ in that **koto** generally refers to the abstract idea of factual knowledge, whereas **no** concerns the workings of one's feelings. Thus, the first of the above examples can be paraphrased as *I forgot about the fact that I had seen it before*, whereas in the second one the speaker absent-mindedly forgot to switch on the TV, or perhaps change channels. The third example implies factual knowledge when **koto** is used, and impressionistic knowledge with **no**. Not surprisingly, verbs like **miru** or **kiku**, having to do with the workings of the senses, are always used with **no** rather than with **koto**:

Michiko-san ga piano o hiku no o kikimashita. *I heard Michiko play the piano.*

Ken-san ga o-sake o nomu no o mimashita. *I saw Ken drink alcohol.*

However, **kiku** can also be used in the sense of *hear about some fact*; in this case, obviously **koto** is required:

Michiko-san ga piano o hiku koto o kikimashita. *I heard that Michiko plays the piano.*

Apart from verbs, this structure is also used with certain adjectives:

Nihongo o kaku koto/no wa muzukashii desu. *Japanese is difficult to write.*

Demo, hanasu koto/no wa yasashii desu. *But it is easy to speak.*

Ano hito wa hashiru no ga hayai desu. *He is a fast runner.* (**hashir.u** *to run*)

Michiko-san wa oyogu no ga jōzu desu. *Michiko is good at swimming.*

3 *Expressing permission with* -te mo i.i

When asking for permission to do something, you attach **mo ii (desu) ka?** (*is it all right if?*) to the **-te** form of the verb:

1 Tabako o sutte mo ii desu ka? *Is it all right if I smoke?*
2 Issho ni itte mo ii desu ka? *May I come with you?*

If you remove the final **-i** from the negative plain form of verbs and add **-kute**, you get a form which can be used to ask for permission ***not*** to do something (*is it all right if I don't . . .*):

3 Zenbu tabenakute mo ii desu ka? *Is it all right if I don't eat it all?*

In questions, the subject is always *I* (or *we*), but in the case of statements giving permission, the subject becomes *you*:

Eiga ni itte mo ii desu. *It is all right if you/You may go to the movies.*
Mada kaeranakute mo ii desu. *It is all right if you don't/You needn't/don't have to come back yet.*

Affirmative answers to the original questions **1–3** would be:

1 Hai, (sutte mo) ii desu.
2 Ē, (itte mo) ii desu.
3 Ē, (tabenakute mo) ii desu.

(For ways of ***withholding*** permission, i.e. prohibiting, see Unit 15).
The **-te mo ii** form can also be used with adjectives of both types, and with nouns, as follows:

-i *adjectives* Heya wa chiisakute mo ii desu ka? O-furo wa atsukunakute mo ii desu ka?	 *Is it all right if the room is small?* *Does it matter if the bath isn't hot?*
na *adjectives* Tenisu wa heta de mo ii desu ka? Hoteru wa shizuka ja nakute mo ii desu ka?	 *Is it all right if I am no good at tennis?* *Is it all right if the hotel isn't quiet?*
nouns Ashita de mo ii desu ka? Nihongo ja nakute mo ii desu ka?	 *Is tomorrow all right?* *Is it all right if it's not Japanese?*

With nouns, a verb is normally implied, so the meaning understood is *Is it all right if we (go, etc.) tomorrow?/Do you mind if I don't (speak/write, etc. in) Japanese?*

4 *Recommending what to do using* [sentence] hō ga i.i

In Unit 8, we saw how the noun **hō** is used in comparisons after nouns and adjectives; after verbs in their plain past tense, the combination **hō ga ii** is used to advise a course of action (*you'd better/you should*):

Hayaku kaetta hō ga ii desu. *You'd better go home quickly.*
Benkyō shita hō ga ii desu. *You'd better do some studying.*

To tell someone what course of action is best ***avoided***, **hō ga ii** is attached to verbs in the plain present-tense negative form:

Kore o tabenai hō ga ii desu. *You'd better not eat this.*
Amari nomanai hō ga ii desu yo. *You shouldn't drink too much.*

5 *Expressing ability to do things with* [verb] koto ga deki.ru/[verb]-re.ru/rare.ru

There are two ways of expressing the idea *to be able to* (*do*) in Japanese.

(*a*) **(A wa) [verb (present plain form)] koto ga dekiru**
This is another **[verb] koto** pattern, now linked to the verb **dekiru**, which here means *to be possible.* Literally, therefore, the pattern means *As for A*, [*doing*] *is possible*, i.e. *A is able to* [*do*].

Nihongo o hanasu	koto ga dekimasu ka?	*Can you speak Japanese?*
Oyogu		*Can you swim?*

Negatives are formed by using the negative form of **dekiru**, **dekinai**:

Sonna ni hayaku aruku	koto ga/wa dekimasen.	*I can't walk so fast.*
Jiru-san wa tako o taberu		*Jill can't eat octopus.*

(Note that either **ga** or **wa** is possible after **koto** in negative sentences.)

(b) [verb]-reru/rareru

As the **koto ga dekiru** forms are rather lengthy, a special verb form known as the potential is usually preferred, although the former expression is sometimes used for greater emphasis. Potential forms are obtained in the following way:

(i) With **-iru/-eru** verbs, replace the final **-ru** with **-rare.ru**:

tabe¦ru	tabe¦rareru	(→taberaremasu, taberareta, etc.)
oki¦ru	oki¦rareru	
mi¦ru	mi¦rareru	

(ii) With **-u** verbs, replace the final **-u** with **-e.ru**:

aruk¦u	aruk¦eru	(→arukemasu, aruketa, etc.)
oyog¦u	oyog¦eru	
yom¦u	yom¦eru	
ka¦u	ka¦eru	
hanas¦u	hanas¦eru	
mats¦u	mat¦eru	

(Verbs like **matsu** are again slightly irregular in that they drop their **s**. See Unit 4.)

(iii) **Suru** and **kuru**

suru	dekiru
kuru	korareru

(Note that all potentials act like **-iru/-eru** verbs.)

Before going on to see how these forms are used in sentences, it may be useful to point out that **kuru** and **iru/-eru** verbs are developing alternative potential forms that are similar to the potentials of **-u** verbs, e.g. **mireru, okireru, koreru**. These non-standard forms are becoming increasingly acceptable (see for example the second sentence on page 182).

Here are examples of sentences with potential forms; note that if the potential verb has an object, it can generally be marked by either **ga** (**wa** for contrast) or **o**.

Mō sukoshi iraremasu ka? *Can you stay a little longer?*
Ashita hayaku okiremasu ka? *Can you get up early tomorrow?*
Watashi wa tako wa taberaremasen. *I can't eat octopus.*
Raishū issho ni ikemasu ka? *Can you come with us next week?*
Nihongo o hanasemasu ka? *Can you speak Japanese?*
Watashi wa piano ga hikemasen. *I can't play the piano.*

Occasionally, the subject is marked by **ni wa** instead of **wa**, which serves to emphasise the ability/non-ability on the part of the subject. In negative sentences, this can be reinforced by using **totemo** ((*not*) *at all*):

Watashi ni wa totemo kono shigoto ga/wa dekimasen. *This job is quite beyond my capabilities.*

Or, in a different word order:

Kono shigoto wa watashi ni wa totemo dekimasen.

In the case of verbs of the type **benkyō (o) suru**, the lengthy **suru koto ga dekiru** is hardly ever used; instead, **suru** is replaced with **dekiru**. Note that before **dekiru**, **tenisu**, etc. takes **ga** (or **wa**, if contrastively used).

Sumisu-san wa tenisu ga dekimasu ka? *Can you play tennis, Smith-san?*
Watashi wa dansu wa dekimasen. *I cannot* **dance** (*although I can do a host of other things!*)
(Kuruma no) unten ga dekimasu ka? *Can you drive* (**unten (suru)**)?

The reason why **kuruma no** (rather than **o**) is used in the last example is that **unten** here is acting as a noun rather than as a verb.

Renshū

1 You are scrutinising a set of photographs of girls with a Japanese acquaintance, who takes the opportunity to inform you about his preferences regarding girlfriends. As he is a domineering character of violent disposition, you are in no mood to disapprove of his tastes, choosing instead to voice approval using relative clauses according to the model:

Rei: Kono onna wa karada ga ōkii kara kirai da.
Watashi mo karada no ōkii onna ga kirai da.

(*a*) Kono onna wa me ga chiisai kara kirai da.
(*b*) Kono onna wa kami ga nagai kara suki da.
(*c*) Kono onna wa iro ga kuroi kara kirai da. (**kuro.i** (here) *sunburnt*)
(*d*) Kono onna wa ashi (*legs/feet*) ga futoi (*fat*) kara kirai da.
(*e*) Kono onna wa zubon (*trousers*) o haku kara kirai da.

2 Using **koto** or **no**, produce Japanese sentences matching the meaning of the English sentences:

(*a*) I forgot to bring the book.
(*b*) I saw Michiko drive a car.
(*c*) I know that Kyoto summers are hot.
(*d*) I heard Anzai-sensei sing.
(*e*) I heard that Anzai-sensei sings.
(*f*) I am a fast reader.

3 Your Japanese boyfriend has a tendency to indulge in various vices, but you, his health-conscious girlfriend, have other ideas. Using **hō ga ii**, provide positive or negative alternatives as required by the cues to your boyfriend's cravings:
Rei: Terebi ga mitai. (Jogingu suru *to go jogging*)—Jogingu shita hō ga ii desu yo!

(*a*) Kēki ga tabetai. (Yasai (*vegetable*) o taberu)
(*b*) Wain ga nomitai. (Arukōru (*alcohol*) o nomu NEG)
(*c*) Pātī ni ikitai. (Hayaku neru)
(*d*) Tabako ga suitai. (Suu NEG)

4 Reply to the requests/offers/invitations in accordance with the cues, explaining that you are unable to comply or accept:
Rei: Soko ni jūsho o kaite kudasai. (Nihongo; kaku)
Watashi wa Nihongo ga kakemasen.

(*a*) Kuruma de kite kudasai. (kuruma; unten suru)
(*b*) Nihongo de hanashite kudasai. (Nihongo; hanasu)
(*c*) Kono oishii tako o dōzo. (tako; taberu)
(*d*) Umi e itte, oyogimashō. (oyogu)
(*e*) Doyōbi ni issho ni tenisu o shimasen ka? (tenisu suru)
(*f*) Bā e nomi ni ikimashō. (sake; nomu)

Language and Society

1 *Idiomatic uses of* dekiru

One idiomatic use of **dekiru** as a potential is seen in the following examples, which are concerned with having/lacking skills:

Nihongo ga dekimasu ka? *Do you know any Japanese?*
Watashi wa piano ga dekimasen. *I can't play the piano.*

These expressions may be said to be alternatives to **Nihongo ga hanasemasu ka?/Watashi wa piano ga hikemasen**.

Apart from its use in potentials, **dekiru** is also commonly used (often in combination with **mada/mō**) in the sense of *to get a job done*:

Gohan wa mō dekimasu ka? *Will dinner be ready soon?*
Hai, mō dekimashita yo. *Yes, it's just ready.*
Mō dekite imasu yo. *It's already prepared.*
Shukudai (*homework*) ga dekimashita. *I've finished my homework.*
Nekutai ga dekite imasu ka? *Is the tie ready?* (*At the cleaners*)

The expression **yoku dekiru** means *to be very able* (**ano hito wa shigoto/benkyō ga yoku dekiru**), whereas **yoku dekimashita** normally means *well done!*. In the **-te iru** form, the same expression has again a somewhat different meaning:

Kono isu wa yoku dekite imasu. *This chair is well made.*
Kono hanashi wa yoku dekite imasu. *This story-line is well thought out.*

2 *Use of potential forms with Japanese food and drink*

Japanese people will often enquire about your *ability* to eat things like raw fish (**sashimi**) and to drink **sake**, rather than asking whether you like them. This may have something to do with the idea that the Japanese way of life is unique and incomprehensible to the Westerner. Note the following stock exchanges:

O-sashimi ga taberaremasu ka?

Ē, taberaremasu./Ē, daijōbu desu./Ē, daisuki desu.
Iie, taberaremasen./Iie, o-sashimi wa chotto . . .

Nihon no o-sake ga nomemasu ka?

Ē, nomemasu. (etc.)
Iie, nomemasen.

sake label

15 Neru mae ni kono kusuri o nonde kudasai *Please take this medicine before you go to bed*

In this unit you will meet various clauses involving time, including *when* and *before*, and learn how to express *must* and *must not* in Japanese. You will also be introduced to two sentence endings equivalent to *It seems* and *Apparently*. Finally there will be some information that we hope you will never need, on being ill in Japan.

Kaiwa

Tomu-san wa saikin karada no chōshi ga warui yō da. Tsukare ga nakanaka torenai shi, yoku kaze o hiitari o-naka o kowashitari suru. Sore de, Anzai-sensei to sōdan shite, Anzai-sensei to onaji daigaku o deta isha ni mite morau koto ni shita. Anzai-sensei ni yoru to, totemo ii isha da sō da. Shinsatsu wa mō hajimatte iru.

Tomu Konogoro dōmo chōshi ga warui n' desu. Asa okiru toki, atama mo nodo mo itai shi, seki mo demasu. Sore ni, shokuyoku ga hotondo arimasen. Shigoto o shite iru toki sugu tsukareru shi.

Isha Ikemasen ne. Sa, ato de ketsuatsu o hakarimasu ga, sono mae ni shatsu o nuide kudasai.

Tomu (*kao ga aoku naru*) Ketsuatsu?

Isha Kinchō shite wa dame desu yo!

saikin *recently*
A wa karada no chōshi ga warui *A is not feeling well* (Lit. As for A, the condition of his body is bad.)
chōshi *condition, state*
[statement] yō da *It seems that [statement]* ● S1
tsukare ga tore.ru *to recover from one's fatigue*

tsukare *fatigue*
tore.ru potential form of **tor.u** *to take, remove* ● Unit 14 S5
o-naka o kowas.u *to have a stomach upset*
onaji *same* ● S2
daigaku o de.ru *to graduate from university*
isha ni mite mora.u *to see/consult a doctor* ● Unit 16 S1
[noun] ni yoru to *according to [noun]*
[statement] sō da *apparently [statement]* ● S3
shinsatsu (suru) *medical examination*
konogoro *recently*
dōmo (here) *somehow*
[verb (plain form)] toki *when [verb]* ● S4
seki ga de.ru *to have a cough*
seki *cough*
shokuyoku (ga nai) *(to have no) appetite*
hotondo [negative] *hardly at all*
Ikemasen ne *That won't do* (an expression of sympathy)
ketsuatsu *blood pressure*
hakar.u *to measure*
mae ni *before* ● S5
nug.u *to take off*
kinchō (suru) *stress, tension*
[verb]-te wa dame da *You etc. must not [verb]* ● S7

True or false?

1 Tomu-san wa konogoro yoku nerarenai.
2 Tomu-san wa yoru seki ga deru.

Kensa ga yatto owatta.

Tomu Dō desu ka? Warui n' deshō ka?
Isha Iie, shinpai shinakute mo ii desu yo. Ketsueki kensa no kekka wa raishū wakarimasu ga, tonikaku daijōbu na yō desu. Tokoro de, Hādo-san wa nannen umare desu ka?
Tomu Sen kyūhyaku gojū-nen desu.
Isha Shōwa nijūgo-nen desu ne. Kore kara karada ni ki o tsukenai to dame desu yo.
Tomu Hai, wakarimashita.
Isha Tabako o suimasu ne. Sore wa yameta hō ga ii desu. O-sake wa?

Tomu	Boku no yō na shigoto wa dōshitemo settai ga ōi desu. O-sake o nonde iru aida wa ii desu ga, tsugi no asa wa . . .
Isha	Dekiru dake, sake mo yamete kudasai. Sore kara, undō mo motto shinakereba narimasen. Ēto . . . (*shohōsen o kaki-nagara*) neru mae ni kono kusuri o nonde kudasai.
Tomu	Nigai kusuri desu ka?

kensa (suru) *check-up*
waru.i (of illness) *serious*
ketsueki kensa *blood test*
ketsueki *blood*
kekka *results*
tonikaku *anyway*
tokoro de [sentence] *by the way [sentence]* (signals change of topic)
nannen umare desu ka? *What is your year of birth?/When were you born?*
umare *birth*
[verb]-nai to dame da *I* etc. *must [verb]* ● S8
A no yō na B *B such as A* ● S1
dōshitemo *inevitably, whether I want it or not*
settai *receptions, entertainment*
[verb (plain form)] aida *while [verb]* ● S6
dekiru dake *as much/far as possible*
undō (suru) *exercise*
[verb]-nakereba naranai *I* etc. *must [verb]* ● S8
shohōsen *prescription*
kusuri o nom.u *to take medicine*
kusuri *medicine*
niga.i *bitter, nasty-tasting*

True or false?

3 Tomu-san wa karada no chōshi ga taihen warui to isha ga itta.
4 Tomu-san wa tabako o yamenakereba naranai.

Structures

1 [statement] yō da *It seems . . .*

This is one of several endings that can be attached after statements

(Structures 4; Unit 17 Structures 3 and 6). **Yō da** is very close to *it seems*. A speaker uses it to imply that he/she is making a statement based not upon actual knowledge, but on objective deductions made on the basis of the available evidence. This is often visual, but not necessarily so. **Yō da** and the other sentence endings are often used when describing the state of mind of someone other than oneself. In the following examples, note the forms which nouns, adjectives and verbs take before **yō da**, both in the present tense and in the past. They are the forms which would normally be found in front of nouns.

nouns Anzai-sensei wa dōmo byōki no Mukashi, koko wa resutoran datta	 yō desu. yō desu.	*Anzai-sensei somehow seems ill.* *Formerly, this seems to have been a restaurant.*
na *adjectives* Michiko-san wa Ken-san ga suki na Saikin made koko wa shizuka datta	 yō desu. yō desu.	*Michiko seems to like Ken.* *It seems that until recently it was quiet here.*
-i *adjectives* Ano mise wa totemo takai Kinō no pātī wa tanoshikatta	 yō desu. yō desu.	*That shop looks very expensive.* *It seems that the party yesterday was enjoyable* **(tanoshi.i).**
verbs Jiru-san wa tsukarete iru Tomu-san wa genki ni natta	 yō desu. yō desu.	*Jill appears to be tired.* *Tom appears to have recovered.*

When there is a negative, it will normally come before **yō da**:

Koko wa mō resutoran de wa nai	yō desu.	*This doesn't appear to be a restaurant any more.*
Ano ringo wa amari oishikunai	yō desu.	*That apple doesn't look very tasty.*

In the examples given above where there was a past tense before **yō da**, the speaker was giving his/her ***present*** impression of something which had already happened. When recalling ***past*** impressions, however, where English would use *seemed* rather than *seems*, **yō datta** is used, and the statement preceding it does not go into the past:

Tomu-san wa senshū byōki no	yō deshita.	*Tom seemed ill last week.*
Kinō Jiru-san wa tsukarete iru	yō deshita.	*Jill seemed to be tired yesterday.*

Before nouns, **yō da** takes the form **yō na**:

tako no yō na aji *a taste* (**aji**) *like octopus*
tsukarete iru yō na me *eyes which look tired*

Kyō wa fuyu no yō na tenki desu. *Today the weather is like winter.*
Koko wa daremo sunde inai yō na tokoro desu. *This is the sort of place which seems to have no-one living in it.*

A common pattern is **[proper noun (A)] no yō na [general noun (B)]**. Here the meaning is similar to *B such as/like A*:

Tomu-san no yō na Igirisujin *an Englishman/Englishmen like Tom*
Furansu no yō na kuni *a country/countries* (**kuni**) *such as France*
Aisukurīmu no yō na tsumetai mono o tabemashō. *Let's eat something cold such as ice-cream.*

Kyōto no yō na furui machi ni sumitai desu. *I want to live in an old town such as Kyoto.*

2 *The adjective* onaji *same*

Onaji works like a **na** adjective at the end of sentences and in forming the negative, but goes straight in front of nouns like an **-i** adjective. The Japanese equivalent for *same as* [*noun*] is **[noun] to onaji**.

Kore wa watashi no kasa to onaji desu. *This is the same as my umbrella.*
Onaji da.
Onaji de wa nai deshō!
Michiko-san no wanpīsu to onaji iro desu. *It's the same colour as Michiko's dress* (**wanpīsu**).

3 [statement] sō da *apparently*

Sō da is a sentence ending similar to **yō da**. It implies that the statement is not the speaker's own opinion, but something which he/she has heard or read. It is equivalent to English *apparently/I hear/they say that* . . . . Like **yō da**, it is often used in talking about the feelings/intentions of other people. In the following examples, note the forms which nouns, adjectives, and verbs take in front of **sō da**, both in the present tense and in the past. They are in fact the plain forms that you would expect to see at the end of sentences in informal speech.

nouns		
Hādo-san no okusan wa Amerikajin da	sō desu.	*Apparently Mr Herd's wife is an American.*
Kinō koko wa sugoi ame datta	sō desu.	*Apparently there was terrific rain here yesterday.*

na *adjectives* Hādo-san no hisho wa totemo kirei da	sō desu.	*They say that Hādo-san's secretary is very pretty.*
Kuruma wa dame datta	sō desu.	*Apparently the car was ruined.*
-i *adjectives* Anzai-sensei wa ima taihen isogashii	sō desu.	*Apparently Anzai-sensei is very busy at the moment.*
Tarō-kun mo ikitakatta	sō desu.	*I hear that Tarō-kun wanted to go too.*
verbs Tanaka-san wa rainen kekkon suru	sō desu.	*I hear that Tanaka-san is getting married next year.*
Suzuki-san wa densha ni noriokureta	sō desu.	*Apparently Suzuki-san missed his train.*

As with **yō da**, negatives tend to precede **sō da**:

Tomu-san wa byōki de wa nakatta sō desu.
Ken-san wa sakana ga suki ja nai sō desu.
Jiru-san wa ano eiga ga mitakunai sō desu.

Sentences ending in **sō da** often begin with **[noun] ni yoru to/yoreba**, *according to* [*noun*], or some other form of words giving the source of your knowledge:

Shinbun ni yoru to, Igirisu no shushō ga rainichi suru sō desu. *According to the newspapers, the British Prime Minister is going to visit Japan* (**rainichi suru**).

Tomodachi kara kiita no desu ga, Tomu-san wa tabako o yameta sō desu. *I heard from a friend that Tom has given up smoking.*

4 toki *when*

Toki is a noun meaning time (e.g. **ano toki** *at that time*), but it is most commonly found where English would use *when/whenever*. The time, or *when*, part of the sentence before **toki**, and the action of the main part of the sentence after **toki**, occur more or less contemporaneously with each other. Nouns, adjectives and verbs occurring before **toki** take the forms which it is usual for them to take before nouns. **Toki** can be followed by **ni** to give a sense of greater precision, and by **wa** to give a sense of contrast, or even by both.

nouns			
Ame no	toki	takushī ni norimasu.	*When it rains, I take a taxi.*
Kodomo no	toki wa	yoku benkyō shimashita.	*When I was a child I studied hard (but I don't now).*
na *adjectives*			
Hima na	toki ni	asobi ni kite kudasai.	*Please call on us whenever you are at leisure* (**hima na**)*/have some spare time.*
Genki na	toki wa	Tomu-san wa yoku o-sake o nomimashita.	*When Tom was well, he often drank (but he doesn't now).*
-i *adjectives*			
Tabako ga suitai	toki ni wa	dō shimasu ka?	*What do you do when you want to smoke?*
Atsui	toki	hotondo neraremasen deshita.	*When it was hot, I was hardly able to sleep.*

verbs			
Michi o wataru	toki	ki o tsukete kudasai.	*Please be careful when you cross the road.*
Nihon ni iru	toki	itsu mo Nihongo de hanashimashita.	*When I was in Japan, I always spoke in Japanese.*

In the above examples, the form before **toki** was the same whatever the tense at the end of the sentence. With verbs, however, it is possible to have past tenses in front of **toki**. An alternative version of the last example would therefore be:

Nihon ni ita toki Nihongo de hanashimashita.

5 mae *before*

We have already met **mae** with reference both to physical position, with the meaning 'in front' (Unit 2 Structures 5), and to telling the time (Unit 6 Structures 5). You will find **mae** working in a similar way with other expressions of time which involve number + counter (e.g. **san-kagetsu mae (ni)** *three months ago/before;* **jū-nen mae (ni)** *ten years ago/before*). You will also find **mae** preceded by **[noun] no**, and by verbs in the present plain form, with a meaning equivalent to English *before*. As with **toki**, **mae** can be followed by **ni** and/or **wa**.

nouns			
Gohan no	mae ni	te o araimashō.	*Let's wash our hands before the meal.*
Shiken no	mae ni	kinchō shimashita ka?	*Were you tense before the exam* (**shiken**)*?*
verbs			
O-furo ni hairu	mae ni	Nihonjin wa karada o araimasu.	*The Japanese wash their bodies before they get into the bath.*
Dekakeru	mae ni	tomodachi ni denwa o kakemashita.	*Before setting out I telephoned a friend.*

Note that **mae ni** or **mae (ni) wa** is also possible in isolation, with the meaning *before* or *formerly*, and that you will also come across **kono mae** *previously/recently* and **sono mae** *before that* (both with or without **ni**/(**ni**) **wa**).

6 aida *between/while*

Like **mae**, **aida** (**ni**/(**ni**) **wa**) is a noun which acts both as a position word and as a time word. As a position word, it is typically found in the pattern **A to B no aida**:

> Nagoya wa Tōkyō to Ōsaka no aida ni arimasu. *Nagoya is in between Tokyo and Osaka.*

As a time word, it can also have a meaning equivalent to *between*:

> Rokuji to shichiji no aida ni nani o shite imashita ka? *What were you doing between* 6 *and* 7 *o'clock?*

More often, however, it is preceded by **[noun] no**, or by a verb, with the meaning *during* or *while*:

> Natsu-yasumi no aida Michiko-san wa mainichi benkyō shimashita. *During the summer holidays, Michiko studied every day.*
>
> Michiko-san ga piano o hiite iru aida, Tarō-kun wa terebi o mite imashita. *While Michiko was playing the piano, Tarō was watching the television.*

In the above examples, the part before **aida** (X) has the same duration as the part afterwards (Y). With **aida *ni***, however, the implication is that Y is of shorter duration, and takes place within the time span of X:

> Natsu-yasumi no aida **ni** Ken-san wa manga o issatsu yomimashita. *During the summer holidays, Ken read one comic book* (**manga**).
>
> Michiko-san ga piano o hiite iru aida **ni**, Tarō-kun wa chokorēto o zenbu tabemashita. *While Michiko was playing the piano, Tarō ate all the chocolate.*

With verbs, **aida** (but not **aida ni**) clearly overlaps with **-nagara** (Unit

11 Structures 6), but unlike **-nagara** it can be used with different subjects in each part, as in the example above and in the second example below:

Tomodachi o matte iru aida shinbun o yomimashita. *I read a newspaper while waiting for a friend.*
Kodomo ga nete iru aida wa totemo shizuka deshita. *It was very quiet while the children were asleep.*

The verb in front of **aida** is usually in the **-te iru** form, but this is not possible with **iru** since it has no **-te iru** form anyway:

Igirisu ni iru aida ni, Bābarī o kaō to omoimasu. *I think I'll buy a Burberry coat* (**Bābarī**) *while I am in Britain.*
Jiru-san ga inai aida Tomu-san wa tabako o takusan suimashita. *Tom did some heavy smoking while Jill was not there.*

Note also the use of the **-i** adjective **nagai** in front of **aida**:

Suzuki-san wa nagai aida Furansu ni imashita. *Suzuki-san was in France for a long time.*

You will also come across **kono aida**, which means *the other day/recently*, and **sono aida**, *during that time/meanwhile*.

7 [verb]-te wa ikenai/dame da *must not [verb]*

This construction literally means [*verb*]*-ing will not do/is no good*. **Ikenai/ikemasen** is a form of the verb **iku**, *to go*, which literally means *cannot go*. As in the **Kaiwa**, it can be used with the sentence ending particle **ne** as an expression of sympathy, but when pronounced in more authoritarian tones it functions as a fairly brusque way of forbidding something:

A Tabako o sutte mo ii desu ka? *Is it all right if I smoke?*
B Iie, ikemasen. *No, you must not.*

In similar contexts **dame da/desu** will have the same effect: you are likely to hear mothers admonishing naughty children with the words, **Dame, dame, dame!** Preceded by **[verb]-te wa, [noun] de wa** and **[adjective]-te/de wa**, both **ikenai** and **dame da** therefore enable you to make prohibitions.

Mite wa dame desu! *You mustn't look!*
Kono saki e haitte wa ikemasen. *No entry beyond this point* (**kono saki**).
Yasui wain de wa dame desu. *Cheap wine won't do.*
Heya ga konna ni kitanakute wa ikemasen! *I won't have the room this dirty* (**kitana.i**)*!*

It is often advisable to avoid this construction, however, as it sounds rather brusque; a softer alternative for verbs would involve the use of **-naide kudasai**, for example.

Note that in informal speech, **-te wa** is contracted to **-cha**, and **-de wa** to **-ja**:

Itcha (=itte wa) dame! *You mustn't tell!*
Koko de asonja (=asonde wa) ikenai! *You can't play here!*

8 [verb]-nakute wa/nai to/-nakereba . . . *must [verb]*

The idea of *you (etc.) must* is expressed in a rather roundabout way in Japanese, by a cluster of patterns. One way is really the opposite of the **-te wa ikenai/dame da** construction introduced above, and literally means *not doing* [*verb*] *will not do/is no good*:

Ashita wa rokuji ni okinakute wa ikemasen. *I must get up at six o'clock tomorrow.*
Motto benkyō shinakute wa dame desu. *You must study more.*

The other ways all basically mean *if you* (*etc.*) *do not* [*verb*], *it won't do*. For the first part of these patterns, you need the negative form of either of two constructions which both mean *if*, and which we will meet later in more detail (Unit 19 Structures 1). For the negative of the **to** form, which is different again from both the *and* **to** (Unit 8 Structures 3) and the quoting **to** (Unit 13 Structures 1), you simply add **to** to the present plain negative:

minai to tabenai to	kakanai to hanasanai to	konai to shinai to

To make the negative **-eba** form of any verb, start with its present plain negative, drop the final **-i**, and add **-kereba**:

miru	mina¦i	mina¦kereba	kaku	kakana¦i	kakana¦kereba
taberu	tabena¦i	tabena¦kereba	hanasu	hanasana¦i	hanasana¦kereba
kuru	kona¦i	kona¦kereba	suru	shina¦i	shina¦kereba

In the case of **-eba**, the pattern is completed by the addition of **ikenai/ikemasen**, **dame da/desu**, or **naranai/narimasen**, which also has a meaning equivalent to *it won't do*. With **to**, you will only find the first two:

Kusuri o {nomanakereba / nomanai to} ikemasen. *You must take your medicine*

Watashi wa mō ikanakereba narimasen. *I must go now.*

Michiko-san ni {iwanakereba / iwanai to} dame desu. *You must tell Michiko.*

Note that these constructions can also be adapted to function with nouns and adjectives:

Kyō ja nakute wa/ja nakereba ikemasen ka? *Must it be today?*

O-furo wa konna ni atsukunakute wa/-nai to dame desu ka? *Does the bath have to be this hot?*

Bōi-furendo wa hansamu ja nakute wa/ja nakereba ikemasen ka? *Does a boy-friend* (**bōi-furendo**) *have to be handsome?*

In informal speech, these patterns are frequently reduced to a contracted form of **-nakute wa**, **-nakucha**, with or without a final **ikenai** etc.:

Mō ikanakucha (=ikanakute wa) (ikenai). *I've got to go now.*

Isoganakucha (=isoganakute wa) (dame da). *You must hurry.*

Renshū

1 Jill and Mrs Anzai are having a gossip. Add **yō desu** to their

statements to make it clear that they are just going by appearances.
Rei: Tanaka-san wa hontō ni kekkon shimasu.
→Tanaka-san wa hontō ni kekkon suru yō desu.

(*a*) Ano atarashii resutoran wa oishii desu.
(*b*) Suzuki-san wa kimasen deshita.
(*c*) Asoko de utte iru konpyūta wa totemo benri desu.
(*d*) Ano wakai Doitsujin wa yūmei na kaisha no shachō desu.

2 Later, Jill and Mrs Anzai repeat each other's gossip to their respective husbands. They therefore add **sō desu** rather than **yō desu**.
Rei: Tanaka-san wa hontō ni kekkon shimasu.
→Tanaka-san wa hontō ni kekkon suru sō desu.

3 The doctor is asking Tom questions. Use the clues in the brackets to construct his possible answers.
Rei: Itsu seki o shimasu ka? (asa okiru/toki; neru/mae ni)
Asa okiru toki seki o shimasu.
Neru mae ni seki o shimasu.

(*a*) O-naka ga itsu itaku narimasu ka? (Hiru-gohan/toki; Nihongo o benkyō suru/mae ni)
(*b*) Itsu undō shimasu ka? (Genki na/toki ni; terebi o mite iru/aida)
(*c*) Itsu tabako o suimasu ka? (Shigoto/mae ni; hataraite iru/aida)
(*d*) O-sake o itsu nomimasu ka? (Tsukarete iru/toki; shigoto ga owaru/kara)

4 Using the **-te mo ii** construction, Tom then asks for permission to continue some of his favourite activities. Unfortunately the doctor uses *must not* constructions in order to refuse permission:
Rei: tokidoki tabako o suu
→Tokidoki tabako o sutte mo ii deshō ka?
Iie, sutte wa ikemasen/dame desu.

(*a*) maiban terebi o miru
(*b*) atsui o-furo ni hairu
(*c*) hanbāgā o taberu
(*d*) yoru osoku made hon o yomu

5 This time Jill has suddenly started to feel ill while at work. Using the **-nakute mo ii** construction, a Japanese colleague tries to persuade her that she doesn't have to fulfil all her commitments. Using *must* constructions, however, Jill refuses to accept this:

Rei: kyō wa gogo oshieru
→Kyō wa gogo oshienakute mo ii deshō.
Iie, oshienakereba narimasen/oshienai to dame desu (etc.)

(*a*) Ginza de Tanaka-san ni au
(*b*) kaimono ni iku
(*c*) ban-gohan o tsukuru (**ban-gohan** *dinner*, *evening meal*)
(*d*) ashita dekakeru

6 Put the following dialogue between two business colleagues into Japanese:

A Where is Mr Suzuki, I wonder?
B He rang up ten minutes ago – apparently he is not feeling well.
A Is that so? Perhaps he ought to see a doctor.
B Anyway we must finish that report.

Language and Society

Being ill in Japan

Health is taken extremely seriously in Japan, as the high status of doctors would suggest. Even minor ailments such as colds are treated with care. In cold weather, it is common for people to gargle (**ugai suru**) on returning home from outside, and some still wear gauze masks (**masuku o kakeru**) for the same reason when outside in the winter. There is also a considerable preoccupation with stomach ailments (**benpi (suru)** *to be constipated*; **geri (suru)** *the opposite!*). The traditional medical system of Chinese origin known as **kanpō** exists alongside the Western one, and it is not unusual to consult both with regard to the same problem.

Chemists in Japan are able to sell quite powerful drugs (such as sleeping pills – **suiminyaku**) without a prescription. If a doctor gives you a prescription, however, you will get it made up at the hospital or surgery rather than at the chemist's. (Note that it is not unusual for medicine in Japan to come in powdered form.) To call an ambulance (**kyūkyūsha**), dial 119.

Note the following additional useful words and phrases:

byōki da *to be ill*
daun suru *to fall ill* (colloquial)
kaifuku (suru) *to recover*
netsu ga aru *to have a temperature*
byōin *hospital*
nyūin (suru) *to enter hospital*
tai'in (suru) *to leave hospital*
shujutsu (suru) *operation*
shujutsu o ukeru *to undergo an operation*
chūsha (suru) *injection*
chūsha o shite morau *to be injected*
kangofu *nurse*
[person] no/o mimai ni iku *to visit someone who is ill*
kusuriya *chemist*

Bayer Aspirins

16 Tetsudatte agemashō ka? *Shall I help you?*

In this unit you will see how imperatives are formed, encounter indirect requests and learn to express the 'giving' and 'doing' of favours; you will also learn how members of the family are addressed and referred to, not only within the family but also when speaking to outsiders.

Kaiwa

Ken-san to Michiko-san wa mae kara no yakusoku de kissaten de atta ga, Michiko-san wa ochitsukanai.

Michiko Ken-san, warui kedo, yōji ga yama hodo atte, amari jikan ga nai no yo.

Ken Nani ka atta no?

Michiko Uchi wa kazoku zen'in byōki da kara, nan demo watashi ni yatte kure to tanomu no. Chichi wa Supo-nichi o katte koi to iu shi, haha ni wa nagai kaimono no risuto o moratte iru shi, otōto made chūmon shite aru rimo-kon kā o totte kuru yō ni iu n' da kara, taihen na no yo.

Ken Mina-san dō shita n' desu ka?

Michiko Otōto ga saisho ni kaze o hiite, sore ga haha ni utsutte, soshite ima wa chichi made daibu warukute, shigoto o yasunde iru no yo.

Ken Michiko-san wa yoku daijōbu da ne.

Michiko Mainichi bitamin-zai o abiru hodo nonde iru no yo!

mae kara *from before, from earlier on*
yakusoku (suru) *promise, date*
[noun] de (here) *because of [noun]*
ochitsuk.u *to settle down, calm down*
yōji *things to do*
yama hodo *heaps* (Lit. *to the extent of mountains*)
nani ka atta no? *Is something wrong?*
uchi *at home; we*
zen'in *everyone*
yar.u = suru
[verb]-te kure *please [verb]* ● S3
tanom.u *to ask (a favour/for help)*
chichi *(my) father* ● LS1
Supo-nichi *a popular sports newspaper* (a contraction of **Supōtsu Nippon**)
katte koi plain imperative of **katte kuru** (*to buy*, Unit 17 S2) ● S2
haha *(my) mother* ● LS1
risuto *list*
mora.u *to receive* ● S1
[person (etc.)] made *even [person (etc.)]*
rimo-kon kā *remote-controlled (model) car*
totte kuru *to fetch* ● Unit 17 S2
[verb (present plain form)] yō ni iu *to tell to [verb]* ● S3
saisho ni *in the beginning, at first*
utsur.u *to spread; be infected*
shigoto o yasum.u *to take time off work, stay at home*
yoku *miraculously, luckily*
bitamin-zai *vitamin pills*
abiru hodo *(drink) vast amounts*

True or false?

1 Michiko-san wa mainichi bitamin-zai o sukoshi nonde iru.
2 Michiko-san wa byōki ni natte inai.

Ken wa sukoshi kangaete ita:

Ken Michiko-san wa taihen da kara, nani ka tetsudatte agemashō ka?

Michiko Hontō? Sore wa tasukaru wa! Jā ne, Shinjuku kara otōto no rimo-kon kā o totte kite moratte mo ii kashira? Kore ga seikyūsho yo.

Ken E, goman-en mo suru n' desu ka?!

Michiko Ē, takai wa yo nē . . . o-kane wa ima watashite okimasu kara ne, yoroshiku o-negai shimasu!

Ken Demo, dō yatte Michiko-san ni watashimashō ka?

Michiko Konban uchi ni irasshai; ban-gohan o gochisō shite ageru kara.

Ken Sore dake wa kanben shite kudasai; boku wa sono kaze o hikitakunai kara. KUSHAN!! (*ōki na kushami o suru*)

Michiko Ara, mō hiite īru kara ii ja nai!

[verb]-te age.ru ● S1
tasukar.u (intransitive) *to be saved, be a help*
seikyūsho *bill*
suru = kakaru (*to cost*)
watas.u *hand over*
watashite ok.u *give* (*for future use*) ● S4
yoroshiku o-negai shimasu *please* ● LS2
dō yatte? *how? in what way?*
irasshai *please come* ● S2
gochisō suru *to treat*
[noun] dake *at least* [*noun*]
kanben (suru) *to spare, let off*
kushan *sound of sneezing*
kushami *a sneeze*

True or false?

3 Michiko-san wa otōto-san no rimo-kon kā o totte kite morau.
4 Rimo-kon kā wa amari takakunai.

Structures

1 *Giving/receiving and doing favours with* ([verb]-te) age.ru/kure.ru/mora.u

In Japanese, there is no single equivalent of the English *to give*; instead, there are two basic verbs of that meaning which are used depending on whether the giving is outgroup (away from the speaker and/or those associated/identified with him) or ingroup (towards the speaker and/or those associated/identified with him). The notion of outgroup/ingroup is not fixed; 'ingroup' can range from one person (the speaker versus the listener) to a whole nation (e.g. Japan versus another country).

The in/outgroup distinction means that the choice of verb will generally make clear who is giving to whom, especially in exchanges between speaker and listener (see below). For this reason the use of personal pronouns such as **watashi** or **anata** etc. is even more redundant with these verbs than is usually the case in Japanese.

Ageru is used when the action of giving is taking place in the direction ingroup→outgroup, that is when the giver is either the speaker or someone associated/identified with him.

Ken-san ni purezento o agemashita. *I gave Ken a present.*
Suzuki-san wa Ken-san ni purezento o agemashita. *Suzuki-san gave Ken a present.*

The same principle applies when you are giving actions rather than things, in other words when you are doing an action for someone. **Ageru** is here attached to the **-te** form of the action (verb) in question:

Ken-san ni o-kane o kashite agemashita. *I lent Ken some money.*
Suzuki-san wa Ken-san ni purezento o katte agemashita. *Suzuki-san bought a present for Ken.*

Notice that the use of **-te ageru** implies that you are doing the other person a favour; for this reason, it may at times be more appropriate, or tactful, to use the verb without **-te ageru**:

Ken-san ni Eigo o oshiete imasu. *I teach Ken English.*
Tetsudaimashō ka? *Shall I help?*

This is particularly the case when you are doing something for someone of higher social standing (see Unit 9 Structures 5; Unit 18 Structures 1):

O-mochi shimashō ka? *Shall I carry it (for you)?*

Kureru is used when the giving/doing of a favour takes place in the direction outgroup→ingroup, that is when the ***receiver*** is the speaker or someone associated/identified with him:

O-kane o kashite kuremasu ka? *Will you lend me (some) money?*

Ken-san wa purezento o kuremashita. *Ken gave me a present.*
Suzuki-san wa Ken-san ni purezento o kuremashita. *Suzuki-san gave Ken a present.*

Ageru can never be used when the speaker is the receiver, nor when the listener is the giver, unless he happens to be a close friend of the speaker; conversely **kureru** can never be used when the speaker is the giver, nor when the listener is the receiver. When giving takes place between third persons, however, either **ageru** or **kureru** may be used, depending on which side the speaker identifies with. Compare two sentences (of identical factual content) given above and repeated here: in the first one, the speaker 'sides' with Suzuki-san, thus treating Ken as outgroup, whereas in the second example the situation is reversed.

Suzuki-san wa Ken-san ni purezento o agemashita.
Suzuki-san wa Ken-san ni purezento o kuremashita.

Morau, on the other hand, means *to receive* an object or a favour; in other words, the action of giving is perceived from the receiving end. The receiver here is ingroup, and the giver, who is marked by either **ni** or **kara**, outgroup:

Haha ni/kara tokei o moraimashita. *I received a watch from my mother.*
Ken-san wa Suzuki-san ni purezento o moraimashita. *Ken received a present from Suzuki-san.*

Depending on the context, **morau** can also mean *to get* in the sense of asking for something (or influencing the giver in some other way):

Suzuki-san ni/kara tokei o morai-nasai. *Get a watch from Suzuki-san.*

When used after **[verb]-te** form, **morau** again has two possible meanings. In other words, depending on the context, the following sentence, which literally means *I received Ken mending my watch*, is equivalent either to *I had my watch fixed by Ken* or to *I got Ken to fix my watch*:

Ken-san ni tokei o naoshite moraimashita.

To convey the former meaning only, **-te kureru** could also be used:

Ken-san ga tokei o naoshite kuremashita. *Ken fixed my watch for me.*

The choice of **-te morau** or **-te kureru** here will often depend on whether the giver or the receiver is the focus of the discourse. The **-te morau** sentence above centres on the receiver *I*, (the speaker, ingroup), whereas in the **-te kureru** sentence the same speaker treats Ken (another person, outgroup) as the main protagonist. In the **-te morau** sentence, therefore, the person actually performing the action of the **-te** verb is indicated by **ni/kara**, not **wa/ga**.

Here are some more examples involving **-te morau**:

Suzuki-san ni/kara kuruma o kashite moraimashita. *I got Suzuki-san to lend me his car.*
Nihonjin ni/kara Nihongo o oshiete moratte imasu. *I am being taught Japanese by a Japanese.*
Tomodachi ni kaimono shite moraimashita. *I had a friend do my shopping for me.*

2 *Imperative forms*

Imperative verb forms are arrived at as follows:

(*a*) **iru/eru** verbs: replace the final **-ru** with **-ro**

ne¦ru	→	ne¦ro
tabe¦ru	→	tabe¦ro
i¦ru	→	i¦ro
oki¦ru	→	oki¦ro

(*b*) **-u** verbs: replace the final **-u** with **-e**

ka¦u	→	ka¦e
kak¦u	→	kak¦e
hanas¦u	→	hanas¦e
mats¦u	→	mat¦e
shin¦u	→	shin¦e
yom¦u	→	yom¦e
yar¦u	→	yar¦e

(*c*) irregular formations:

suru	→	shiro
kuru	→	koi
kudasaru	→	kudasai
nasaru	→	nasai
irassharu	→	irasshai

(*d*) plain negative imperatives
These are formed by attaching **na** to the plain present form:

okiru	na	*don't get up!*
kau	na	*don't buy it!*
kuru	na	*don't come!*

You are unlikely to use these forms yourself in direct speech, as they are too brusque for normal use between adults. You may, however, hear them used, e.g. by husbands addressing their wives or children, or among schoolboys, who may soften their impact by adding **yo**: **hayaku okiro yo!** (get up, quick!); **naku na yo** (*don't cry!*). Females generally avoid these forms, using **[verb]-te** (Unit 8 Structures 5) instead, often with **yo**: **hayaku okite yo!/nakanaide yo!** Imperative forms are, however, commonly used in indirect requests, and it is mainly for this reason that you need to become familiar with them.

3 *Direct and indirect requests*

In Unit 8 Structures 5 we saw how to make formal requests using **-te kudasai**; less formal requests can be made by using **kure** instead of **kudasai**, and 'orders' are given by using the imperative form:

katte kudasai	*please buy (it) for me*
katte kure	*buy (it) for me*
kae	*buy (it)*

Kudasai and **kure** are in fact imperative forms themselves, the former an irregular formation from **kudasaru**, the latter a regular imperative of **kureru**. Requests using **kudasaru/kureru** always carry the implication that the speaker would like something done ***for his/her benefit***, whereas imperatives not involving **kudasaru/kureru** plainly tell another person what to do.

Indirect (or 'reported') requests are used to inform a third person about what you have been asked, told, or requested to do by someone else, or what you have asked other people to do. You already know how to report others' statements by means of **to iu** (Unit 13 Structures 1), and in fact **iu** (and occasionally some other verbs, such as **tanomu**) can also be used to report indirect requests when attached to the request, either positive or negative, with the help of the 'quoting' **to**:

Haha wa watashi ni katte kure to iimashita. *Mother asked me to buy it.*
Haha wa watashi ni ochitsuke to iimashita. *Mother told me to calm down.*
Haha wa hairanaide kure/hairu na to iimashita. *Mother told me not to go in.*

Note that **kiku** cannot be used, since it only means *ask a question*, not *ask* in the sense of *request*.

The actual request made by your mother may well have been **katte kudasai** or **ochitsuki nasai** or perhaps, **katte kite** in the positive, or **hairanaide kudasai**, etc. in the negative, but in reported requests we are concerned with reporting the gist of what was said rather than the actual words. (If necessary, that can be rendered by means of a direct quote.) For this reason it is customary to 'reduce' the request itself to its simplest form by discarding any elements that may have been originally present for reasons of politeness only.

Indirect requests can also be formed by using **[verb (present plain form)] yō ni** in front of verbs of requesting such as **iu**, this time without the particle **to**:

Haha wa watashi ni iku yō ni iimashita. *Mother told me to go.*
Haha wa watashi ni ikanai yō ni iimashita. *Mother told me not to go.*
Jiru wa Ken ni hayaku kaeru yō ni iimashita. *Jill told Ken to come home early/quickly.*
Watashi wa tomodachi ni o-kane o kashite kureru yō ni tanomimashita. *I requested a friend to lend me some money.*

Watashi wa tomodachi ni ikanai yō ni tanomimashita. *I requested my friend not to go.*

Note that again **kureru** is used if the implication is one of doing the speaker a favour.

4 *Fine-tuning verbs by attaching* ok.u *to* [verb]-te

Oku is one of several verbs, such as **ageru**, etc. in Structures 1 (see Unit 17 Structures 2 for others), that can be attached to the **-te** form of verbs to provide extra shades of meaning. **Oku** on its own means *to put/place*, but used after other verbs it indicates that the action of the verb is performed in preparation or readiness. Note the effect of adding **oku** in the following:

O-kane o watashimashita. *I handed over the money.*
O-kane o watashite okimashita. *I gave him the money (for future use, i.e. to enable him to pay the bill with it).*

Similarly:

Nihon no tomodachi ni denwa o shite okimashita.
Ashita no kēki o tsukutte okimashita. (**tsukur.u** *to make*)
Kurisumasu no purezento o mina katte okimashita.

The first sentence implies, for instance, that you rang your Japanese friend to inform him of someone's impending visit to Japan, the second that you have already organised the cakes for tomorrow's party, and the third, that you have already bought all your Christmas presents. Sentences ending in **-te oku** are often highly dependent on the context for their interpretation, but perhaps not as much as is the case in English, where one would often say *I rang my Japanese friend*, *I have made tomorrow's cake*, or *I have bought all the Christmas presents*, without giving any indication that this is done in preparation or readiness. In other words, **-te oku** makes the situation more explicit than is normally the case in English.

Renshū

1 Taking consideration of the meaning, use appropriate forms of

ageru, kureru or **morau** to complete the sentences below:
Rei: Chichi wa watashi ni nekutai o____mashita.→kure

(*a*) Kono hon wa chichi ga katte ____ta n' desu yo.
(*b*) Watashi ga tetsudatte ____mashō.
(*c*) Chichi kara Rōrusu-roisu o ____nasai.
(*d*) Nihonjin kara Eigo o oshiete ____te imasu.
(*e*) Kodomo ni kono rajio o naoshite ____mashō.
(*f*) Michiko-san ga o-kane o kashite ____mashita.

2 Your friend takes an unusual degree of interest in other people's affairs; to satisfy his curiosity, tell him about various requests that have been made to you during the course of the day, using first the **to iu**, then the **yō ni iu** pattern.
Rei: Chichi: 'Hayaku oki nasai'→Chichi ga hayaku okiro to/okiru yō ni iimashita.

(*a*) Haha: 'Asa-gohan o amari takusan tabenaide kudasai.'
(*b*) Haha: 'Daidokoro o tetsudai nasai.'
(*c*) Sensei: 'Nōto (*notebook*) o wasurenaide kudasai.'
(*d*) Tarō: 'Motto nome yo.'
(*e*) Tarō: 'Mada kaeranaide kure.'

3 Fill in the appropriate kinship terms in the following exchanges between an ingroup and outgroup person (read Langage and Society first!):
Rei: ______ wa imasu ka? – Iie, ______ wa chotto dekakete imasu. (Father)→Otōsan; chichi.

(*a*) (*Photo*) Kono kata wa ______ desu ka? – Iie, ______ ja arimasen. Otōto desu. (Elder brother)
(*b*) (*Photo*) Kore ga ______ desu.—Hē, ______ ja nai n' desu ka? Wakai desu ne! (Mother; elder sister)
(*c*) ______ mo issho ni ikimasu ka? – Iie, ______ wa benkyō______ ga atte, ikenai n' desu. (Younger brother)
(*d*) ______ wa o-genki desu ka? – Ē, ______ wa genki desu ga, ______ wa amari genki ja arimasen. (Grandmother; grandfather)

Language and Society

1 *Kinship terms of address and reference*

In Unit 1 Language and Society 2 we saw some examples of terms of address and reference, noting that **okusan**, for instance, can be used for both referring to and addressing someone else's wife (outgroup), whereas for one's own wife (ingroup) **kanai** is used in conversation with outgroupers.

Different forms are also used in addressing and referring to those members of the speaker's family who are senior to him/her:

Relation	*Address*	*Reference* (*in speech with outgroupers*)
grandfather	(o-)jī-san	sofu
grandmother	(o-)bā-san	sobo
father	(o-)tō-san	chichi
mother	(o-)kā-san	haha
elder brother	(o-)nī-san	ani
elder sister	(o-)nē-san	ane
younger brother	*NAME*	otōto
younger sister	*NAME*	imōto

It is obvious that a hierarchical relationship exists between oneself (the speaker) and senior members of one's family; hence, such members are addressed by a kinship term with **-san** attached. Junior members, however, are addressed by their personal name. If the speaker is male, the address is likely to be by name only (e.g. **Tarō**), but females may use **Tarō-san** (or the diminutive **Tarō-chan**). When you refer to members of your own family in speech with outsiders, any such distinctions become obliterated in that everyone is referred to without **-san**. Towards outsiders, then, members of one's own family are referred to in a uniformly modest fashion. This is, incidentally, also true for reference to the company president by an employee when talking to outsiders: **shachō** is used, without **-san** (company presidents are, however, also addressed as **shacho** by their subordinates). For reference in conversation with ingroupers, the same forms as those used for address are generally used; below are some examples:

Onēsan, nani ka tabemono wa nai ka?	*Isn't there anything to eat, sis'?* (ingroup address)
Ane wa mada kaette kite imasen.	(outgroup reference)
Otōsan, onēsan wa doko desu ka?	(ingroup address and reference)

When addressing or referring to members of an outgroup family, the corresponding terms are as follows (in formal situations, **-san** is replaced by **-sama**; **okusan** too becomes **okusama**):

Relation	*Address*	*Reference*
grandfather	ojī-san	ojī-san
grandmother	obā-san	obā-san
father	otō-san	otō-san
mother	okā-san	okā-san
elder brother	onī-san	onī-san
elder sister	onē-san	onē-san
younger brother	otōto-san	otōto-san
younger sister	imōto-san	imōto-san

In other words, the most formal set of terms is used throughout, regardless of considerations of seniority.

2 O-negai shimasu *and some related expressions*

In Unit 4 Structures 3 we saw that **[noun] o o-negai shimasu** indicates that one asks for the object the noun refers to. **(Yoroshiku) o-negai shimasu** can also be used in reply to someone's offer to help, and **o-negai da/desu (kara)** to reinforce a request:

Tetsudaimashō ka?→(Yoroshiku) o-negai shimasu. *Yes, please.*

O-negai desu. Issho ni kite kudasai. *Please/I implore you, come with me.*
O-negai da kara, katte kudasai. *Please buy it for me.*

(Yoroshiku) o-negai shimasu is also used on its own to confirm a request that has been made, or help that has been offered earlier. Sometimes it is repeated again when the person who made the request or was offered help leaves.

Note that **dōzo** can be used in the sense of *please*, as in **Dōzo, koko ni o-namae o kaite kudasai** (*please, write your name in this space*), but cannot be used in the same way as **yoroshiku o-negai shimasu**, as it tends to be used with offers rather than requests:

O-cha o dōzo. *Please have some tea.*
Issho ni itte mo ii desu ka? *May I come with you?*
– Dōzo. *Please do.*

Dōzo also often accompanies gestures, such as a waiter showing you the way (*this way, please*), or someone letting you through the door first.

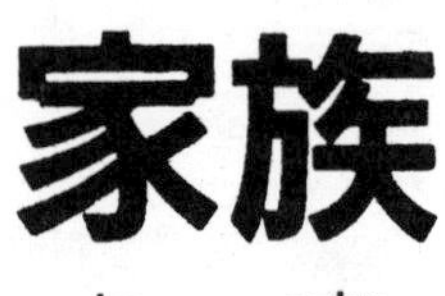

17 Suzuki-san wa hikōki ni noriokure-sō desu *It looks as if Suzuki-san will miss the plane*

In this unit you will learn how to express intention and conviction and see some more uses of the **-te** form. You will also meet indirect questions, and some more sentence endings with the idea of *seems*. In addition, there will be some words and phrases to do with airports and air-travel.

空港
kū kō

Kaiwa

Tomu-san to Suzuki-san wa kokusai-kaigi de Honkon e iku koto ni natte iru. Hisho no Yamada-san wa Tomu-san o miokuru tsumori de issho ni Narita made kita. Futari wa chekku-in kauntā no mae de Suzuki-san o matte iru.

Tomu Suzuki-san wa osoi ne. Ato jūgofun de chekku-in ga owatte shimau darō?

Yamada Asa ichiban no shinkansen de Sendai kara kuru to iu koto deshita kara, mō Narita ni tsuite iru hazu desu ga . . . Yamanaka Māketingu ni denwa shite mimashō ka?

Tomu Sō da ne. Chanto notta ka dō ka shirabete kudasai.

Yamada Ja, chotto denwa shite kimasu.

Tomu O-negai shimasu.

kokusai *international*
kaigi *conference*
Honkon *Hong Kong*
miokur.u *to see off*

[verb (present plain form)] tsumori de *with the intention of doing [verb]* ● S1
Narita (kokusai kūkō) *Narita (International Airport)*
chekku-in kauntā *check-in counter*
ato [jūgofun] de *in [fifteen minutes'] time*
[verb]-te shima.u *to [verb] completely* ● S2
asa ichiban no shinkansen *the first bullet train in the morning*
[statement] to iu koto deshita *the arrangement was that [statement]*
[place] ni tsuk.u *to arrive at [place]*
[statement] hazu da *should/is likely to [statement]* ● S3
[verb]-te miru *to try doing [verb]* ● S2
ka dō ka *whether or not* ● S4
shirabe.ru *to investigate*
[verb]-te kuru *to go and [verb]* ● S2

True or false?

1 Yamada-san mo Honkon e iku koto ni natte iru.
2 Suzuki-san wa asa ichiban no shinkansen ni noranakatta ka mo shirenai.

Gofun gurai shite kara, Yamada-san ga kaette kuru.

Yamada Hisho no hanashi ni yoru to, Suzuki-san wa pasupōto ga nakanaka mitsukaranakute noriokureta sō desu.

Tomu Yappari sō ka. Demo, dōshite renraku shite kure-nakatta n' darō.

Yamada Awatete ita kara, machiawase no koto o wasureta rashii desu.

Tomu Tonikaku, boku ga saki ni chekku-in nado sumashita hō ga yosa-sō da ne.

Yamada Ē, Suzuki-san wa hikōki ni mo noriokure-sō desu kara ne!

pasupōto *passport*
mitsukaranakute *being unable to find* (Lit. *being not found*)
mitsukar.u (intransitive) *to be found*
[verb]-nakute ● S5
Yappari sō ka? *That's what happened after all, is it?/As I thought* (note that there is no rising intonation with the **ka** here)
yappari = yahari

renraku (suru) *contact, communication*
awate.ru *be flustered/in a hurry*
machiawase *meeting, rendezvous*
[noun] no koto *about [noun]*
[statement] rashi.i *it seems [statement]* ● S6
sumas.u *to finish, get over with*
[verb]-ta hō ga yosa-sō da *It seems that I'd better [verb]*
yosa-sō da = [ii]-sō da ● S7
hikōki *aeroplane*
[-masu base**]-sō da** *to be likely to [verb]*

True or false?

3 Suzuki-san wa Tomu-san ni renraku shiyō to shita.
4 Tomu-san wa Suzuki-san o matanaide chekku in suru koto ni shita.

Structures

1 [verb (plain present form)] tsumori da *expressing intentions*

Tsumori is a noun meaning *intention.* In the pattern **A wa [verb (present plain form)] tsumori da**, it is generally used as a way of expressing one's own intentions, and asking questions about the intentions of the person you are talking to. Intentions expressed in this way are stronger and less tentative than intentions expressed using **[verb]-(y)ō to omou** (Unit 13 Structures 7).

> Watashi wa rainen Nihon e iku | tsumori desu. *I intend to go to Japan next year.*
> Dō suru | tsumori desu ka? *What do you intend to do?*

To express past intentions, simply put **da** into the past tense. In the past, the intentions of other people can also be described:

> Kinō haha ni denwa suru|tsumori deshita ga, wasuremashita. *I meant to ring my mother yesterday, but I forgot.*

Sugiura-san wa Tanaka-san to kekkon suru | tsumori datta keredomo, dame deshita. *Sugiura-san intended to marry Tanaka-san, but it didn't work out.*

This construction is often found in the middle of sentences in the form **A wa [verb] tsumori de** (the **-te** form of **da**), with a meaning equivalent to *with the intention of*:

Bōi-furendo ni ageru tsumori de, takai nekutai o kaimashita. *I bought an expensive tie, with the intention of giving it to my boy friend.*

Also note the use of **sono** in front of **tsumori**, as in the following:

A Kore o zenbu taberu n' desu ka? *Are you going to eat all of this?*
B Ee, sono tsumori desu. *Yes, that is my intention./Yes, I am.*

2 *More fine-tuning of verbs using the* -te *form*

In Unit 16 Structures 1 and 4, various patterns were introduced which involved the verbs **ageru**, **kureru**, **morau** and **oku** following the **te** form of other verbs. **Shimau**, **miru**, **kuru**, and **iku** can function in a similar way.

(*a*) **[verb]-te shimau** ***to [verb] completely***
By itself, **shimau** is usually used in the sense of *to put away* (e.g. **Futon o shimaimashita ka?** *Have you put away the futon?*), and is also found in the plain past as an expletive used by men when they realise that they have made a mistake of some kind: **Shimatta!** *Damn!*. With the **-te** form of other verbs it basically emphasises the fact that the action of the other verb is (or soon will be) completed. In its most straightforward use, it is therefore equivalent to *do something completely/finish doing it/end up doing it*:

Yatto owatte shimaimashita! *At last it's all done.*
Hayaku tabete shimai nasai! *Hurry up and finish your meal!*
Ato ichijikan de zenbu tsukutte shimau kara, sore made matte kudasai. *I will finish making them all in an hour, so please wait till then.*

Suzuki-san wa o-sake o nomi-sugite nyūin shite shimaimashita. *Suzuki-san drank so much that he ended up in hospital.*

Shimau is also used after the **-te** forms of actions which have been (or soon will be) completed with startling speed or with inconvenient/drastic results. In all these cases, there is no fixed English equivalent since the nuance is likely to be conveyed by intonation as much as by any particular word.

Mō zenbu nonde shimaimashita ka? *Have you already drunk it all?*
Shachō ni itte shimaimasu yo! *I'll tell the boss!*
Ken-san wa sara o otoshite shimaimashita. *Ken went and dropped a plate.*
O-kane o zenbu tsukatte shimaimashita. *I've gone and used* (**tsuka.u**) *all the money.*
Kyō no shinbun mo sutete shimatta n' desu ka? *Have you thrown away* (**sute.ru**) *today's newspaper as well?*
Satō-san wa mō dekakete shimaimashita. *Satō-san has already left.*
Suzuki-san wa pasupōto no koto o sukkari wasurete shimaimashita. *Suzuki-san completely* (**sukkari**) *forgot about his passport.*

In informal situations, you will often hear **-te shimau** contracted to **-chau**, or **-jau** in the case of verbs whose **-te** form ends in **-de**:

Sensei ni misetchau (=misete shimau) yo! *I'll show it to teacher!*
Ara, mata machigatchatta (=machigatte shimatta)! *Oh no, I've gone and made another mistake* (**machiga.u**)*!*
Are o mō yonjatta (=yonde shimatta) no? *Have you finished reading that already?*

(*b*) **[verb]-te miru** ***to try doing [verb]***
This pattern is used when the action of the verb in the **-te** form is performed in order to find out what the result will be; in other words, when English uses *try doing* rather than *try to do* (**-(y)ō to suru**, Unit 13 Structures 8):

Ano o-mise de kiite mimasu. *I'll try asking at that shop* (*to see if they know/to see if they have any*).

Denki o tsukete mite kudasai. *Try switching on (the power/lights* **denki**) *(to see if it will work).*

Note the use of combinations such as **tabete miru** and **kite miru** where English is likely to use *try* by itself:

Kore wa tako desu ga, tabete mimasen ka? *This is octopus – won't you try eating some/won't you try it (to see whether you like it or not)?*

Michiko-san no kimono o kite mimashita. *I tried wearing/tried (on) Michiko's kimono (to see what it felt like/if it fitted)*

The appropriate form of **-te miru** is often used in front of **-tai** and **-(y)ō to omou** to make the speaker's expression of his/her wishes or intentions seem more tentative, and therefore less assertive:

Ichido Yōroppa e itte mitai to omoimasu. *I should like to visit Europe once/one day* (**ichido**).

Kono Nihongo no hon o yonde miyō to omotte imasu. *I am thinking of reading this Japanese book.*

(*c*) **[verb]-te kuru** ***and*** **[verb]-te iku**

The two basic verbs of motion join with the **-te** forms of other verbs in three different ways, **kuru** being used when the action is going on in the direction of the speaker, and **iku** when it is going on in a direction away from the speaker, as is normally the case with **kuru** and **iku**.

(i) ***Describing the direction of the action***

In this use **kuru** and **iku** are combined mainly with other verbs involving movement, and serve to indicate the direction of the movement:

Inu ga hashitte kimashita. *A dog came running up.*

Nanji ni kaette kimasu ka? *What time will you be back?*

Kaidan o nobotte ikimashō. *Let's climb* (**nobor.u**) *the stairs* (**kaidan**).

Note the way in which they combine with **motsu** to form **motte kuru/iku**, *to bring/take (something)*, and with **tsure.ru** to form **tsurete kuru/iku**, *to bring/take (someone)*:

Kamera o motte kimashita ka? *Have you brought your camera?*

Wain o motte ikimashō. *Let's take some wine.*

Tomodachi o tsurete kite kudasai. *Please bring a friend.*
Otōto o tsurete itte mo ii desu ka? *Is it all right if bring my (younger) brother along?*

Also note **totte kuru**, *to fetch* (*something*):

Ken-san wa Tarō-kun no rimo-kon kā o totte kite kuremashita. *Ken fetched Tarō's model car* (*for Michiko*).

Also note the expression **denwa ga kakatte kuru** (*to receive a telephone call*) in which **-te kuru** is combined with **denwa ga kakaru**, *a telephone call is made*, the intransitive equivalent of **denwa o kakeru**):

Denwa ga kakatte kimashita yo. *There was a telephone call for you.*

Other verbs of motion, **kaeru** in particular, will combine with the **-te** form of verbs in a similar way:

Kodomo ga hashitte kaerimashita. *The child ran home.*
Michi o aruite watarimashita. *I walked across the road* (**watar.u** *to cross*).
Imōto o tsurete kaerimashita. *I took my* (*younger*) *sister home.*

(ii) ***Doing something and then coming/going***
You have already met the combination with **kuru** in the phrase **itte kimasu** (Unit 3 **Kaiwa**, Language and Society 1) and in commands in Unit 16. The idea is that the speaker, or someone else, performs the action of the verb in the **-te** form, and then comes to where the speaker is now. In the present, it is usually equivalent to English *go and do something*:

Sugu itte kimasu. *I'll be back in a second.*
Chotto tegami o dashite kimasu. *I'll just go and post a letter.*
Matchi o katte kite kudasai. *Please go and buy some matches* (**matchi**).

In the past, it is used to refer to something which you did before coming to where you are now:

Senshū wa chotto Pari e itte kimashita. *I had a quick trip to and from Paris last week.*
Gohan o tabete kimashita. *I ate a meal before I came/I've just eaten.* (A useful way of refusing an offer of food!)

Kippu o wasurete kimashita! *I've forgotten my ticket/I've left my ticket behind!*

With **iku**, however, the idea is that the speaker, or someone else, does something and then goes away from where the speaker is now:

Gohan o tabete ikimashō. *Let's have a meal and then go/Let's eat before we go.*
Ara, otōsan wa pasupōto o wasurete ikimashita! *Oh dear, father's forgotten his passport (and gone)/left his passport behind!*

(iii) ***Describing actions which take place over time***
With **kuru** this combination is used to indicate either that something has begun, or that an event which started to come about some time before is still going on. Often the implication is that you have only just noticed it. **Kuru** is usually in the past tense.

Ame ga futte kimashita. *It has started raining.*
O-naka ga suite kimashita. *I've started to feel hungry.*
Kyū ni samuku natte kimashita. *It's suddenly turned cold.*

With **iku**, it is rarer, and refers to an event which will start in the present and go on from there. **Iku** is likely to be in the present tense.

Kore kara dandan atatakaku natte iku deshō. *I expect that it will gradually* (**dandan**) *grow warmer from now on.*

3 [statement] hazu da *expressing convictions*

Hazu da is used to express convictions/expectations with regard to past, present or future situations which have some objective backing (as opposed to **darō**, which tends to be more subjective, see Unit 6 Structures 2). The speaker is not sure about the statement but has, or had, evidence that it is, or was, likely to be so or to occur. The statement might concern a natural occurrence, something which happens regularly, or something which is scheduled to happen. **Hazu da** is therefore equivalent to English *is likely/supposed/meant/should/ought to* (*happen/have happened*). It is found after nouns, adjectives, and verbs in the forms which these generally take in front of nouns:

nouns Ken-san wa jūroku-sai desu kara, kōkōsei no hazu desu. Kinō wa yasumi datta hazu desu ga, kaisha ni ikanakereba narimasen deshita.	 *Ken is sixteen (years old* **-sai**) *so he should be a high-school student* (**kōkōsei**). *Yesterday should have been a holiday, but I had to go to the office/to work.*
na *adjectives* Tomu-san wa Nihon ni nagaku sunde iru kara, Nihongo ga jōzu na hazu desu ga . . . Koko wa shizuka datta hazu desu ga . . .	 *Tom has been living in Japan for a long time so his Japanese ought to be good, but . . .* *This place was supposed to be quiet . . .*
-i *adjectives* Jūnigatsu desu kara, Igirisu wa mō samui hazu desu. Motto yasukatta hazu desu.	 *It's December, so Britain is likely to be cold by now.* *It should have been much cheaper.*
verbs Tanaka-san wa kyō Yōroppa kara kaette kuru hazu desu. Michiko-san wa ima gakkō de benkyō shite iru hazu desu. Kono hon wa mō yonda hazu deshō.	 *Tanaka-san is meant to be coming back from Europe today.* *Michiko-san is supposed to be studying in school now.* *You are meant to have read this book already, aren't you?*

Also note the use of **sono** and **sonna** in front of **hazu**:

A Hādo-san wa ashita kara Honkon e iku koto ni natte imasu ne. *Mr Herd is going to Hong Kong from tomorrow, isn't he?*

B Hai, sono hazu desu. *Yes, that is what is meant to be happening.*
A Tanaka-san wa kaisha o yameta sō desu. *They say that Tanaka-san has left her job.*
B Iie, sonna hazu wa arimasen! *Surely that can't be right!*

4 *Reporting questions*

In reporting questions, the same basic principles are followed as in reporting statements (Unit 13 Structures 1), with the original question going into the plain form. **Kiku** is the most straightforward verb for asking questions, but **tazune.ru**, which has a similar meaning, is also used. Note that the quoting **to** can be omitted after **ka**:

'Nanji ni dekakemasu ka?' *What time are you setting out?*
→Nanji ni dekakeru ka (to) Yamada-san ni kiite okimasu. *I'll ask Yamada-san what time she is setting out.*
'Ikura haraimashita ka?' *How much did you pay?*
→Ikura haratta ka (to) Anzai-san ni tazunete kudasai. *Please ask Anzai-san how much she paid.*

Japanese adopts the same strategy whenever a question is buried in a sentence. With verbs other than **kiku** and **tazuneru**, however, the quoting **to** is never used after **ka**:

Dare ga denwa o kaketa ka shitte imasu ka? *Do you know who telephoned?*
Pasupōto o doko ni oita ka oboete imasen. *I don't remember where I left my passport.*

When there is no question word in the sentence, such as **nanji**, **dare**, etc., **ka dō ka** (*whether or not*) is often used instead of **ka** by itself:

Michiko-san ga iku ka dō ka kikimashita ka? *Did you ask whether Michiko was going or not?*
Tanaka-san ga kekkon suru ka dō ka shirimasen. *I don't know whether Tanaka-san will get married or not.*
Eiga ga omoshirokatta ka dō ka oshiete kudasai. *Please tell me whether the film was interesting or not.*

Finally, note that it is usual to omit **da** (but not **datta**) before **ka**:

Sugiura-san wa donna hito ka shitte imasu. *I know what sort of person Sugiura-san is.*
Sore wa hontō ka dō ka shirabemashō. *Let's investigate whether or not that is true.*
Kyonen wa howaito Kurisumasu datta ka dō ka oboete imasu ka? *Do you remember whether or not we had a white Christmas* (**howaito Kurisumasu**) *last year?*

5 [verb]-nakute/-naide: *two negative* -te *forms*

All verbs have two negative **-te** forms, except for **aru**, which has only **nakute**. (The negative **-te** form of **da** is **ja/de (wa) nakute**, see **Kaiwa**, Units 12 and 13.) In Unit 8 Structures 5 you were introduced to the **-naide** form. In addition to its use in expressing negative requests, this form is used in the middle of sentences, usually with a meaning equivalent to *without -ing* in English:

Yūbe nenaide benkyō shimashita. *Last night, I studied without sleeping.*
Tarō-kun wa sensei ni nani mo iwanaide uchi e kaerimashita. *Tarō went home without saying anything to the teacher.*

You met the other, **-nakute**, form in Unit 14 Structures 2 and Unit 15 Structures 8. In addition to its use in the **-nakute mo ii** and **-nakute wa ikenai** patterns, this form is also used in joining sentences. The subjects of the two sentences can be different, and the first one often gives the reason for the second (Unit 13 Structures 4):

Motto mae ni renraku shinakute, dōmo sumimasen. *I am sorry I did not contact you earlier.*
Jikan ga nakute komatte imasu. *I'm in trouble because I've haven't any time.*
Dare mo minakute yokatta desu. *I'm glad no-one saw.*

6 [statement] rashii: *it seems/apparently*

Rashii is an **-i** adjective which is added on to statements and has implications similar to both **yō da** (Unit 15 Structures 1) and **sō da** (Unit 15 Structures 4); in other words, **rashii** is used by a speaker to indicate that what he or she is saying is based on information obtained visually and/or from what has been heard or read. In the following examples, note the forms which nouns, adjectives, and verbs take before **rashii**, both in the present tense and in the past:

nouns Koko wa kanari ii hoteru rashii desu. Suzuki-san no otōsan wa yūmei na haiyū datta rashii desu.	*This looks like quite* (**kanari**) *a good hotel.* *Apparently, Suzuki-san's father was a famous actor* (**haiyū**).
na *adjectives* Kono terebi wa dame rashii desu. Wakai toki kanojo wa kirei datta rashii desu.	*It looks as if this television is no good.* *They say she was pretty when she was young.*
-i *adjectives* Ano eiga wa totemo omoshiroi rashii desu. Kyonen no fuyu wa samukatta rashii desu.	*That film seems very interesting.* *It appears that the winter was cold last year.*
verbs Tomu-san wa asatte Honkon kara kaette kuru rashii desu. Suzuki-san wa yatto pasupōto ga mitsukatta rashii desu.	*It seems that Tom will return from Hong Kong the day after tomorrow* (**asatte**). *It seems that Suzuki-san has at last found his passport.*

When there is a negative, it will normally come before **rashii**:

Soto wa amari atatakakunai rashii desu. *It doesn't look very warm outside* (**soto**).

Suzuki-san wa hikōki ni norenakatta rashii desu. *Apparently Suzuki-san was unable to get on the aeroplane.*

7 [adjectives/verbs]-sō da *it seems (to me)*

When added to adjectives and verbs, **-sō da** indicates that what you are saying is based on a personal, primarily visual, impression which may or may not be shared by other people. It is distinguished from **sō da** meaning *apparently* (Unit 15 Structures 4) by the fact that it combines with non-final forms of both adjectives and verbs, to make what are pronounced as single words.

With adjectives, **-sō da** is equivalent to *it seems/looks* (*to me*) in English. **Na** adjectives drop **na** in front of **-sō da**, the most common combination being with **genki na**:

Kyō wa genki-sō desu ne. *You look well today.*
Ano torakku wa totemo jōbu-sō desu. *That lorry* (**torakku**) *looks really strong* (**jōbu na**).

-i adjectives drop their final **-i**:

Kono sūpu wa hontō ni oishi-sō desu. *This soup looks really delicious.*
Sono ōbā wa atataka-sō desu ne! *Your overcoat* (**ōbā**) *looks warm!*

-sō da is particularly common with adjectives of emotion, such as **ureshi.i** (*happy*), **kanashi.i** (*sad*), **sabishi.i** (*lonely*), and **genki na** (which can mean *cheerful*), when used in describing the feelings of others. Such descriptions must be based on the personal evaluation of the speaker, since we can never know what someone else is really feeling:

Ureshi-sō desu ne! *You're looking happy!*
Michiko-san ga inai kara, Ken-san wa chotto sabishi-sō desu. *Ken seems a little lonely because Michiko isn't there.*

Ii and **nai**, the negative plain form of **aru**, have similar, irregular, forms when combined with **-sō da**: **yosa-sō da** and **nasa-sō da**.

Jiru-san wa atama ga yosa-sō desu. *Jill looks intelligent.*
Ano gakusei wa o-kane ga amari nasa-sō desu. *That student* (**gakusei**) *doesn't seem to have very much money.*

With verbs, **-sō da** tends to be used when you detect signs that an action is about to occur; it is therefore equivalent to *it looks* (*to me*) *as if it is likely to/going to/about to*. **-sō da** follows the **-masu** base of verbs.

Ame ga furi-sō desu ne. *It looks like rain.*
Ki o tsukete yo! Hon ga zenbu ochi-sō desu! *Look out! The books are all about to fall!*
Michiko-san mo korare-sō desu. *It looks as though Michiko will be able to come too.*

To refer to past impressions, **-sō da** becomes **-sō datta**:

Ano resutoran wa taka-sō datta kara, hairimasen deshita. *That restaurant looked expensive, so we didn't go in.*
Tomu-san wa kaze o hiki-sō deshita. *It looked as if Tom was going to catch a cold.*

To form the negative with combinations with adjectives, it is possible simply to turn **-sō da** into **-sō de wa nai/nakatta**:

Tomu-san wa genki-sō de wa arimasen deshita. *Tom didn't look well.*
Kono hon wa amari omoshiro-sō de wa arimasen. *This book doesn't look very interesting.*

It is also possible to use their usual negative forms and turn **nai** into **nasa-sō da**:

Tomu-san wa genki ja nasa-sō deshita. *Tom didn't look very well.*
Kono hon wa amari omoshirokunasa-sō desu. *This book doesn't look very interesting.*
Tarō-kun wa tanjōbi ni purezento o iroiro moratta keredomo, amari ureshiku nasa-sō deshita. *Tarō got all sorts of presents on his birthday, but he didn't look very happy.*

In the case of verbs, however, the negative is formed by turning **-sō da** into **-sō mo nai/nakatta**, the resultant combination being fairly emphatic: *there's no sign of/no way that.*

Kyō wa owari-sō mo nai kara, kaerimashō. *There's no sign of our finishing today, so let's go home.*
Zenbu tabe-sō mo arimasen. *There's no way we're going to eat it all.*

-sō da can also occur in front of nouns, in the form **-sō na**, and adverbially, in the form **-sō ni**:

genki-sō na kodomo *a healthy-looking child*
ame ga furi-sō na hi *a day which looks like rain*

Tarō-kun wa ureshi-sō ni aisukurīmu o tabemashita. *Tarō happily (looking happy) ate the ice cream.*
Repōto ga owari-sō ni narimashita. *The report is nearly finished.*

Renshū

1 The following are extracts from conversations. Complete the replies by using the words in brackets, providing an appropriate verb, and adding **tsumori desu**.
Rei: A Nanji ni dekakeru n' desu ka?
B (rokuji)→Rokuji ni dekakeru tsumori desu.

(*a*) **A** Itsu Sapporo e ikimasu ka?
B (raishū)
(*b*) **A** Ashita nani o suru n' desu ka?
B (eiga)
(*c*) **Jiru** Konban benkyō suru deshō?
Ken (Iie, Michiko)
(*d*) **Anzai-san no okusan** Konban Ken-san ni au n' desu ka?
Michiko Iie (hon)

2 Put the verbs into the **-te** form and add **shimau**, **miru**, **kuru** or **iku** as appropriate.
Rei: Kore wa oishii desu yo. Tabemasen ka?
→Tabete mimasen ka?

(*a*) **A** Bīru o zenbu nomimashita!
B Kaimashō ka?
(*b*) Sukiyaki o uchi de tsukuritai desu.
(*c*) Yamada-san wa mainichi eki made arukimasu.
(*d*) Hādo-san wa mō hikōki ni norimashita.
(*e*) Kore kara dandan samuku naru deshō.

3 Indicate that the following statements have some objective basis in fact by substituting **hazu desu** for **deshō** etc.

Rei: Tanaka-san wa rainen kekkon suru deshō.
→Tanaka-san wa rainen kekkon suru hazu desu.

(*a*) Kyō wa nigatsu nijū kunichi deshō.
(*b*) Kono hanbāgā wa oishi-sō desu.
(*c*) Ano hoteru wa shizuka ka mo shiremasen.
(*d*) Pasupōto ga mō mitsukatta deshō.
(*e*) Kaigi wa raishū deshō.

4 Change the following into indirect questions by adding the sentence endings indicated in the brackets. Remember to use **ka dō ka** where necessary.
Rei: Suzuki-san wa doko ni imasu ka? (kiite kudasai)
→Suzuki-san wa doko ni iru ka kiite kudasai.

(*a*) Kinō nan-bon nomimashita ka? (oboete imasen)
(*b*) Michiko-san ga mada matte imasu ka? (shitte imasu ka?)
(*c*) Sukiyaki ni satō (*sugar*) o iremasu ka? (wasuremashita)
(*d*) Hikōki wa nanji ni tsukimasu ka? (shirabemashō)
(*e*) Hādo-san ga tabako o yamemashita ka? (wakarimasen)

5 Put the verb in brackets into the appropriate negative **-te** form.
Rei: Mado o (akeru) kudasai. →Mado o akenaide kudasai.

(*a*) Pen o (tsukau) mo ii desu.
(*b*) O-kane o (watasu) heya o demashita.
(*c*) Kaze o (hiku) yokatta desu.
(*d*) Takushī ga nakanaka (kuru) aruku koto ni shimashita.
(*e*) Uchi e (kaeru) kaisha de nemashita.

6 Tanaka-san has been looking unwell recently. Complete these worried snippets of gossip about her by adding **rashii desu** or **-sō desu** etc. as indicated.
Rei: (Sugiura-san to kekkon shimasen) rashii desu.
→Tanaka-san wa Sugiura-san to kekkon shinai rashii desu.

(*a*) (amari genki de wa arimasen) -sō desu.
(*b*) (kao-iro ga amari yoku arimasen) rashii desu.
(*c*) (saikin nakimashita) -sō ni narimashita.
(*d*) (yūbe neraremasen deshita) rashii desu.
(*e*) (itsumo kanashii) -sō desu.

Language and Society

Airports and Air-travel in Japan

More and more Japanese are using air-travel to go abroad every year, but the relatively long distances between Tokyo and the two extremes of the Japanese archipelago mean that domestic flights are also heavily used: the Tokyo-Sapporo route is one of the busiest, if not the busiest, air route in the world. It is very common for a traveller to be accompanied to the airport and seen off (**miokuru**), and also to be met (**mukaeru**) on his/her return. English will of course be spoken on international flights (**kokusai-bin**, as opposed to **kokunai-bin** (*domestic flights*)) and at international airports, but here are some more words and phrases which might be of use:

suchuādesu *air-hostess*
[number]-bin *flight [number]*
chakuriku (suru) *landing (of airplane)*
ririku (suru) *taking-off (of airplane)*
nyū(koku)kan(ri) *immigration control*
zeikan *customs*
nyūkan/zeikan de tsukamar.u *to be caught by immigration control/customs*
jisa *time difference*
[number]-jikan no jisa *a time difference of [number] hours*
jisa-boke o shite iru *to be suffering from jet-lag*
jisa-boke ga naotte iru/naotta *to be/have recovered from jet-lag*

18 Irashite itadakemasen deshō ka? *Might you be able to come?*

In this unit you will encounter honorific and humble speech levels, and see how to put these to use in telephone conversations. There are also some more expressions of contrast and purpose, and you will find some information on when and how Japanese enjoy having parties.

Kaiwa

Jiru-san no seito datta Tanaka-san kara mukashi no kurasu no menbā no dōsō-kai no koto o shiraseru tame ni denwa ga kakatte kita.

Tanaka	Moshi-moshi. Hādo-sensei no o-taku desu ka? Watakushi Tanaka to mōshimasu ga, Jiru-sensei irasshaimasu deshō ka?
Tom	Hai, chotto o-machi kudasai; ima yonde mairimasu kara.
Tanaka	Osoreirimasu.
Jiru	Moshi-moshi. O-matase itashimashita.
Tanaka	Tanaka de gozaimasu. Taihen go-busata shite orimasu.
Jiru	A, Tanaka-san? O-hisashiburi desu nē. O-genki desu ka? Kekkon no hinichi wa mō kimatta n' desu ka?
Tanaka	Hinichi wa mada desu keredo, o-shōgatsu ni mata go-renraku itashimasu kara . . . Tokoro de kyō denwa itashimashita no wa reinen no kurasu-kai no ken de gozaimasu ga, konkai mo irashite itadakemasen deshō ka? Minna mo zehi to mōshite orimasu.

Jiru Watakushi mo zehi sanka shitai n' desu ga, itsugoro no yotei desu ka?

Tanaka Ichiō jūnigatsu yokka o kangaete orimasu ga, ikaga deshō da?

Jiru Jūnigatsu yokka nē . . . chotto o-machi ni natte, techō o mite kimasu kara.

Tanaka Hai, o-negai shimasu.

seito *pupil*
kurasu *class*
menbā *member*
dōsō-kai *class reunion, alumni meeting*
[noun] no koto o shirase.ru *to inform about [noun]*
[verb (plain present form)] tame ni *in order to [verb]* ● S3
watakushi formal equivalent of **watashi** ● S2(*c*)
mōshimasu (mōs.u) humble equivalent of **iu** ● S1(*c*)
irasshaimasu (irassharu) honorific equivalent of **iru** (and **iku/kuru**, see Unit 3, **yoku irasshaimashita**) ● S1 (*c*)
mairimasu (mair.u) humble equivalent of **iku/kuru** ● S1 (*c*)
osoreirimasu *I would be much obliged* ● LS2
itashimasu (itas.u) humble equivalent of **suru** (see Unit 9, **o-matase shimashita**) ● S1
de gozaimasu (de gozaru) formal equivalent of **desu** ● S2
go-busata shite orimasu stock phrase to apologise for neglecting to call or write ● LS2
o-hisashiburi desu *it's been a long time* ● LS2
hinichi *date*
kimar.u (intransitive) *to be decided* (see Unit 14 **kime.ru**)
reinen *yearly*
kurasu-kai *class reunion*
[noun] no ken *about [noun]* (more formal than **[noun] no koto**)
konkai *this time*
irashite alternative form of **irasshatte** ● S1(*c*)
zehi (irashite kudasai) (*please*) *do* (*come*) ● LS2
orimasu (or.u) humble equivalent of **iru** (see Unit 11) ● S1(*c*)
sanka [suru] *to take part*
yotei [suru] *schedule, plan*
itsugoro no yotei desu ka? *when is it planned for?*
ichiō *for the time being, tentatively* ● LS2
ikaga formal equivalent of **dō** ● S2(*b*)

True or false?

1 Tanaka-san no kekkon no hinichi wa mō kimatta.
2 Jiru-san wa kurasu-kai ni sanka shitakunai desu.

Jiru Moshi-moshi. O-matase shimashita. Jūnigatsu yokka wa chotto tsugō ga warui yō desu. Demo ne, mō hitotsu hakkiri shinai no. To iu no wa, shujin no shiriai no kata to issho ni dekakeru koto ni natte iru n' desu ga, sono go kakunin shite nai no. Da kara ne, sore o shirabete moratte, ato de mō ichido o-denwa shimasu.

Tanaka Sore wa dōmo, sumimasen. Kochira kara itashimashō ka?

Jiru Ie, jikan ga hakkiri shinai kara, watashi kara shimasu wa. Jā, mata nochi hodo.

Tanaka Shitsurei itashimasu.

Jiru Sayonara.

Shibaraku shite kara, Jiru-san kara denwa ga aru.

Jiru Moshi-moshi, Tanaka-san desu ka? Hādo desu.

Tanaka A, sensei, konban wa.

Jiru Ano ne, shirabete moratta keredo, yahari dame deshita.

Tanaka Sore wa zannen desu – minna mo tanoshimi ni shite ita no ni. (*sukoshi kangaeru*) Sore ja, mata hoka no hi o kangaete, go-renraku shimasu kara, yoroshiku o-negai itashimasu.

Jiru Gomen nasai ne. Senpō wa chanto kakunin shite ita no ni, shujin wa sono toki yotte ite, zenzen oboe ga nakatta mitai. Mattaku ne, kochira made hazukashiku natte shimaimasu wa!

True or false?

3 Jiru-san wa jūnigatsu yokka wa tsugō ga yokunai.
4 Shujin no shiriai no hito wa kakunin shite inakatta.

tsugō *circumstances; convenience*

tsugō ga warui *to be inconvenient* (**tsugō ga ii** *to be convenient*)

mō hitotsu [negative] *not very* (=**amari [negative]**)
to iu no wa *that is to say*
shiriai *acquaintance*
kakunin (suru) *confirmation*
mō ichido=**mata**
kochira kara *from this end*
nochi hodo formal equivalent of **ato de**
zannen na *to be too bad, a pity* (see **zannennagara**, Unit 14)
([occasion] o) tanoshimi ni suru *to look forward* (*to* [*occasion*])
[statement] no ni *even though, despite* [*statement*] ● S4
senpō *the other party/person*
yo.u *to get drunk*
oboe ga nai *to have no memory/recollection*
mitai (da)=informal **yō da** ● Unit 22 S1(*j*)
mattaku (ne) (emphatic) *really!*
hazukashi.i *to feel ashamed*

Structures

1 *Honorific and humble forms*

Honorific and humble expressions are largely concerned with verbs, i.e. people's actions. The actions of people who are perceived as being of high social status are customarily expressed by using 'honorific' verb forms, whereas the same speaker will use 'humble' forms with regard to his own actions when conversing with such people. In Unit 16 we saw how the in/outgroup distinction accounts for the choice between **ageru** and **kureru**; the same distinction may be applied to the choice between honorific and humble forms: humble forms are used for ingroup actions (i.e. when the speaker and members of his group are the subject), honorific forms for outgroup actions (i.e. when the listener and his group, or persons talked about are the subject). If the humble verb is transitive, the object will either be the outgroup person himself or something associated with him – one of the effects of this distinction is therefore to clarify the subject and/or object of the verb, which are often not made explicit in any other way.

Like **ageru/kureru**, honorific and humble forms are very much like two sides of a coin in that a speaker who uses honorific forms towards someone else will normally also employ humble forms about himself. Note, however, that the person being addressed will often talk back at a different level of speech (for instance, without using honorific/

humble forms) where there is a marked difference in social status, etc. There has already been some information on speech levels between shop attendants and customers in Unit 9 Language and Society 2, and we saw some instances of humble forms there and elsewhere (Units 10 and 11).

Apart from social status (in Japan, medical doctors and teachers of any kind are typical groups with high status), other factors such as seniority, social distance (lack of intimacy) and the degree of formality of the situation also contribute to the choice of speech levels. In Japan, telephone conversations are perceived as being fairly formal situations (except when they take place between people who are very intimate) – so people will sound more formal on the telephone than when conversing otherwise.

There are a number of regular processes by which honorific and humble forms of verbs may be obtained.

(*a*) ***Regular humble forms***

In Unit 9, we saw that the combination **o-[-masu** base**] suru** produces a humble form. To make the expression even humbler, **itasu** can be used instead of **suru**. Note that, although never the subject, the action involves the outgroup person in some way, often as the beneficiary of the action (occasionally, as in the first example below, as the benefactor):

o-kari-shimasu/itashimasu (*I*) *will borrow* (*it, from you, etc.*)
o-yobi-shimashō/itashimashō *Let* (*me*) *invite* (*you*)
o-mise-shimasu/itashimasu (*I*) *will show* (*you*)

Most **[noun] (suru)** verbs, in particular those derived from Chinese rather than Western languages, have **go-[noun] suru** as their humble form:

go-renraku shimasu/itashimasu (*I*) *will contact* (*you*)
go-chūmon shimashō/itashimashō ka? *Shall* (*I*) *order* (*it, for you*)?

Some, however, use **o-** rather than **go-**:

o-denwa shimasu/itashimasu (*I*) *will ring* (*you*)
o-yakusoku shimasu/itashimasu (*I*) *promise* (*you*)

(*b*) *Regular honorific forms*

There are two regular processes available. The more formal of these involves **o-[-masu** base**] ni naru**, or **go-[noun] ni naru** for most **(noun) suru** verbs:

> o-machi ni narimasu ka? *Will (you) wait?*
> mō o-kaeri ni narimasu ka? *Are (you) leaving already?*
> o-yomi ni narimashita ka? *Have (you) read (it)?*
> go-chūmon ni narimasu ka? *Will (you) order it?*

It is also possible to use **nasaru** instead of **ni naru**. This is less common, and used mainly by women:

> o-machi nasaimasu ka?
> o-yomi nasaimashita ka?
> go-chūmon nasaimasu ka?

Desu can sometimes, but not always, replace **ni naru/nasaru**. Often it is equivalent to a **-te iru** form:

> o-machi desu da?/o-machi ni natte imasu ka? *Are (you) waiting?*
> o-kaeri desu ka?/o-kaeri ni natte imasu ka? *Are (you) back?/ Are (you) leaving?* (the latter only with **desu**)
> o-dekake desu ka?/o-dekake ni natte imasu ka? *Is he/she out?/Are (you) going out?* (the latter only with **desu**)

The second, less formal process involves passive forms and will therefore be introduced in Unit 21.

(*c*) *Irregular humble and honorific forms*

Some common verbs, such as **suru**, have special humble and honorific equivalents, as in the following chart (regular forms used where no special forms exist are given in rounded brackets; note that some humble and honorific forms have more than one meaning, while, on the other hand, there is a choice of humble/honorific equivalents for the same verb in some cases):

Verb	*Humble*	*Honorific*	*Meaning*
au	o-me ni kakar.u	(o-ai ni naru)	*to meet*

Verb	*Humble*	*Honorific*	*Meaning*
aru 	 (motte or.u)	(o-ari da) (o-mochi da)	*to be there/* *to have*
iru	or.u	irassharu/ o-ide ni naru/ orare.ru	*to be there*
iku	mair.u	irassharu/ o-ide ni naru	*to go*
kuru	mair.u	irassharu/ o-ide ni naru	*to come*
suru	itas.u	nasaru	*to do*
iu	mōs.u/ mōshiage.ru*	ossharu	*to say, be called*
miru	haiken suru	go-ran ni naru	*to see, look at*
kari.ru	haishaku suru	(o-kari ni naru)	*to borrow*
kiru		o-meshi ni naru	*to put on (clothes)*
taberu/ nomu	itadak.u	meshiagar.u/ agar.u	*to eat/to drink*
omou	zonji.ru	(o-omoi ni naru)	*to think*
shiru	zonjiage.ru*/ zonji.ru	go-zonji da	*to know*

*Being the politer of each pair, **mōshiageru** and **zonjiageru** are used only in the sense of *to say **to someone*** and *to know **a person***, respectively, whereas **mōsu** can also refer to one's own name, and **zonjiru** to the knowledge of facts).

Note that **nasaru, irassharu** and **ossharu** are like **kudasaru** in that their **-masu** form is not **nasarimasu** etc. but **nasaimasu**, **irasshaimasu** and **osshaimasu**, and their imperative forms are **nasai**, **irasshai** and **osshai**.

As seen from the example in the **Kaiwa**, the **-te** form of **irassharu** (**irasshatte**) is sometimes shortened to **irashite**, especially by women.

Opposite are some typical question-answer exchanges between people of equal standing involving some of the above pairs.

Watashi no shashin o goran ni narimashita ka? – Hai, haiken shimashita. *Have you seen my photo? – Yes, I have.*
Nan to osshaimasu ka? – Tanaka to mōshimasu. *What is your name* (Lit. *what are you called*)? – *My name is Tanaka.*
Dōzo, meshiagatte kudasai. – Hai, itadakimasu. *Please have some food. – Thank you, I will.*
Okāsama wa irasshaimasu ka?—Hai, orimasu. *Is your mother at home?—Yes, she is.*
Ashita nanji ni irasshaimasu ka?—Sanji ni mairimasu. *What time will you come tomorrow?—At three o'clock.*

Unlike the **o-/go-[-masu** base**] suru** humble forms, the action of many of the above humble verbs does not have to involve an outgroup person: e.g. **oru** is mostly used in the sense of *I/he/she/we* (ingroup) *am/is/are here*, without implying that *I/he* etc. are at the house of a person of high status. The exceptions are **o-me ni kakaru**, **mōshiageru**, **haiken suru**, **haishaku suru**, and **zonjiageru**, which are limited in the same way as regular humble forms.

As **oru/irassharu** and **orareru** are the humble/honorific equivalents of **iru**, and **mairu/irassharu** those of **kuru/iku**, it is possible to increase the formality of a sentence involving **-te iru** or **-te kuru/iku** by substituting their respective humble/honorific forms, as appropriate:

Jūnigatsu yokka o kangaete orimasu. *I have December the* 14*th in mind.*
Shujin wa kaette orimasu. *My husband is back.*
Suzuki-san o go-zonji desu ka? Hai, zonjiagete orimasu. *Do you know Suzuki-san? Yes, I do.*
Sensei wa o-kaeri ni natte irasshaimasu ka? *Is sensei back?*
Yonde mairimasu. *I will call her.*
Kaimono ni itte mairimasu. *I'm going out shopping.*
Hayaku kaette irasshai. *Please come home soon.*

There are a few irregular expressions that are essentially euphemisms; some of these verbs can be used for the actions of both ingroup and outgroup persons (in case of ingroup, in their **-masu** form; for outgroup, often in their **o-[masu** base**] ni naru** form; or for ingroup only, with humble forms being unavailable in most cases):

neru	**yasumu** (*rest*)	o-yasumi ni naru
kuru	**mieru** (*become visible*) (outgroup only) This expression is only used for third persons (for ***addressing*** outgroup, **irassharu** is used) **ukaga.u** (*call*) (ingroup only) **agaru** (*enter a house*) (ingroup only)	o-mie ni naru
kiku	**ukagau**; **o-ukagai suru** (humble) (both ingroup only)	
shinu	**nakunar.u** (*pass away*)	o-nakunari ni naru

Ingroup examples:

Shujin wa mō yasumimashita. *My husband has already gone to bed.*

Yūbe nakunarimashita. *She died last night.*

Ashita ukagaimasu. *I shall call upon you tomorrow.*

Chotto o-ukagai shitai desu ga . . . *I hope you won't mind my asking you, but . . .*

O-shirase suru tame ni agarimashita. *I have come to inform you.*

Outgroup examples:

Yukkuri o-yasumi ni natte kudasai. *Please have a good night's sleep.*

Kyō o-kyaku-san ga miemasu. *A guest* (**kyaku**) *is coming today.*

O-mie ni narimashita. *They are here.*

Sensei ga sengetsu o-nakunari ni narimashita. *Sensei passed away last month.*

(*d*) ***Humble and honorific forms of* ageru/kureru/morau**

As we saw in Unit 16, **ageru** and **morau** are used by ingroup only; they can therefore be expected to have humble equivalents for formal situations:

ageru sashiage.ru

morau itadaku (the humble form for **taberu/nomu** is therefore in fact the humble form of **morau** *to receive*)

Kono hon o sashiagemasu. *I would like to give you this book.*
Sensei kara tegami o itadakimashita. *I have had a letter from sensei.*

Expressions involving **-te ageru/morau** can also be made more formal by substituting these humble forms:

kite moraitai desu→kite itadakitai desu→irasshatte itadakitai desu *I would like you to come.*

Ageru is used towards a listener of equal or slightly lower status; for intimate people and people of clearly lower status, as well as pets etc., **yaru** is used (**inu ni mizu o yarimashita** *I gave the dog water*). Witness the following examples in rising order of formality:

oshiete yaru/yarimasu→oshiete agemasu→oshiete sashiagemasu *I will teach/show you*

When asking politely if the listener would do something for you or join you in some activity, the potential form of **itadakimasu** is generally used in question form, with the literal meaning *can I receive your doing . . . ?*); to make this even politer, **itadakemasu deshō ka** or **itadakemasen deshō ka** may be used:

Kono hon o kashite itadakemasu ka? *Could you possibly lend me this book?*
Issho ni kite itadakemasu ka? *Would you mind coming with me?*
O-namae to go-jūsho o koko ni kaite itadakemasu deshō ka? *Would you be so kind as to write your name and address here?*
Nichiyōbi ni irashite itadakemasen deshō ka? *Could you perhaps come on Sunday?*

At a less polite level, **moraeru** can be used:

O-kane o kashite moraemasu ka? *Can you lend me some money?*

As we saw in Unit 16, **kureru** has **kudasaru** as its formal equivalent. This is an honorific form. Because **kureru** is used with outgroup subjects only, it has in fact no humble form.

(*e*) ***An idiomatic expression:* o-denwa mōshiageru**
Although you will usually hear **(o-)denwa o shimasu/itashimasu/sashiagemasu**, also note **o-denwa mōshiageru**, a very formal humble equivalent of **denwa (o) suru**. Note that it is not possible to use **mōsu** instead of **mōshiageru**.

Although **o** can be used after **o-denwa**, it is more often omitted; this is characteristic of formal language and occurs with other particles such as **wa**, as in the **Kaiwa**: **Jiru-sensei irasshaimasu ka?/Watakushi Tanaka to mōshimasu ga, . . .**

2 *Other formal expressions*

Humble and honorific expressions are clearly distinguished by the fact that the former are used only with regard to the speaker and his group, and the latter with regard to the listener or to third persons.

Recall that in Unit 2 Language and Society 1 we saw that **o-/go-** can also indicate this distinction (**o-tegami** *your letter*), but at other times will simply give the conversation a politer, more formal ring (**o-sake**).

(*a*) **Desu** *and* **de gozaimasu**
The use of **desu** and **-masu** (rather than using plain forms) at the end of a sentence etc. also has a formal effect (recall also the use of **deshō** instead of **desu** to make very polite questions—Unit 6 Structures 2); this can be heightened further by using **de gozaimasu** instead of **desu** (**-masu** does not have a more formal equivalent; instead, the verb to which it is attached is converted to a humble/honorific one where possible).

Kyō wa nichiyōbi de gozaimasu.

De gozaimasu is used in expressions such as **sō de gozaimasu ka** or **sayō de gozaimasu ka?** (*indeed?*). It is also common in statements about ingroup members:

Tanaka de gozaimasu. *I am Tanaka.*
Shujin de gozaimasu. *This is my husband.*

It is, however, never used with regard to an outgroup person; for such cases, **de irasshaimasu** (the honorific equivalent of **desu**) is sometimes used in formal situations, such as on the telephone.

Hādo-sensei de irasshaimasu ka? *Is that Herd-sensei?*
Okāsama wa taihen o-genki de irasshaimasu. *His/your mother is very energetic.*

(*b*) **Arimasu** ***and*** **gozaimasu**

When referring to objects, **gozaimasu** may be used for both in- and outgroup as a very formal equivalent of **arimasu** (although for outgroup, the honorific **o-ari desu/deshō** can also be used):

Atarashii o-sakana ga gozaimasu yo. *We have some fresh fish.*
Ima o-jikan gozaimasu/o-ari desu ka? *Would you have time now?*

(*c*) ***Formal equivalents of nouns:*** **hito→kata**; **dō→ikaga**; **watashi→watakushi**; **koto→ken** ***etc.***

These may be divided into three types: nouns such as **kata** can be used only about outgroup and are therefore honorific (much like referring to outgroup relations, see Unit 16 Language and Society 1), whereas **watakushi** is a humble expression. **Ikaga** and **ken** are expressions that are used in formal situations without necessarily referring to any person (in practice, however, **ikaga**, being a question word, almost invariably refers to outgroup).

Gaikoku no kata mo irasshaimasu ka? *Are there any foreigners, too?*
Kono kata ga Hādo-san no okusama desu. *This lady is Herd-san's wife.*
Watakushi Tanaka to mōshimasu. *My name is Tanaka.*
Bīru wa ikaga desu ka? *Would you like some beer?*
Go-ryokō no ken de go-renraku o mōshiagete orimasu ga. *I am contacting you about your trip.*

3 *Indicating purpose and reason with* tame (ni)

We saw in Unit 7 Structures 2 that before **iku/kuru** etc., purpose can be expressed by **[-masu** base**] ni**. In a more general way, however, purpose is expressed by the noun **tame (ni)** after both the present plain form of verbs and **[noun] no:**

Nihongo o narau tame ni Nihon ni ikimasu. *I will go to Japan in order to learn* (**nara.u**) *Japanese.*
Jogingu o suru tame ni hayaku okimashita. *I got up early to do my jogging.*
Shinsatsu no tame ni shatsu o nuide kudasai. *Please take off your shirt for the examination.*
Shigoto no tame ni Nihon ni kimashita. *I have come to Japan to work.*

When attached to nouns referring to people and countries etc., **tame ni** means *for* (*the benefit of*) [*noun*]:

Sensei no tame ni purezento o kaimashō *Let's buy a present for sensei.*
Ken-san no tame ni pātī ga shitai desu. *I'd like to throw a party for Ken.*
Kuni no tame ni shita koto desu. *It's something I did for my country.*

Note that before **desu**, **tame** is used without **ni**:

Nan no tame ni kita n' desu ka? *What have you come for?*
Ryokō no uchiawase no tame desu/ryokō no uchiawase o suru tame desu. *In order to make travel arrangements* (**uchiawase**).

When **tame ni** is attached to adjectives, and verbs that indicate a state (**aru/iru**) or are in the **-te iru** or **-ta** form, it indicates a reason: **tame** here has a more formal/official ring than **kara**:

Dōshite konna ni osoi n' desu ka? Densha ga okureta tame desu. *Why are you so late? On account of the train running late.*
Yotte ita tame ni oboe ga arimasen. *Because I was drunk I don't remember.*
Ii gakkō ga chikaku ni aru tame ni koko ni sunde imasu. *We live here because there is a good school nearby.*
Kurasu ga ōkii tame ni amari renshū dekimasen. *I don't get much practice* (**renshū (suru)**) *because the class is big.*

4 [statement] no ni *to indicate contrast*

In Unit 5 Structures 4 we saw that **ga** can signal a contrast (*but*); **no ni** is stronger in that it expresses a pronounced contrast (*although/despite*). **No ni** is attached to the same forms as **n' da/desu** (Unit 7 Structures 5). Compare the meanings of the pair of sentences below:

Kēki ga atta ga, kaimasen deshita. *There was some cake, but I didn't buy any.*
Kēki ga atta no ni, kaimasen deshita. *Although there was some cake, I didn't buy any.*

Here are some more examples with **no ni**:

O-kane ga amari nai no ni, eiga ni itta. *Although I haven't got much money, I went to the cinema.*
Kanojo wa kirei na no ni, dare mo kekkon shitagaranai. *Despite her beauty, no one wants to marry her.*
Yotte ita no ni, yoku oboete iru. *Although he was drunk, he remembers well.*

Sometimes the order of the two sections is reversed (this can also be done in English):

Yoku oboete iru nē, yotte ita no ni. *You remember well, don't you, despite having been drunk.*

Because of its stronger impact **no ni** can be used at the end of a sentence in emphatic past-tense statements lamenting a missed opportunity:

Minna mo tanoshimi ni shite ita no ni. *Everyone was hoping so much that you'd come!*
Ikitakatta no ni. *I really wanted to go!*
Aitakatta no ni. *I wanted to see you so much!*

Renshū

1 Conduct a telephone conversation with a senior friend/colleague (Tanaka Yōji-san, male, or Yōko-san, female) on the following lines (if possible, get a friend to play the other part; swap parts once you are fluent and confident in the first one);

(*a*) Ring up and confirm that you are connected to the right people. —His/her mother answers.
(*b*) Identify yourself and ask if your friend/colleague is home. —He/she is, and the mother calls him/her.
(*c*) Thank the mother (in advance) for calling him/her to the phone.
(*d*) He/she comes to the phone, saying his/her given name. You identify yourself to him/her, and say hello. Then ask if he/she is free to join you in going to see a film on Saturday.
(*e*) He/she thanks you for your invitation and asks you to wait because he/she needs to check his/her diary.
(*f*) He/she thanks you for holding the line. He/she is unfortunately not free on Saturday.
(*g*) You suggest Sunday as an alternative. – On Sunday, he/she is free.
(*h*) You say that you will pick him/her up at his/her place on Sunday at 5 o'clock, and ask how that suits him/her. – Yes, he/she will be waiting for you.
(*i*) You say good bye.—He/she says good bye.

2 You (Clive Baker) are having a conversation with a stranger at a party celebrating the publication of a book by your **sensei**. Fill in the blank sections of the questions or replies for the exchanges below as suggested by the cues:
Rei: Sensei no hon (o) o-mochi desu ka? – Hai, ______.
→Hai, motte orimasu.

(*a*) Shinbun de sensei no shashin (o) go-ran ni narimashita ka? Hai, ______.
(*b*) (Tanaka-san o) ______ ka? – Iie, zonjite orimasen.
(*c*) Shitsurei desu ga, Sumisu-san de irasshaimasu ka? – Iie, watashi wa ______.
(*d*) Bēkā-san wa raishū no pātī ni mo ______ ka? – Hai, mairu tsumori desu.

3 You have recently arrived in Urawa (near Tokyo), and your inquisitive landlady is determined to find out all about your reasons in deciding to come to Japan, and anything else that incites her curiosity. Answer her cross-examination-type questions using **tame ni** or **tame desu.**

Rei: Nan no tame ni Nihon ni kita n' desu ka (Nihongo o narau)
→Nihongo o narau tame desu./Nihongo o narau tame ni kimashita.

(*a*) Nan no tame ni Nihongo o narau n' desu ka? (Nihon no kaisha ni tsutomeru)
(*b*) Dōshite Nihon no kaisha ni tsutometai n' desu ka? (O-kane ga ii)
(*c*) Nan no tame ni Urawa ni kita n' desu ka? (Nihonjin no tomodachi ga sunde iru)
(*d*) Nan no tame ni itsu mo sonna ni hayaku okiru n' desu ka? (Shichiji no nyūsu (*news*) o miru)
(*e*) Dōshite yūbe anna ni osoku kaette kita no desu ka? (Tomodachi to nonde ita)
(*f*) Dōshite watashi to hanashitagaranai n' desu ka? (Urusai! (*annoying*))

4 Form a catalogue of missed opportunities/unwise decisions by linking the **no ni** sections with the sections appropriate to complete the sentences:

1 Sono kimono wa takai no ni	(*a*) arimasen deshita.
2 Jikan ga atta no ni	(*b*) kaimashita.
3 Omoshiroi eiga na no ni	(*c*) pātī ni ikimasen deshita.
4 Hayaku kippu o kai ni itta no ni	(*d*) okiraremasen deshita.
5 Yūbe hayaku neta no ni	(*e*) mimasen deshita.

Language and Society

1 *Parties*

Such gatherings are generally held away from the home, at eating or drinking places. Apart from class reunions (**kurasu-kai** or **dōsō-kai**), common occasions are gatherings called **konpa** (from English *company*!) where university students eat and drink with their teachers (who will often foot the major part of the bill). Company employees often go out in the evenings in small groups, but large-scale company gatherings mostly take place within the framework of large-scale outings.

In addition, there are two or three occasions in the year when most Japanese go out to get drunk with their colleagues. These are:

Hanami (*cherry-blossom viewing*) in spring, when hordes of Japanese get drunk on the weekend under the blossoms, leaving behind tons of rubbish and empty bottles.

Bōnen-kai, the end-of-year parties, which take place in November/December, when most drinking places of decent size are booked solid for the purpose.

Shinnen-kai, the New Year parties that take place after the New Year holidays in January.

Of course, there is a great deal of singing on all these occasions.

2 *Some useful expressions used in formal language*

One feature of Japanese language used on formal occasions is the 'roundabout' expression; this is of course also found in English (e.g. *Would you mind if I open the window?*).

Such expressions are felt to be more considerate because they are vaguer and less direct, and therefore do not unduly narrow down the addressee's choice. Instead of **itsu/nanji?**, **ikura?** and **ato de**, for instance, expressions like **itsugoro/nanjigoro?** (*about when?*), **ikura hodo/ikahodo?** (*about how much?*) and **nochi hodo** (*later*, Lit. *some time after*) are used:

Nanjigoro o-ukagai shimashō ka? *When would you like me to come?*
Nochi hodo o-ai shimashō *I'll see you later.*

It is useful to be able to use some stock phrases that are used on formal occasions; when someone calls another person to the telephone for you, for instance, it is customary to say **osoreirimasu**; before hanging up **shitsurei (ita)shimasu**; and when ringing someone you haven't talked to for some time, **go-busata shite (or)imasu** (*Sorry I haven't been in touch*). **O-hisashiburi (desu)** (see Unit 2 Language and Society 2) can be used in reply to **go-busata shite imasu**, especially by people of higher status.

19 Moshi o-kane ga attara, Igirisu e itte mitai wa *If I had the money, I'd like to go to Britain*

In this unit, you will be introduced to various ways of expressing the conditional (*when/if* in English), and related patterns for giving and requesting advice and for expressing both hope and regret. You will also meet another use of **-te mo** and various ways of saying *only*. In addition, there will be some information on the weather in Japan and the Japanese yearly cycle.

ame

Kaiwa

Tsuyu ga hajimatta. Mainichi no yō ni ame ga furu shi, shikke ga ōi kara, ki o tsukenai to, tabemono ya fuku nado ni kabi ga haeru. Michiko-san ga Hādo-san-tachi no ie no mado kara mite iru.

Michiko Tsuyu wa hontō ni iya da wa! Ame ga yandara doko ka e dekakete mo ii n' da keredo . . . Igirisu ni wa nai deshō – konna tenki.

Ken Igirisu wa tsuyu wa nai ka mo shirenai keredo, ichinenjū ame bakkari desu yo.

Michiko Sō kashira. Tonikaku, moshi o-kane ga attara, Igirisu e itte mitai wa.

Ken Michiko-san ga ikitai to iu nara, kondo no o-shōgatsu ni boku-tachi ga Igirisu ni kaeru toki, issho ni ikanai? Fuyu da to, kōkūken ga ikura ka yasuku naru kara.

Michiko Demo, go-ryōshin wa nan to ossharu kashira. Watashi no yō ni hajimete gaikoku ni iku hito o tsurete iku no wa taihen deshō?

Ken Kitto yorokobu to omou yo.
Michiko (*kōfun shita koe de*) Sō? Ja, uchi ni kaettara, sugu chichi to haha ni kiite miru wa.

tsuyu *the rainy season* (June/early July) ● LS1
mainichi no yō ni *as if every day; almost every day*
shikke ga ōi (sukunai) *humidity is high (low)*
shikke *humidity*
[verb (present plain form)] to *if [verb]* ● S1(*a*)
[noun] ni kabi ga haeru *mould grows on [noun]/[noun] grows mouldy*
kabi *mould*
hae.ru *to grow, sprout*
mado kara miru *to look out of a window*
yandara -tara form of **yam.u**
yam.u (intransitive) *to stop, cease* (→**yameru** transitive)
[verb]-tara *if [verb]* ● S1(*b*)
ichinenjū *all through the year/all year round*
[noun] bak(k)ari da *It's/there's nothing but [noun]* ● S2
moshi *if*
[verb (plain form)] nara *if [verb]* ● S1(*c*)
kondo no [noun] (here) *next/this [noun] coming*
kōkūken *air tickets*
ikura ka *a little, somewhat*
ryōshin *parents*
hajimete *for the first time*
kōfun (suru) *excitement*
koe *voice*

True or false?

1 Michiko-san wa Igirisu e itta koto ga nai.
2 Michiko-san wa denwa de otōsan to okāsan ni kiite miru.

Yoru, Michiko-san wa otōsan to okāsan ni sono hanashi o suru.

Michiko Ato de Ken-san no okāsan mo zehi issho ni irasshai to itte kuremashita shi . . .
Okusan Sore wa kotoba dake no hanashi ka mo shiremasen yo.
Anzai Izure ni shite mo, wakai onna no ko ga hitori de Yōroppa ni itte wa ikemasen!
Michiko Hitori ja nai deshō. Hādo-san-tachi ga tsuite iru kara.

Anzai Tsuite ite mo dame!

Okusan Onna no tomodachi to issho nara ii n' da keredomo . . .

Michiko (*gakkari shite*) Ken-san ni imōto ga ireba yokatta no ni. (*kyū ni mata akaruku natte*) Demo, okāsan wa Ken-san no okāsan no tomodachi na n' deshō. Okāsan mo issho ni ikeba dō kashira?

Anzai (*atama ni kite*) Sonna kane wa nai!

Okusan (*atama ni kite*) Kinjo no sūpā de pāto o shite kasegimasu.

Anzai Kimi ga inai aida, ore wa dō suru n' da?

Okusan Tarō no sewa demo sureba?

Anzai (*akirete*) Jā, kimatta. Minna de ikō!

Sore wa kotoba dake no hanashi ka mo shiremasen *She might have been only saying that* (**kotoba dake no hanashi** *talk that is only words*)

[noun] dake *just/only [noun]* ● S2

izure ni shite mo *either way/in any case*

onna *woman, female*

onna no ko *girl*

hitori de *by oneself/on one's own* ● S3

tsuk.u (here) *to accompany/attend one*

tsuite ite mo dame! *it's no good even if they're with you* ●S4

gakkari suru *become disappointed*

Ken-san ni imōto ga ireba yokatta no ni *If only Ken had a younger sister*

[verb]-eba *if [verb]* ● S1(*d*)

[verb]-eba yokatta no ni *if only [verb]* ● S5

akaru.i *bright, cheerful*

atama ni kuru *to become angry (the blood comes to your head)*

sūpā *supermarket*

pāto *part-time work*

kaseg.u *to earn (money), work (for money)*

kimi *you* (used mainly by men towards wives/girlfriends or other men of equal or lower status) ● Unit 22 S1(*e*)

ore *I* (used by men in informal situations; has masculine connotations) ● Unit 22 S1(*e*)

[noun] no sewa (suru) *help/care for, looking after [noun]*

akire.ru *to be amazed/disgusted/at your wit's end*

minna de *all together*

True or false?

3 Michiko-san wa issho ni ikanai hō ga ii darō to Ken-san no ryōshin ga itta.
4 Anzai-sensei wa hitori de Tarō-kun no sewa ga shitai rashii.

Structures

1 [verb/noun/adjective] to, -tara, nara and -eba: *the conditional*

(*a*) **[verb/noun/adjective] to**
This pattern has already come up in relation to ways of expressing the idea of *must* in Japanese (Unit 15 Structures 8). The verb or, more rarely, adjective in front of **to** is in the present plain form, either positive or negative, whatever the tense of the main clause. (Nouns and **na** adjectives before **to** take **da**.)

When the main clause is in the present tense, **to** indicates that the main clause is the natural, inevitable, or habitual consequence of the situation/action in front of **to**:

Migi e magaru to, ginkō ga arimasu. *If you turn* (**magar.u**) *right* (**migi**), *you'll find a bank.*
Hayaku nenai to, ashita nebō shimasu yo. *If you don't go to bed early you'll oversleep tomorrow.*
O-sake o nomu to, dō narimasu ka? *What happens to you when you drink (alcohol)?*
Shikke ga ōi to, kabi ga sugu haemasu ne. *When humidity is high, things soon get mouldy don't they?*

To is generally used in making objective statements of fact, and not when the main clause involves the will of the speaker, or the making of suppositions, requests and commands.

When the main clause is in the past tense, **to** indicates that the action in the main clause took place immediately after the action in the **to** clause. It is more common in written than in spoken Japanese:

Beddo ni hairu to, sugu nemashita. *No sooner had I got into bed* (**beddo**) *than I went to sleep.*

Michiko-san no hanashi o kiku to, Hādo-san-tachi wa yorokonda. *On hearing what Michiko had to say, the Herds were overjoyed.*

(b) [verb/noun/adjective]-tara

This is formed by adding **-ra** to the plain past forms (negative as well as positive) of both adjectives and verbs (and nouns):

na *adjectives* (*and nouns*)	genki da→ genki dattara/de nakattara shizuka da→ shizuka dattara/ de nakattara
-i *adjectives*	atsui→ atsukattara/atsukunakattara ii→ yokattara/yokunakattara mitai→ mitakattara/mitakunakattara
-iru/-eru *verbs*	miru→ mitara/minakattara taberu→ tabetara/tabenakattara
-u *verbs*	kaku→ kaitara/kakanakattara hanasu→ hanashitara/hanasanakattara
irregular verbs	kuru→ kitara/konakattara suru→ shitara/shinakattara

In more formal situations, you will also come across **-tara** forms of verbs which are made from the **-mashita** form, such as **mimashitara**.

The use of **-tara** indicates that the action or situation in the *when/if* clause will be finished or complete before the action or situation in the main clause takes place. The relationship between the two clauses is temporal rather than logical. Unlike **to, -tara** can therefore be used in subjective situations, and when making requests or commands. Here are some examples when the main clause is in the present tense:

Koko made kitara, hitori de kaeremasu. *Once I have got this far, I can get back by myself.*

Ashita ame dattara, uchi de terebi o mimashō. *If it rains tomorrow let's watch television at home.*

Samukattara, mado o shimete kudasai. *If you feel cold, please shut the window.*

Yokattara, kore o dōzo. *Please take this if you would like it.*

Hontō ni benkyō shitakattara, mata kite kudasai. *Please come again, when you really want to study.*

Michiko-san ga konakattara, omoshirokunai deshō. *It won't be any fun, will it, unless Michiko comes.*

-tara with the main verb in the past implies that the situation or action in the main clause followed the **-tara** clause in time, but was not an intended consequence, and may have come as a surprise:

Michiko-san wa chi o mitara, kyū ni ki o ushinaimashita. *When she saw the blood* (**chi**), *Michiko suddenly fainted* (**ki o ushina.u**).

Kesa okitara, yuki ga futte imashita. *When I got up this morning it was snowing.*

Uchi ni kaettara, dare mo imasen deshita. *When I returned home, there was no-one there.*

(*c*) **[verb/noun/adjective] nara**

Verbs and **-i** adjectives take the plain form in front of **nara**, while nouns and **na** adjectives drop **desu**. The part of the sentence before **nara** usually involves an assumption or supposition about something actual in the present, or about something which may occur in the future. The equivalent in English would be *If it is the case that/If as you say . . . .* The main clause involves a statement, request, command or question which depends on the part in front of **nara** being true:

Tomu-san wa Igirisujin nara, kuriketto ga wakaru hazu desu. *If Tom is British, he should understand cricket* (**kuriketto**).

Sore ga hontō nara, komaru deshō ne. *If that's true, we'll be in trouble, won't we.*

Sonna ni muzukashii nara, tetsudatte agete mo ii desu yo. *If it's that difficult, I don't mind helping you.*
Tarō-kun ga iku nara, watashi wa ikimasen. *If Tarō is going, I won't go.*

Unlike **-tara** (and **to**), with **nara** the main clause does not have to follow the *if/when* clause in terms of time:

O-furo ni hairu nara, hayaku hairi nasai. *If you're going to have a bath, have it quickly.*
Konban karē o taberu nara, igusuri o nonde okimashō *If we're going to eat curry this evening, let's take some digestive tablets beforehand.*
Nihonjin to kekkon suru nara, mazu Nihongo o benkyō shinakereba ikemasen. *If you're going to marry a Japanese, you must first study the language.*

With nouns **nara** sometimes acts as an emphatic **wa**:

Watashi nara hitori de anna tokoro e ikimasen. *I wouldn't go to such a place alone (if I were you).*
Michiko-san nara daijōbu deshō. (*If it's*) *Michiko* (*she*) *will be all right.*

Sore nara is often equivalent to *in that case*:

Sore nara, ashita Hādo-san-tachi ni denwa o shimashō. *In that case, let's telephone the Herds tomorrow.*

(*d*) **[verb/noun/adjective]-eba**

The positive **-eba** form of verbs is made by dropping the final **-u** and adding **-eba**:

-iru/-eru *verbs*	miru → mireba taberu → tabereba
-u *verbs*	kaku → kakeba hanasu → hanaseba
irregular verbs	kuru → kureba suru → sureba

Note what happens to verbs ending in **-tsu**, such as **matsu**:

matsu	→	mateba

The negative **-eba** form of verbs has already come up in connection with *must* (Unit 15 Structures 8); the **-eba** form of **-i** adjectives (negative as well as positive) is made in the same way, by dropping the final **-i** and adding **-kereba**:

minai	→	minakereba
kakanai	→	kakanakereba
atsui	→	atsukereba/atsukunakereba
oishii	→	oishikereba/oishikunakereba
mitai	→	mitakereba/mitakunakereba

Note that **ii** becomes **yokereba**. With nouns and **na** adjectives, **da** becomes **de areba/de nakereba**:

ame da	→	ame de areba/de nakereba
shizuka da	→	shizuka de areba/de nakereba

-eba indicates the circumstances under which the situation or action in the main clause will be possible:

Ame ga fureba, suzushiku naru deshō. *If it rained it would get cooler.*

Jikan ga areba, mata kite kudasai. *Please come again, if you have the time.*

Ano hon ga omoshirokereba, watashi mo yomu ka mo shiremasen. *If that book is interesting, I may read it too.*

In modern spoken Japanese, it is less common than the other conditional forms, and occurs mainly in more formal speech and in certain set constructions, the most common of these being **-nakereba narimasen/ikemasen**.

(*e*) ***More uses***

-tara and **-eba** are often used in asking for and giving advice, with the literal meaning *If it/you . . . , then . . .* :

Dō shitara/sureba, kaze ga naorimasu ka? *What should I do for my cold to get better?*
Shibaraku uchi o denakattara/denakereba, naoru deshō. *It should get better if you don't leave the house for a while.*
Kono hon o yondara/yomeba, wakaru deshō. *You would understand if you read this book.*

-tara/-eba, ii deshō ka? (Lit. *If . . . , do you suppose it is good?*) and **-tara/-eba, dō deshō ka?** (Lit. *If . . . , how would it be?*) are also used in asking for/offering advice (see also **hō ga ii** Unit 14 Structures 3):

Dō shitara/sureba, ii deshō ka? *What should I do?*
Kusuri o nondara/nomeba, dō deshō ka? *How about taking some medicine?*

In informal situations, you will also come across suggestions phrased like Mrs Anzai's in the **Kaiwa**:

Tarō no sewa demo sureba/shitara? *How about looking after/Why not look after Tarō or something?*

In polite situations, the **-tara/-eba** form of **yoroshi.i**, an honorific form of **ii**, is fairly common when you are urging someone to do something:

Yoroshikattara/Yoroshikereba, kochira de shibaraku o-yasumi ni natte kudasai. *Please rest here for a little if it would please you.*

You will also come across polite suggestions consisting of **-tara/-eba dō/ikaga deshō ka?**:

O-suwari ni nattara/narimashitara/nareba dō deshō ka? *How about sitting down?*
Mō sukoshi meshiagattara/meshiagarimashitara/meshigareba ikaga deshō ka? *How about a little more?*

. . . to/-tara/-eba ii desu is also used to express hopes, again with the literal meaning *If . . ., it will be good.*

Pasupōto ga hayaku mitsukaru to/mitsukattara/mitsukareba ii desu ne. *I hope the passport turns up quickly.*
Hontō ni Igirisu ni ikeru to/iketara/ikereba ii desu ne. *Wouldn't it be lovely if I really was able to go to Britain!*

Hikōki ni noriokurenai to/noriokurenkattara/noriokurenakereba ii desu ga ne. *I hope he's not late for the plane.*

Another pattern in which **-eba**, or **-tara**, can be found is given in Structures 5.

(*f*) Summary

Clearly all four conditional forms overlap to a certain extent, **nara** being the most easily distinguished, and **-tara** being the most common. The difference between **to**, **-tara** and **-eba** might best be illustrated by a comparison of the following:

1 Yukkuri hanasu to, wakarimasu.
2 Yukkuri hanashitara, wakarimasu.
3 Yukkuri hanaseba, wakarimasu.

1 describes my general competence at Japanese: *When you speak slowly, I understand.* 2 refers to a specific situation. You have asked me if I understand you, and I reply that *If you speak slowly I will understand.* In 3 you have asked what you should do for me to understand you. I tell you that *Provided you speak slowly, I'll understand.*

Finally, note that **moshi** used with any of these conditional words, normally right at the beginning of the sentence, will emphasise the idea of *if*:

Moshi yukkuri hanashitara, wakaru deshō. *If you were to speak slowly, I would probably understand.*

2 bak(k)ari, dake *and* shika*: only*

These three particles are often, but not always, equivalent to English *only*. **Shika** is probably the closest to English usage since **[noun] shika** implies *only* [*noun*] *and nothing else*, even though more was expected. **Shika** always takes a negative verb. The particles **wa**, **ga** and **o** are usually omitted with **shika**, but other particles precede it:

Tomodachi ga futari shika kite kuremasen deshita. *Only two friends came.*

Hyaku-en shika arimasen. *I have only 100 yen* (*but I need more*).

Suzuki-san wa Nihongo shika dekimasen. *Suzuki-san can only speak Japanese.*
Pan shika tabemasen deshita. *I ate only bread.*
Tomodachi ni shika iimasen deshita. *I told only my friends.*

Note the pattern **[verb (present plain form)] shika nai**:

Matsu shika arimasen. *All we can do is wait.* (Lit. *There is only waiting.*)

Shika is never found in front of **da/desu**, and cannot be used where the final verb is going to be in the negative anyway.

The basic meaning of **dake** is *extent*, and it is used where *only* refers more to an exact limit which has not been exceeded. It is less emphatic than **shika**, and often translates as *just* as well as *only*. With counters and amounts in general, **dake** means *only* in the sense of *just/exactly*:

Hyaku-en dake agete kudasai. *Please give me just* 100 *yen* (*that is all I need*).
Sukoshi dake tabemashita. *I ate just a little.*

After nouns, **dake** is equivalent to *just/only/at least*; **o** and **ga** are replaced, and other particles follow:

Tomodachi dake kureba, ii desu. *I hope that only friends will come.*
Kono shigoto dake shite kaerimashō. *Let's do just this job and then go home.*
Tabako dake wa yamete kudasai. *Please give up smoking at least.*

Unlike **shika**, dake can be used in front of **da/desu**, and when the verb is already in the negative:

Hoshii no wa kimi dake desu *You are the only thing I want.*
Jiru-san wa tako dake tabemasen. *The only thing Jill doesn't eat is octopus.*

Note that either present or past plain forms of verbs can precede **dake**:

Kaze o hiite iru dake da kara, shinpai shinakute mo ii desu. *There's no need to worry since it's only a cold.*
Tomodachi to eiga o mi ni itta dake desu. *I simply went to see a film with a friend.*

You will also find **[noun] dake no [noun]**:

Kore wa tomodachi dake no pātī desu. *This is a party for friends only.*
O-kane dake no mondai de wa arimasen. *It's not a problem of money alone.*

Bakari refers to an approximate extent or limit. With counters, it implies that a rough guess is being made, and is therefore equivalent to *about*:

Tomodachi ga jūnin bakari kimashita. *About ten friends came.*
Nijikan bakari machimashita. *I waited about two hours.*

With nouns, **bakari** (and the more emphatic **bakkari**) overlaps with **dake** and has connotations of *exclusively/nothing but/only/just*. **O** and **ga** are usually replaced, and other particles follow:

Suzuki-san wa konogoro o-sake bakari nonde imasu. *Recently Suzuki-san has been drinking nothing but alcohol.*
Kore wa kami bakari de tsukurimashita. *I made this with paper only.*

Like **dake**, it can be used where **shika** cannot:

Watashi bakari de wa arimasen. *It's not only me.*

The pattern **[verb (past plain form)] bakari da** means *I* (*etc.*) *have just* [*verb*]:

Kaette kita bakari desu. *I have just got back.*
Tarō wa o-furo ni haitta bakari desu. *Tarō has just got into the bath.*

3 hitori de *by oneself*

Hitori, *one person*, can mean *alone*:

A Issho desu ka? *Are you with someone* (*together*)*?*
B Iie, hitori desu. *No, I'm alone.*

However, when you are ***doing*** something alone, in other words, when an adjective or verb comes at the end of the sentence, **de** must be added:

Hitori de daijōbu desu ka? *Are you all right by yourself?*
Yūbe hitori de terebi o mimashita. *Yesterday evening I watched television alone.*

Note a similar use of **de** in **futari de, sannin de** etc., for doing things in a twosome, threesome etc.; **minna de**, for doing things all together, as at the end of this **Kaiwa**; and **zenbu de** for giving the price of everything together (Unit 9 **Kaiwa**):

Sannin de takushī ni norimashita. *The three of us got in a taxi.*

4 *More on* -te mo

In Unit 14 Structures 2, we met **-te mo ii** as a way of giving and asking permission. **Te mo** is found with other adjectives, and with verbs as well, with the meaning *even if*:

Mado o akete mo atsui desu. *It's hot even if we open the window.*
Ken-san ga itte mo watashi wa ikimasen. *I won't go even if Ken goes.*
Tomodachi ga nakute mo heiki desu. *I don't mind* (**heiki na**) *even if I have no friends.*
Takakute mo kaimasu. *I'll buy it even if it's expensive.*

When there is an interrogative, such as **dare** or **nani**, in the **-te mo** clause, it has a meaning equivalent to [*question word*]*-ever* . . . :

Dare ga kite mo watashi wa kamaimasen. *I don't care* (**kamaimasen**) *whoever comes.*
Nani o tabete mo Michiko-san wa futorimasen. *Michiko doesn't get fat whatever she eats.*
Kono bīru wa ikura nonde mo oishii desu. *This beer tastes delicious however much you drink.*

5 [verb/noun/adjective]-tara/-eba . . . no ni *if only*

A **no ni** clause (Unit 18 Structures 4) preceded by **-tara** or **-eba** can be used to express regret, in a pattern which literally means something like *Although X would happen/would have happened if* . . . , (*it won't/didn't*), and which is equivalent to English *If only* . . . :

Motto renshū shitara/sureba, sugu jōzu ni naru no ni. *If only you practised more, you would soon improve.*

Kuru mae ni tegami o kaitara/kakeba, mondai ga nakatta no ni. *If only you had written a letter before you came, there wouldn't have been any problem.*
Tabako o suwanakattara/suwanakereba, seki ga sugu naoru no ni. *If only you didn't smoke, your cough would soon get better.*
Genki dattara, watashi mo minna to issho ni iketa no ni. *If only I hadn't been ill, I would have been able to go with everyone too.*

-eba ii/yokatta no ni, literally *Although it would be/would have been good if . . .*, is equivalent to *If only . . .* with no main clause, or a plaintive *I wish . . .*:

Ieba, ii no ni. *If only/I wish you would tell me.*
Denwa sureba, yokatta no ni. *If only/I wish you had telephoned.*
Michiko-san no tanjōbi o wasurenakereba, yokatta no ni. *If only/I wish I hadn't forgotten Michiko's birthday.*

Renshū

1 Using the conditional **to** for objective statements of fact, Jill explains various aspects of life in Britain to Mrs Anzai. Complete her sentences as shown by the example.
Rei: Ichigatsu no Rondon wa (yoru ni naru) (samui)
Ichigatsu no Rondon wa yoru ni naru to, samui desu.

(*a*) (takushī de iku) (Tokyo yori takai)
(*b*) (Igirisujin ni michi o kiku) (shinsetsu ni oshiete kureru) [**michi o kiku** *ask the way*]
(*c*) Igirisu de wa (kurejitto kādo ga aru) (benri da) [**kurejitto kādo** *credit card*]
(*d*) (oto o tate-nagara sūpu o nomu) (shitsurei da) [**oto o tateru** *make a noise;* **shitsurei na** *rude*]
(*e*) (hajimete hito ni au) (akushu suru) [**akushu suru** *to shake hands*]

2(*a*) Tom has just returned from his trip to Hong Kong. Yamada-san has a list of things he must do, but Tom has already planned his day. Using the conditional **-tara** with its temporal sense, he informs her of his schedule, which starts with his customary cup of coffee. Complete his sentences as shown by the example.

Rei: (kōhī o nomu) (kaigi no repōto o kaku)
Kōhī o nondara, kaigi no repōto o kakimasu.

1 (kaigi no repōto o kaku) (sore o Igirisu ni okutte morau)
2 (repōto o Igirisu ni okutte morau) (hiru-gohan o taberu)
3 (hiru-gohan o taberu) (gorufu ni iku)
4 (gorufu kara kaette kuru) (Igirisu ni denwa o suru)
5 (Igirisu ni denwa o suru) (uchi ni kaeru)

(*b*) Yamada-san, however, has other plans. Using **-eba dō deshō ka?** she offers Tom useful advice on how he can, in fact, fit much more into his day. Construct her sentences as in the example.
Rei: (kōhī o nomi-nagara repōto o kaku)
Kōhī o nomi-nagara repōto o o-kaki ni nareba dō deshō ka?

1 (hiru-gohan o hayaku taberu)
2 (kyō no gorufu o yameru)
3 (yoru osoku made shigoto suru)
4 (ashita hayaku kaisha ni kuru)

3 Put the adjectives/verbs in brackets into appropriate conditional forms.
Rei: Shigoto ga (owaru), asobi ni kite kudasai.
Shigoto ga owattara, asobi ni kite kudasai.

(*a*) Massugu (iku), eki ga arimasu. [**massugu** *straight ahead*)
(*b*) Tenki ga (ii), doko ka e ikimashō.
(*c*) Denwa o (kakeru), ima kaketa hō ga ii desu.
(*d*) Motto (hansamu na), Satō-san to kekkon shita ka mo shiremasen.
(*e*) Michiko-san ga mitai to (iu), misete agete mo ii desu yo.

4 In the course of a drinking session, Anzai-san has become rather maudlin. Using **[verb/adjective]-tara/-eba . . . no ni** patterns, he sees his life as a series of disasters. (When the second part of the sentence is not specified, use **ii/yokatta** as appropriate before **no ni**.)
Rei: Chichi ga kanemochi (da), kodomo no seikatsu ga motto (raku na) [**kanemochi** *rich* (*man*); **raku na** *comfortable*]
Chichi ga kanemochi dattara, kodomo no seikatsu ga motto raku datta no ni.

(*a*) Supōtsu ga (jōzu na), gakkō de ninki ga (aru) [**ninki ga aru** *to be popular*]

(*b*) Daigaku de motto benkyō (suru)
(*c*) Terebi ga motto (omishiroi), maiban nomiya de sake o (nomanai)
(*d*) Kanai ga itsumo monku bakari (iwanai) [**monku o iu** *to complain*]

5 Add **bakari**, **dake or shika** as appropriate to the gaps indicated by brackets in the following sentences:
Rei: Gofun ( ) machimasen deshita.
Gofun shika machimasen deshita.

(*a*) Tarō-kun wa benkyō shinaide, terebi ( ) mite imasu.
(*b*) Hitotsu ( ) de ii desu.
(*c*) Ano kodomo wa hiragana ( ) kakemasen.
(*d*) Muzukashii no wa kono hon ( ) de wa arimasen.
(*e*) Tabako o yameru ( ) arimasen.

Language and Society

1 *The Japanese and their weather*

The weather (**tenki**) is a convenient topic of conversation among strangers and acquaintances in Japan. The differences between the seasons are sharp. Spring (**haru**) and autumn (**aki**) are the most pleasant, the first being associated with the cherry blossom (**sakura**), and the second with the autumn leaves (**kōyō**/**momiji**). These, and other seasonal signs, will feature in general conversation, and in news broadcasts, etc. The Japanese summer (**natsu**) is less pleasant: first comes the rainy season (**tsuyu**) in June/early July, then comes a period of hot and humid weather, described as **mushiatsu.i**, about which everyone complains and which lasts until early September. Summer and early autumn also coincide with the typhoon (**taifū**) season. The winter (**fuyu**) is short and mild in the south of Japan but grows longer and more severe as you go north. Note that the word **tenki** itself refers to weather rather than temperature, so that it is described as **ii**/**warui**, etc. but not **atsui**/**samui**, etc.

Here are some useful expressons:

ame/yuki ga furu/yamu *rain/snow falls/stops*
ōame/ōyuki *heavy rain/snow*
tsumetai/ii kaze ga fuk.u *a cold/pleasant wind blows*
kumori/hare (desu) (*it is*) *cloudy/sunny*
tsuyu-iri/tsuyu-ake *the beginning/end of the rainy season*
tenki ni naru *to turn fine*
Kyō wa ii/iya na o-tenki desu ne! *What lovely/horrible weather it is today!*

2 *The Japanese yearly cycle*

References to this have already come up in various Language and Society notes. Every area has its own festivals (**matsuri**), but the major yearly celebrations fall at the beginning of the year (**o-shōgatsu**) and in mid-August (**o-Bon**). At the New Year everyone has about a week off, which would traditionally be spent at home, with visits to relatives, one's seniors at work, and a Shinto shrine or Buddhist temple. Increasingly, however, families are choosing to spend this period at hotels, and the young are going abroad. At New Year, children are given **o-toshidama**, gifts of money in small envelopes, by their parents and visitors to the house, and by those whom they go to visit. In April come the cherry blossoms, and the start of the financial and school years. This is also the time when school and university graduates enter companies. At the end of April/beginning of May there is Golden Week. O-Bon, when the ancestors are thought to come back to the family home, is a time for people to travel back to their ancestral home and visit their family graves. Increasingly it too is being used as an ordinary holiday. Autumn has its autumn leaves, and December the preparations for New Year, and Christmas. Late June/early July and December, which coincide with the two bonus payments of the year, are also times for ritual gift-giving, to teachers of one's children, to one's superiors at work, and, increasingly, to relatives. The summer gifts are known as **o-chūgen** and the winter ones as **o-seibo**, but the contents are the same: gift-wrapped boxes of towels, soap, tinned food, whisky etc., which are often not delivered personally but by the store where they are ordered.

20 Waseda ka Keiō o ukesaseru tsumori desu *We intend to get him to take the entrance exams to Waseda or Keiō*

This unit is mainly concerned with how to talk about making/allowing people to do things. You will also find some information on further in/outgroup expressions, and encounter a female way of ending sentences.

教育

kyō iku

Kaiwa

Anzai-sensei no okusan wa kinjo no Hayashi-san no okusan to tachibanashi o shite iru. Hanashi ga dandan kodomo no kyōiku-ron ni natte, futari wa notte kite iru.

Hayashi Uchi no Takashi wa benkyō ga yoku dekiru kara, shōrai wa Waseda ka Keiō o ukesaseru tsumori desu.

Anzai Ima wa dō nasatte irassharu n' desu ka? Juku ni kayowasete iru n' deshō?

Hayashi Ē, mochiron; datte, imadoki juku ni ikanai to, hoka no ko ni okurete shimaimasu kara ne!

Anzai Sō kashira? Uchi no ko wa ikasenai yō ni shite imasu ga.

Hayashi Demo, katei kyōshi o tsukete irassharu deshō?

Anzai Ē, mā, chanto benkyō saseru tame ni wa tokidoki chekku shite kureru hito ga hitsuyō desu wa ne; demo, shū ikkai shika kite moratte imasen yo.

Hayashi O-taku no botchan wa yoku o-deki ni naru kara nē . . . Izure wa Tōdai o o-uke ni naru n' deshō?

Anzai Iie, sonna tsumori wa nakutte yo. Gaikoku no daigaku ni demo ikaseyō to kangaete iru n' desu.

Hayashi Hē, sō desu ka? Ja, ojōsan mo?

Anzai Sō desu ne . . . Shujin wa shōrai, Rondon de shigoto suru koto ni naru ka mo shiremasen kara, sono toki ni wa watakushi-tachi mo tsuite iku tsumori desu.

Hayashi Ii desu nē . . . ja, gaikokugo perapera ni natte kaette irassharu wa nē, kitto. Watashi-tachi wa sonna zeitaku na koto wa dekinai kara, koko de hosoboso to yaru shika arimasen.

Anzai Ara, sonna koto o osshatte . . . ojōsan ni mo iroiro na o-keikogoto ya supōtsu o sasete irassharu no ni.

Hayashi Ie, mā, hon no sukoshi dake desu wa. O-hana ni o-cha deshō? Sore ni piano to tenisu gurai desu yo.

Anzai Taishita mono ja arimasen ka. Tokoro de, kaigai ni ryokō saseru kimochi wa arimasen no?

Hayashi Ie, abunai kara shinpai de ne . . . hen na otoko ni demo tsukamattara komaru kara. Sore yori hayaku o-kanemochi no Nihon no kata to kekkon sasetai desu yo!

kinjo *neighbourhood*
tachibanashi *a chat 'standing up'* (in the street etc.)
kyōiku *education*
ron *argument, discussion*
nor.u *to get warmed, excited*
shōrai *future, in the future*
Waseda, Keiō famous private universities in Tokyo
[noun] ka [noun] *[noun] or [noun]*
[educational institution] o uke.ru *to take entrance exams for [educational institution]*
ukesase.ru *to get/allow to take* ● S1
juku *after-school (private) cramming institution*
[place] ni kayo.u *to visit regularly, commute to [place]*
mochiron *of course, naturally*
datte *you see*
imadoki *at this time, nowadays*
hoka no [noun] *other [noun]*
ko *child*
[noun] ni okure.ru *to fall behind/be late for [noun]*
[verb (present plain form)] yō ni suru *to make a point of doing [verb]* ● S2

katei *household, home*
kyōshi *instructor, teacher*
katei-kyōshi *private instructor, tutor*
tsuke.ru (here) *to hire*
chekku (suru) *to check*
shū ikkai = shū ni ikkai *once a week*
hitsuyō (na) *necessary*
o-taku no *your* ● LS2
bot-chan (*your*) *son* ● LS1
izure (wa) *anyhow, some day, in due course*
nakutte = arimasen ● LS 2
o-jō-san (*your*) *daughter* ● LS1
tsuite iku *to go along with*
perapera (*speak*) *effortlessly, fluently*
zeitaku (na) *extravagant, luxurious*
hosoboso (to) (*live*) *in poverty, barely make ends meet*
yar.u (here) *to live*
keikogoto *feminine accomplishments* (such as flower arranging)
hon no *just* (*a little etc.*)
o-hana *flower arranging*
[noun] ni [noun] [*noun*] *and* [*noun*] ● S3
o-cha (here) *the tea ceremony*
[noun] gurai *just* [*noun*], *no more* ● Unit 22 S3
taishita mono (desu etc.) *that's something/fantastic!*
kaigai *abroad*
tsukamar.u (intransitive) (here) *to fall into someone's clutches*
sore yori *rather than that*
kanemochi no [person] *rich* [*person*]

True or false?

1 Hayashi-san no musuko wa juku ni kayotte iru.
2 Anzai-san wa musuko o Tōdai ni hairaseru tsumori da.

Structures

1 *The causative (or permissive):* [noun] wa [noun] ni [causative verb] [noun] wa [noun] o [causative verb]

These patterns are used when making, or allowing, someone to do something.

(*a*) ***Formation of causative/permissive verbs***

(i) **-iru/-eru** verbs: replace the final **-ru** with **-sase.ru**

ki¦ru	→	kisaseru
oki¦ru	→	okisaseru
ne¦ru	→	nesaseru
tabe¦ru	→	tabesaseru

(ii) **-u** verbs: replace the final **-u** with **-ase.ru** (note the irregular forms with verbs such as **matsu** and **kau**, and recall the formation of the negative).

kak¦u	→	kakaseru
oyog¦u	→	oyogaseru
hanas¦u	→	hanasaseru
mats¦u	→	mataseru
shin¦u	→	shinaseru
yom¦u	→	yomaseru
kaer¦u	→	kaeraseru
ka¦u	→	kawaseru

(iii) Irregular verbs:

kuru	→	kosaseru
suru	→	saseru

All plain causative forms thus end in **-(s)ase.ru**; this ending changes like any other regular **-iru/-eru** verb.

Causative structures have two protagonists, a 'causer' (or 'permitter') marked by **wa** or **ga**, and a 'causee' (or 'permittee'), marked by **o** or **ni**. In Japanese, these are both almost always animate, mostly human. English expressions like *the wind made the windows clatter* are therefore not generally found. As indicated above, there are two basic causative structures; in their full, unabbreviated form they are distinguished according to the use of either **ni** or **o** to mark the person who is caused or permitted to do something. Let us call them **ni-** and

o-causatives, although in actual speech these particles are often not present, being 'understood' from the context.

(*b*) ***Causatives of intransitive verbs***

With the causative of an intransitive verb, it is normally possible to use either **o** or **ni** to indicate the causee; when **o** is used, the implication is that the causee is being ***forced*** to do something; when **ni** is used, the implication is that he is ***allowed*** to do something.

Sensei wa	gakusei o/ni	kaerasemashita.
Okāsan wa	musume o/ni	kaimono ni ikasemashita.

The differences in meaning can be captured in English translations:

The teacher sent the student home/allowed the student to go home.
The mother made/let the daughter (**musume**) *go shopping.*

With certain situations, however, it is unusual to find **ni**:

	Kodomo o	hayaku nesasemashō. *Let's put the children to bed early.*
Watashi wa	hito o	shinasete shimaimashita. *I caused someone's death/ killed someone* (e.g. in a traffic accident).
Okāsan wa	musuko o	juku ni ikasete imasu. *The mother is sending her son to a crammer.*

All of the above situations are under normal circumstances understood to take place against the will of the causees (although there may be children who do want to go to bed early on nights when their parents go out).

(*c*) ***Causatives of transitive verbs***

With transitive verbs, **ni** rather than **o** is used to indicate the causee, regardless of whether it is a question of permitting or forcing. This is because such verbs will already have an object, followed by **o**, as in the following examples:

Watashi wa	musume ni	ryōri o	tsukurasete imasu. *I am getting/allowing my daughter to do the cooking.*
O-isha-san wa	shujin ni	o-sake o	nomasemasen. *The doctor won't allow my husband to drink.*

The first sentence could be interpreted in two ways, *allowing her to cook* or *making her cook*; only the context can reveal which of the two is intended.

Below are some pairs of examples. Note that the follow-up sentence or answer omits the causer, or the causee, or, more usually, both of them, since they are understood:

Watashi wa kodomo ni miruku o takusan nomasete imasu.
Demo, niku o/wa amari tabesasemasen.
I feed the child lots of milk, but not much meat.

Botchan ni mainichi terebi o nanjikan misasete imasu ka?
Terebi wa amari misasemasen ga, hon o yoku yomasemasu.
How many hours a day do you let your boy watch TV?
I don't let him watch much TV, but I give him a lot to read.

Ano ko no ryōshin wa kodomo ni zenzen atarashii omocha o kawasemasen ne.
Ē, demo, amai mono wa yoku kawasete iru yō desu yo.
Those parents never let their children buy any new toys (**omocha**), *do they?*
No, but they frequently seem to let them buy sweets (**ama.i** *sweet*).

Konya kodomo ni nani o tabesasemasu ka?
Piza o tabesaseyō to omotte imasu ga . . .
What are you going to feed the children tonight (**konya**)?
I'm thinking of giving them pizza (**piza**).

Note that the use of the causative/permissive is usually only appropriate where the causer/permitter is in a position of authority over the causee/permittee. When the causee is someone of higher status than the causer, for instance if you have got a teacher to come to your party, or persuaded your dad to buy you a Rolls Royce, **-te**

morau/itadaku should be used:

Sensei ni pātī ni kite itadakimashita.
Chichi ni Rōrusu-roisu o katte moraimashita.

[Causative]-te kudasai is used to offer your services in the sense of *allow me to . . . .* Because you are asking for permission, **ni** is clearly the appropriate particle to indicate the causee (i.e. the speaker), if mentioned, here:

Watashi ni unten sasete kudasai. *Allow me to drive.* (usual driver tired, drunk etc.)
Watashi ni harawasete kudasai. *Please let me pay* (**hara.u**). (restaurant)

The same form is used in asking for permission to have/do something:

Watashi ni mo hitotsu tabesasete kudasai. *May I have one, too?*
Watashi ni mo yomasete kudasai. *Please let me read it, too.*
Sukoshi yasumasete kudasai. *Can I rest a little?*
Kangaesasete kudasai. *Let me think about it.* (Note that this can be a polite way of saying *No*!)

2 Yō ni suru *and* yō ni naru

Like **koto ni suru** (Unit 13 Structures 3), **yō ni suru** is also used after verbs (i.e. actions) in their present plain form; the meaning is *do one's best to do, make a point of doing*:

Konban hayaku neru yō ni shite kudasai. *Be sure to go to bed early tonight.*
Jūji made ni kaeru yō ni shite kudasai. *Be sure to be back by* 10.
Konban amari nomanai yō ni shimasu. *I'll try not to drink too much tonight.*
Hayaku owaru yō ni shimashō ne. *Let's make a point of finishing early.*

Yō ni suru can also be attached to verbs in their causative forms, meaning *be sure to make someone does/does not do something*:

Kodomo ni terebi o misasenai yō ni shite imasu. *I'm trying to prevent the children from watching TV.*
Kodomo ni yoku undō saseru yō ni shite kudasai. *Try and get the children to take regular exercise.*

Kodomo ni mainichi sankai ha o migakaseru yō ni shimashō. *Let's get the children to brush their teeth three times a day.*

Unlike **suru**, which implies a conscious effort, **naru** implies that something comes about naturally (see **koto ni naru** Unit 13 Structures 3). With the present plain form of verbs **yō ni naru** indicates that the activity to which it is attached has come about as a result of a natural development (such as children's growing up):

Kodomo ga gakkō ni iku yō ni narimashita. *The children are going to school now.*
Musume ga tsutomeru yō ni narimashita. *Our daughter works now.*

When attached to a potential form, the implication is that the ability or skill has been acquired over some length of time (through effort, practice etc.):

Akachan ga arukeru yō ni narimashita. *Baby* (**akachan**) *can walk now.*
Oyogeru yō ni narimashita. *I can swim now.*
Nihongo no shinbun ga yomeru yō ni naritai. *I want to get to the stage where I can read a Japanese newspaper.*

3 *Signalling an addition with* ni/sore ni

When items are enumerated, they can be joined by **to** (which indicates that each and every one is being mentioned) or **ya (nado)**, which signals that only a representative selection is given. **Ni** implies that you are making a mental list of items, which will not necessarily be exhaustive (when listing items in this way, Japanese will often count using the fingers of one hand, bending them from the thumb down for 1 to 5, and unbending them again for 6 to 10):

A Dezāto wa nan' datta n' desu ka? *What was for dessert?*
B Kōhī ni chīzu ni kēki ni chokorēto . . . tabesugite shimaimashita yo. *Coffee, cheese, cake, chocolates – I ate far too much.*
A Kinō no pātī ni wa dare ga kita n' desu ka? *Who came to yesterday's party?*
B Jiru-sensei ni Tomu-san ni Anzai-san-tachi . . . takusan kimashita yo. *Jiru-sensei, Tom-san, the Anzais – lots of people.*

As with **shi** (Unit 12 Structures 3), by using **sore ni** to start a new sentence, it is possible to extend an enumeration over two sentences (to make it more dramatic, or as an afterthought):

Yūbe nomisugite, atama ga itai desu. *I've a headache, having had too much to drink last night.*
Nani o nonda n' desu ka? *What did you have?*
Bīru ni wain ni uisukī . . . Sore ni shanpen (**champagne**) deshita yo. *Beer, wine, whisky . . . and champagne, too!*

Renshū

1 You are a Japanese boy who is as lazy as they come, although not everyone is aware of this trait of yours as you are very skillful in delegating others to do your chores. In reply to your mother's questions, make sentences with causative forms or **-te morau** as appropriate to the status of your 'victim':
Rei: Heya o sōji shimashita ka? (Onēsan) – Onēsan ni shite moratta.

(*a*) Gyūnyū o chanto kai ni ikimashita ka? (Imōto)
(*b*) Shukudai o shimashita ka? (Katei-kyōshi)
(*c*) Watashi no tabako o katte kimashita ka? (Otōto)
(*d*) Gakkō ni tegami o kakimashita ka? (Otōsan)
(*e*) O-sara o araimashita? (Tomodachi *junior/same age*)

2 A recent medical check-up requires your husband to take better care of his health; as he is rather weak of will, your Japanese doctor is putting you in charge, telling you the things you should encourage him to do/prevent him from doing. Change the statements as shown in the model to causative requests, using either **-te/-naide kudasai** or **yō ni suru**:
Rei: O-sake o nomanai. – O-sake o nomasenaide kudasai.
or O-sake o nomasenai yō ni shite kudasai.

(*a*) Mainichi sanpo suru (*to stroll*).
(*b*) Tabako o suwanai.
(*c*) Amai mono o tabenai.
(*d*) Yasai ya sakana o yoku taberu.
(*e*) Asa made terebi o minai.

3 Put the following into Japanese, using **yō ni naru/suru**, as appropriate:

(*a*) Be sure to get up early tomorrow morning.
(*b*) Grandpa eats a lot now. (after illness)
(*c*) I can speak a little Japanese now.
(*d*) Be sure not to be late tonight.
(*e*) I want to get to the stage where I can buy a Rolls Royce.

Language and Society

1 *The use of* botchan *and* ojōsan

These are used to address and refer to outgroup sons and daughters. It is possible to make them even more formal by using **botchama** and **ojōsama**, or less formal with **musuko-san** and **musume-san**. For reference only, you can use **musuko** and **musume** about your own offspring, although for sons humble expressions such as **segare** are available. Such forms reflect the tendency to act in a self-abasing manner towards outgroupers on formal occasions (compare expressions such as **tsumaranai mono desu ga ...** *this is something insignificant/trifling* when giving a present, or **nani mo arimasen ga ...** *there is nothing at all* when asking a guest to start eating a meal you have spent many hours preparing).

Ojōsan is also used to address young, unmarried women in the sense of *Miss*: like **okusan**, it is always used on its own, never attached to a name.

Note also that both **botchan** and **ojōsan** can be used in comments about sons and daughters to indicate that they were brought up in sheltered circumstances, knowing little about the harsh conditions of the real world.

2 Uchi/o-taku *for in/outgroup*

These expressions literally mean *our house* and *your house*:

Uchi ni kaeritai. *I want to go home.*
Uchi ni kimasen ka? *How about coming to my/our place?*

O-taku wa atarashii desu ne. *Your house is new, isn't it.*
O-taku ni kūrā (*air-conditioner*) ga arimasu ka? *Do you have air-conditioning?*

They can also be used in the sense of *you* and *I/we*:

Uchi wa sonna o-kane wa arimasen. *We don't have that kind of money.*
O-taku wa sono hon o yomimashita ka? *Have you read that book?*

Uchi and **o-taku** can also be linked to other nouns with **no** to indicate the idea of *my/our* and *your*:

Uchi no kuruma wa furui desu. *Our car is old.*
Uchi no musuko wa supōtsu ga tokui desu. *Our son is good at sports.*
O-taku no inu wa yoku taberu ne! *Your dog eats lots!*
O-taku no ojōsan wa kirei desu ne. *Your daughter is pretty, isn't she.*

3 *Female use of* -(t)te(yo) *after statements or questions*

This use of the **-te** (doubled to **-tte** in the case of **-i** adjectives, including **nai**) form where a man would use an ordinary **desu/-masu** or plain-form ending is one of the most noticeable characteristics of stereotype female role-playing expected from (or assumed to be expected from) a well-bred Japanese lady, along with high-pitched intonation and the use of slightly emphatic endings such as **wa** and **no**. **Yo** can be attached for emphasis.

Watashi wa sonna o-kane ga nakutte. *I don't have that sort of money.*
Sonna hima wa nakutte yo. *I don't have that much time!*
Issho ni itte mo yokutte? *Is it all right if I come with you?*
Anata, dansu ga dekite? *Can you dance?*

21 Boku wa saifu o toraremashita
I've had my wallet taken

In this unit, you will learn how to suffer in Japanese and how to be made to suffer, through the use of the passive and causative passive forms of verbs. You will also meet another way of expressing reasons and some information about the police and crime in Japan.

Kaiwa

Hādo-san-tachi wa saikin amari un ga yoku nai. Ken-san wa kono mae gakkō de yakyū-bu no kyaputen ni erabareta no ni, ashi ni kega o shite shibaraku shiai ni derarenai. Soshite senshū Jiru-san wa shigoto no kaeri ni ame ni furarete, hidoi kaze o hiite shimatta. Sore dake de wa nai. Kesa Tomu-san wa Shinjuku-eki de suri ni saifu o torareta. Keisatsu ni todokete kara kaisha ni itta keredomo, dōmo shūchūryoku ga nai. Shigoto o shinaide Yamada-san ni hanashi o shite iru.

Tomu	Saifu ni wa o-kane dake ja nakute, kyasshu kādo ya gaikokujin-tōrokusho mo haitte ita no de iroiro tetsuzuki o saserareta. Konna ni isogashii no ni.
Yamada	Komarimashita wa ne. Ginkō ni kyasshu kādo ga nusumareta koto o shirasemashita ka?
Tomu	Un, kōban kara denwa sasete moratta.
Yamada	Atarashii no ga sugu dekiru deshō. Tokoro de, okusama wa ikaga desu ka?
Tomu	O-kage sama de mō sukkari genki ni natte, kesa boku yori hayaku okite hisashiburi ni gakkō e dekaketa.

Yamada Yokatta desu ne. Demo okusama wa netsu ga atte, nete irashita to osshaimashita ne. Okusan ni byōki ni narareru to, Nihonjin no otoko no hito wa taihen komaru yō desu yo – kaji ga zenzen dame da kara. Shachō wa ikaga deshita ka?

Tomu Jitsu o iu to, honto ni taihen datta. Gohan o tsukurasareta shi, sōji ya sentaku mo saserareta.

Yamada Botchan wa nani mo tetsudatte kurenakatta n' desu ka?

Tomu Sara-arai shika dekinai kara, amari yaku ni tatanakatta.

(*Denwa ga naru.*)

Tomu Denwa ka? Kaigi-chū da to itte kudasai. Ima no chōshi da to, nani mo deki-sō mo nai kara.

(*Yamada-san wa juwaki o toru tame ni tonari no heya ni iku ga, awatete modotte kuru.*)

Yamada Okusama de irasshaimasu. Wasuremono o nasatta no de tochū de o-taku ni o-kaeri ni narimashitara, daidokoro no mado ga aite ite, o-mawari-san ga soto de matte ita rashii desu. Ano . . . shachō, shikkari nasatte kudasai. Kondo wa dorobō ni haira reta sō desu.

Tomu Tsuite 'nai nā!

[person] wa un ga ii (warui) *[person] has good (bad) luck*
un *luck*
yakyū-bu *baseball club*
bu *division, section*
kyaputen *captain*
erabare.ru *to be chosen* ● S1
erab.u *to choose, select*
[person] o [position] ni erabu *to choose [person] to be [position]*
[part of body] ni kega o suru *to injure [part of body]*
kega *injury*
shibaraku *for a while*
shiai ni de.ru *to take part in a match*
shiai *match, game*
kaeri ni *on the way home/back*
ame ni furare.ru *to be rained on/caught in the rain* ●S1(*b*)
hido.i *terrible*
suri ni saifu o torare.ru *to have one's purse/wallet taken by a pickpocket* ● S1(*a*)
suri *pickpocket*
saifu *purse, wallet*

keisatsu *the police*
todoke.ru *to report, notify*
shūchūryoku *power of concentration*
shūchū (suru) *concentration*
-ryoku *power*
[person/place] ni/to hanashi o suru *to talk to/make conversation with [person/place]*
[noun A] dake ja nakute, [noun B] mo . . . *not only [noun A] but also [noun B] . . .* ● S2
kyasshu kādo *cash card*
gaikokujin-tōrokushō *alien registration card*
tōroku (suru) *registration, entry*
[sentence] no de *[sentence] and so* ● S3
tetsuzuki o saserare.ru *to be made to go through formalities* ● S4
tetsuzuki [o suru] *[to go through] formalities, procedure*
nusum.u *to steal*
kōban *police box* ●LS
[causative]-te morau *to be allowed to [verb]* ● S5
hisashiburi ni *for the first time in a while, after an interval*
okusan ni byōki ni narare.ru *to be inconvenienced through the illness of one's wife* ● S1(*b*)
otoko no hito *man/men*
kaji *housework*
jitsu o iu *to tell the truth*
sentaku (suru) *washing (clothes* etc. *not dishes)*
yaku ni tatsu *to be a help/useful*
nar.u (*intransitive*) *to ring (bells, telephones,* etc.)
[noun]-chū *in the middle of/during [noun]* ● S6
juwaki o tor.u *to pick up the receiver*
juwaki *telephone receiver*
modor.u *come/go back* (to where you were before rather than to where you belong, which is **kaeru**)
wasuremono o suru *to forget something*
wasuremono *something forgotten/left behind*
tochū de *halfway, on the way*
o-mawari-san *policeman*
shikkari suru *to take a grip on oneself/be strong*
dorobō ni hairare. ru *to have one's house entered by a burglar/be burgled* ● S1(*b*)
dorobō *burglar*
tsuite iru *to be having a lucky streak* (idiom)

True or false?

1 Tomu-san no saifu ni o-kane ga nakatta.

2 Tomu-san wa keisatsu no hito ni ginkō ni denwa o shite moratta.
3 Ken-san wa sentaku o saserareta.

Structures

1 *The passive:* [noun] wa [noun] ni [passive verb]

In Japanese, the passive works in two distinct ways, only one of which is similar to the passive in English. Its basic function is the same, however, in that it allows an event to be seen from the point of view of the person or thing affected by it (the 'patient') rather than from the point of view of its actual instigator (the 'agent').

The passive is formed by replacing the final **-u** of both **-iru/-eru** and **-u** verbs with **-are.ru**. Note that in the case of **-iru/-eru** verbs, the passive is in fact identical in form to the potential (Unit 14 Structures 4), and that verbs such as **matsu** and **kau** again have irregular forms.

taber¦u	→	taber¦areru
oshier¦u	→	oshier¦areru
mir¦u	→	mir¦areru

kak¦u	→	kak¦areru
hanas¦u	→	hanas¦areru
mats¦u	→	mat¦areru
shin¦u	→	shin¦areru
yom¦u	→	yom¦areru
kaer¦u	→	kaer¦areru
ka¦u	→	kaw¦areru

The passives of the two irregular verbs are formed as follows:

kuru	→	korareru
suru	→	sareru

It may seem strange that verbs such as **shinu**, **kaeru**, and **kuru** should have passive forms since *to die*, *to return* and *to come* certainly do not in English, but this relates to the 'indirect' or 'adversative' passive, which is not found in English. Like causatives, passive endings behave like normal **-eru** verbs.

(*a*) ***'direct' passives***
These function similarly to the passive in English.

(i) The passive is used in order to avoid mention of the agent, either so that the sentence can be framed in an impersonal way, or because the agent is not known:

Kono hon wa hiroku yomarete imasu. *This book is being widely* (**hiroku**) *read.*
Kuruma ga nusumareta! *The car has been stolen!*

(ii) The passive is used because the event is seen not from the point of view of the agent, but from the point of view of the patient. Very often the patient will have been inconvenienced in some way. (When the event involves the receiving of a favour, **-te morau** is likely to be used instead, see Unit 16 Structures 1.) The agent is indicated by **ni** or, if inanimate, by **de**:

Watashi wa ano kodomo ni warawaremashita. *I was laughed at by that child.*
Tarō-kun wa sensei ni homeraremashita. *Tarō was praised* (**home.ru**) *by the teacher.*
Ano tsukue wa enpitsu de rakugaki sarete iru. *That desk has had graffiti* (**rakugaki [suru]**) *written on it with a pencil.*

Note that, as in English *I was sent a present*, it is possible for passive verbs in Japanese to have objects:

Haha wa Nihon kara hon o okuraremashita. *My mother was sent a book from Japan.*
Tomu-san wa saifu o nusumaremashita. *Tom had his purse stolen.*
Anzai-sensei wa dare ka ni michi o kikarete, okurete shimaimashita. *Anzai-sensei was late because he got asked the way by someone.*

Note also that there is a tendency to avoid passive constructions where the patient would be inanimate. Alternative patterns would be:

(i) the use of an intransitive verb (Unit 12 Structures 1)

Kono ie wa itsu dekimashita ka? *When was this house built?*
Terebi ga naotte imasu. *The television has been mended.*

(ii) the use of **-te aru** (Unit 12 Structures 2)

Doa ga shimete arimasu. *The door has been shut.*
Tarō-kun no purezento wa kakushite arimasu. *Tarō's presents have been hidden.*

(iii) the use of an **A wa B ga** type construction, where **wa** replaces **o**, making the sentence into a statement about **A**, the patient of the (active) verb (Unit 10 Structures 3(*d*)).

Kono terebi wa chichi ga naoshimashita. *This television was mended by my father.*
Kono shashin wa watashi ga torimashita. *This photograph was taken by me.*

(*b*) ***The 'indirect' or 'adversative' passive***
This has no straightforward English equivalent. The action of the passive verb is not aimed directly at the patient, which is always animate, but is perceived to affect the patient in some way. The agent of the passive, indicated by **ni**, must be mentioned in the sentence unless clear from the context.

In most cases, these 'indirect' passives involve intransitive verbs. In the **Kaiwa** we have **ame ni furarete** instead of **ame ga futte**, to express the fact that Jill accidentally got caught in the rain, and subsequently became ill; later on, we have **okusan ni byōki ni narareru to** instead of **okusan ga byōki ni naru to** because Yamada-san is focussing on the inconvenience caused to Japanese husbands when their wives become ill, rather than on the suffering of the wives themselves; and finally **dorobō ni hairareta** instead of **dorobō ga haitta**, although it is Tom's house which has been entered by the burglar rather than Tom himself. The following examples involve similar cases of 'indirect' inconvenience and suffering on the part of the subject of the passive verbs:

Michiko-san wa tomodachi ni korarete, Ken-san ni aemasen deshita. *Michiko was unable to meet Ken because some friends had come.*
Kodomo no toki, Suzuki-san wa otōsan ni shinaremashita. *Suzuki-san's father died when Suzuki-san was still a child.*
Yūbe tonari no akachan ni nakarete, zenzen neraremasen deshita. *I was kept awake last night by (unable to sleep because of) the crying of the baby next door.*

This pattern is also possible with transitive verbs:

Imōto ni piano o hikarete, tegami o kaku koto ga dekimasen deshita. *I couldn't write a letter because my younger sister was banging away on the piano.*
Michiko-san wa Ken-san no tame ni tsukutta kēki o Tarō-kun ni taberaremashita. *Tarō ate the cake which poor Michiko had made for Ken.*

(*c*) ***The passive as an honorific***
As was stated in Unit 18 Structures 1(*b*), the passive form of the verb can also function as an honorific. In this use the passive form behaves just like an active form. Since it is less formal than the **o-[-masu** base] **ni naru** form, it is used more frequently by men than by women:

Itsu Nihon ni koraremashita ka? *When did you come to Japan?*
O-sushi o taberaremasu ka? *Do you eat sushi?*
Mainichi shinbun o yomaremasu ka? *Do you read a newspaper every day?*

Orareru, one of the irregular honorifics of **iru**, is in fact the passive of the irregular humble form **oru**:

Kasa o motte oraremasu ka? *Do you have an umbrella?*

2 [noun A] dake de/da wa/ja naku(te), [noun B] (mo) *not only [noun A], but also [noun B]*

This tends to occur more often in Japanese than in English, **nakute** being more colloquial than **naku**. **A** can be an adjective or verb as well as a noun. Nouns follow straight in front of **dake**; adjectives and verbs take the forms which they generally have in front of nouns:

Jiru-san wa Eigo dake de naku, Furansugo mo oshiemasu. *Jill teaches French as well as English.*
Ken-san wa hansamu na dake ja nakute, atama mo ii desu. *Ken is not only handsome but also intelligent.*
Tomu-san wa suri ni saifu o torareta dake de wa naku, dorobō ni mo hairareta no desu. *Not only did Tom have his wallet stolen by a pickpocket; he was also burgled.*

Note that **dake** can be replaced by **bakari**.

3 *Linking sentences with* no de: *because/and so*

This works in a similar way to **kara** (Unit 6 Structures 4), but tends to be more limited in its use, since it should really only be used to refer to objective situations. The reason part, that is the part before **no de**, should be an actual fact, so that you will be unlikely to find **darō/deshō no de**. The final part of the sentence is unlikely to involve requests (e.g. **itte kudasai**), suggestions (e.g. **ikimashō**), or wishes (e.g. **ikitai desu**). Nouns, adjectives and verbs in front of **no de** take the same forms as they would in front of **n' desu/da**; in other words, **da** in front of **no de** becomes **na**. In very formal situations, **-masu** forms will be found.

Michiko-san wa byōki na no de, nanimo tabenai deshō. *Since Michiko is ill, she probably won't eat anything.*
Tenki ga totemo yokatta no de, sanpo ni ikimashita. *I went for a walk because it was such nice weather.*
Ame ga futte iru no de, mada dekakenai hō ga ii desu. *It is raining, so we had better not set out yet.*

Unlike **kara**, it is unusual to find a **no de** clause by itself, in reply to a question for example.

4 *The causative passive:* [noun] wa [noun] ni [causative passive]

This is used when an animate subject is made to do something against his/her will. The causative passive is formed simply by turning the causative form of the verb (Unit 20 Structures 1) into the passive:

(*a*) **-iru/-eru** verbs: the causative ending **-saseru** is converted to **-saserare.ru**, and replaces the final **-ru** as before:

tabe	ru	→	tabe	saserareru
oshie	ru	→	oshie	saserareru
mi	ru	→	mi	saserareru

(*b*) **-u** verbs: the causative ending **-aseru** becomes **-aserare.ru**, and replaces the final **-u** as before:

kak.u	→	kak.aserareru
hanas.u	→	hanas.aserareru
mats.u	→	mat.aserareru
yom.u	→	yom.aserareru
kaer.u	→	kaer.aserareru
ka.u	→	kaw.aserareru

For all **-u** verbs except those like **hanas.u**, there is an alternative, shorter, causative passive ending formed by replacing the final **-u** with **-asare.ru**:

kak.u	→	kak.asareru
mats.u	→	mat.asareru
yom.u	→	yom.asareru
kaer.u	→	kaer.asareru
ka.u	→	kaw.asareru

(*c*) irregular verbs:

kuru	→	kosaser.areru
suru	→	saser.areru

The causative passive functions like any normal 'direct' passive:

Ken-san wa muri ni Eikoku no uta o utawasaremashita. *Ken was forced to sing a British song against his will* (**muri ni**).
Tarō-kun wa okāsan ni gakkō e ikaseraremashita. *Tarō was made to go to school by his mother.*
Michiko-san wa okāsan ni yasai o tabesaseraremashita. *Michiko was made to eat the vegetables by her mother.*

5 *Being given/asking for permission to do something:* [causative]-te morau

In Unit 20 Structures 1, we saw that **[causative]-te kudasai** could be used in offering one's services or in asking for permission to do something:

Pen o tsukawasete kudasai. *Please let me use (your) pen.*

[causative]-te morau (Lit. *to receive being allowed to* [*verb*]) is really an extension of this use of the causative:

Pen o tsukawasete moraimashita. *I was allowed to use* (*someone's*) *pen.*

Toshokan de furui hon o yomasete moraimashita. *I was allowed to read old books at the library* (**toshokan**).

The person from whom you receive permission is indicated by **ni**:

Tomodachi ni atarashii pen o tsukawasete moraimashita. *I was allowed by a friend to use his/her new pen→A friend let me use his/her new pen.*

Hādo-san ni shitsumon o takusan sasete moraimashita. *I was allowed by Hādo-san to ask/Hādo-san let me ask lots of questions* (**shitsumon o suru**).

This pattern is often used to express a sense of gratitude for favours received even if you did not actually ask for permission:

Hādo-san-tachi no uchi de Igirisu-ryōri o tabesasete moraimashita. *I was given the opportunity to taste British cooking at the Herds' house.*

Hādo-san-tachi to issho ni Yōroppa e ikasete moraimashita. *The Herds kindly let me go to Europe with them.*

It is also used in formal situations as a way of informing the listener that you are going to do something, often by way of confirming something that has already been discussed:

De wa, asu made kangaesasete moraimasu. (*With your permission*) *I'll think it over till tomorrow then.*

Mata o-denwa sasete moraimasu. *I shall telephone again.*

It can also be used to indicate that you will accept someone's offer. In such cases, the more humble **itadaku** may well replace **morau**:

Ja, o-saki ni o-furo ni hairasete itadakimasu. *I'll use the bath first then.*

A Kore o dōzo. *Please have some.*

B Ja, sukoshi tabesasete moraimasu. *Thank you, I'll have a little.*

A O-agari kudasai. *Please come in.*

B De wa, agarasete itadakimasu. *Thank you, I will.*

Note also the use of **[causative]-te moraitai/itadakitai desu** (Lit. *I want to receive being allowed to* [*verb*]) and **[causative]-te moratte/itadaite mo ii/yoroshii desu/deshō ka?** (Lit. *May I receive being allowed to* [*verb*]*?*) as indirect ways of asking for permission:

Chotto o-tearai ni ikasete itadakitai desu ga . . . *I wonder if it would be all right if I just went to the toilet?* (usually abbreviated to **Chotto o-tearai ni**)
Shashin o torasete moratte mo ii deshō ka? *Is it all right if I take a photograph* (*of you, or something belonging to you*)*?*
Ashita mata denwa o sasete itadaite mo yoroshii deshō ka? *Would it be all right if I were to telephone you again tomorrow?*

6 [noun]-chū *in the middle of/during [noun]*

When **-chū** is added to nouns which indicate some sort of action, it means that the action is in progress. Here are some common occurrences:

eigyō-chū *open* (Lit. *in the middle of operation*)
junbi-chū *closed* (Lit. *in the middle of preparations*)
(Both of the above are signs used by restaurants etc.)
hanashi-chū *engaged/on the telephone*
shiyō-chū *engaged/in use* (*of a toilet etc.*)
kōji-chū *work in progress* (frequent road-sign etc.)
koshō-chū *out of order* (sign on machines)

Renshū

1 In talking to the husband or wife of Katō-san, a colleague, you use **-te kudasaru** to describe with seeming gratitude the various ways in which he or she has been interfering in your affairs. Later on, in talking to a friend, you complain about the very same activities, using the **[passive]-te komarimashita**.

Rei: senshū uchi ni kita
→Katō-san wa senshū uchi ni kite kudasaimashita.
→Katō-san ni senshū uchi ni korarete komarimashita.

(*a*) kinō tegami o yonda
(*b*) o-miai no shashin o mita
(*c*) yūbe denwa o kaketa
(*d*) pātī no toki itsumo soba ni ita (**soba ni** *by* (*my*) *side*)
(*e*) nomiya de tonari ni suwatta

2 Select the appropriate reason in the first column for each sentence in the second column and join them using **kara** or, when appropriate, **no de**.
Rei: D + U
→Tōkyō wa kuruma ga ōi (desu) kara/ōi no de, takushī yori chikatetsu no hō ga hayai desu.

A	O-kane ga arimasen deshita.	U	Takushī yori chikatetsu no hō ga hayai desu.
B	Kore wa benri desu.	V	Nonde mite kudasai.
C	Ame ga futte imasu.	W	Takusan tsukutte okimashita.
D	Tōkyō wa kuruma ga ōi desu.	X	Nanimo kaimasen deshita.
E	Kore wa oishii desu.		
F	Kodomo wa yoku tabemasu.	Y	Yoku tsukaimasu.
		Z	Takushī de ikimashō.

3 (*a*) Help Tom to complain about the terrible life of the Tokyo businessman, by using the causative passive to talk about what they are forced to do, as in the example:
Rei: asa hayaku kaisha e iku
→Asa hayaku kaisha e ikaseraremasu/ikasaremasu.

1 osoku made hataraku
2 nagai repōto o yomu
3 fukuzatsu na wāpuro o tsukau (**fukuzatsu na** *complicated*; **wāpuro** *word-processor*)
4 atsukute mo sūtsu o kiru (**sūtsu** *suit*)
5 gogo tokidoki gorufu o suru

(*b*) As revision practice, now help him to complain by using one of the *must* constructions to talk about what they have to do:
Rei: asa hayaku kaisha e iku
→Asa hayaku kaisha e ikanakereba narimasen/ikanakute wa ikemasen.

4 You are telling an acquaintance about a trip to Japan where you visited a factory to which he/she had introduced you. To indicate your sense of the favour received, use **[causative]-te morau** in describing what you were allowed to do rather than what you did:

Rei: Kōjō-chō no o-taku de Nihon-ryōri o tabemashita. (**kōjō** *factory*; **[noun]-chō** *head of* [*noun*])
→Kōjō-chō no o-taku de Nihon-ryōri o tabesasete moraimashita.

(*a*) Heya o tsukaimashita.
(*b*) Kōjō o jiyū ni mimashita. (**jiyū ni** *freely*)
(*c*) Kōjō no setsumei o kikimashita. (**setsumei (suru)** *explanation*)
(*d*) Bideo o torimashita. (**bideo** *video*)

5 Put into **-masu** form Japanese:

(*a*) Suzuki-san didn't have an umbrella so he got caught in the rain.
(*b*) Tarō was made to drink some bitter-tasting medicine by the doctor.
(*c*) Jill teaches not only English but also German.

Language and Society

kei

satsu

The Police and Crime in Japan

Japan is famous for the safety of its streets at night, although it is equally famous for its organised crime and gangsters (**yakuza**). The police are fairly visible. Police boxes (**kōban**) will be found at regular intervals on major streets, particularly near cross-roads, and are good places to ask for directions if you are lost. Policemen (**keikan**) and women (**fujin-keikan**) are colloquially referred to as **o-mawari-san** or, by the more ruffianly, as **porikō**. To telephone the police in an emergency, you should dial 110 (**hyakutō-ban o mawas.u**).

Foreigners are expected to carry their passport or alien registration card (in the case of longer residents) with them at all times, and you may be asked to show this to a policeman – if you are walking alone at night, for example. Also remember that in Japan pedestrians as well as cars have to obey traffic lights!

Here are some more useful words and phrases:

keisatsu o yonde kudasai *please call the police*
keisatsu-sho *police station*
patokā *police* (i.e. *patrol*) *car* (colloquial)
keimu-sho *prison*
keimu-sho ni hairu *to go to jail*
hannin *criminal*
tsukamae.ru *to catch*
taiho (suru) *arrest*
sur.u *to pick pockets*
yūzai *guilty*
muzai *not guilty*
muzai desu *to be not guilty*

22 Chotto tetsudatte yo *Give me a hand, won't you?*

This unit reviews and sums up the major characteristics of informal Japanese. There is also some revision and expansion of known structures, and practice in converting formal sentences into informal ones, and vice versa. Some information on dialects (and their use in informal Japanese) and common insults is found in Language and Society.

Kaiwa

Hādo-san ikka wa chikaku kuni ni kaeru koto ni natta no de, Anzai-sensei wa kyō Hādo-san-tachi o ie ni yonde iru. Ato ichi, nijikan de sōbetsukai ga hajimaru koto ni natte iru no de, Michiko-san wa isoide sōji o shite iru. Tokoro ga, jibun no heya de benkyō shite ita Tarō-kun wa shukudai ga umaku itte inai . . .

Tarō	Nēsan, chotto shukudai tetsudatte yo.
Michiko	Dame yo, ima sōji de isogashii n' da kara! Itsu dasareta shukudai na no, sore?
Tarō	Senshū no mokuyōbī na n' da kedo.
Michiko	Dattara, nan de motto hayaku yatt' okanai no?! Saigo no saigo made hōtt' oku n' da kara . . . Mattaku mō!
Tarō	Nēsan no kechi! Chotto gurai nara ii ja nai ka!
Michiko	Dame da-ttara! Kochi ga tetsudatte moraitai kurai.
Tarō	Jā, boku ga sanjuppun sōji o tetsudattara, nēsan ga kawari ni sanjuppun shukudai tetsudatte kureru?
Michiko	Sō ne, sore dattara kangaete mo ii wa ne.

Tarō	Kangaeru dake ja dame da. Chanto yakusoku shite yo.
Michiko	Wakatta, wakatta. Yakusoku sureba ii n' deshō?
Tarō	Kitto da ne?
Michiko	Un, kitto yo.
Tarō	Jā, nani suryā ii no?
Michiko	Sō ne . . . mazu kono sōjiki de ikkai o zenbu sōji shite moraimashō ka.
Tarō	Jōdan ja nai yo, zenbu da nante. Nēsan wa sono aida nani su' n' da yo?
Michiko	Atashi tsukareta. Chotto yasumō. Kantoku shite ageru wa.
Tarō	Ya da yo, sonna no. Boku ga zenbu yaru koto ni naru ja nai ka! (*sōjiki o hōridasu*)
Michiko	Āra, shukudai tetsudatte hoshii n' ja nakatta no! Kore jā chotto nē . . .
Tarō	Wakatta yo. Yaryā ii n' darō?

ikka *household, family*
chikaku (here) *in the near future*
kuni (here) *one's country*
ichi, ni [counter] *one or two [hours etc.]*
sōbetsukai *farewell party*
tokoro ga [sentence] *however [sentence]*
umaku iku *to go well* (**uma.i** *tasty; skilful; good*)
nēsan informal variant of **o-nē-san**
dattara *in that case*
dasare.ru *to be given* (of homework)
nan de *why* = **dōshite**
saigo no saigo *the very last*
  saigo *last*
hōtt' oku = **hōtte oku** *to leave* (**hōr.u** *to throw*) ● S1(*c*)
mattaku mō! *stronger version of* **mattaku** *really!*
kechi (na) *stingy; mean*
  nēsan no kechi *what a mean person you are, sis!* (see **nēsan no baka**) ● LS1
[sentence]-ttara *I tell you [sentence]* ● S1(*i*)
kotchi (here) *I* ● S1(*e*)
kurai (here) *if anything, rather* ● S3
suryā contraction of **sureba** ● S1(*c*)
sōji-ki *vacuum cleaner*
jōdan ja nai (Lit. *it's no joke*) paradoxically, *you must be joking!*
nante ● S4
su' n' da = **suru n' da** ● S1(*c*)
atashi (fem) = **watashi** ● S1(*e*)

kantoku (suru) *to supervise*	**āra** exaggerated version of **ara**
ya (na)=iya (na)	**-te hoshii=-te moraitai**
hōridas.u *throw down*	

True or false?

1 Tarō no shukudai wa kinō deta bakari da.
2 Tarō wa sōjiki o tsukawanaide sōji o suru.

(*Sanjuppun tatte kara*)

Tarō Ā, ā. Taihen datta, nēsan! Kore jā ichijikan tetsudatte morawanai to awanai.
Michiko O-tsukare-sama! Sā, o-cha ireru kara, yasunde ne.
Tarō O-cha nanka ii kara, hayaku tetsudatte yo!
Michiko Jā, tsumetai Karupisu demo dō? Asedaku ja nai no . . .
Tarō Wakatta, ja ippai tsukutte.
Michiko Kōri dono gurai ireru?
Tarō Tekitō de ii kara, hayaku shite yo!
Michiko Hai!
Tarō Ē?! Nan dai, kono koppu wa? Bakemono mitai ni dekai ja nai ka!
Michiko Māmā, nodo ga kawaita n' deshō? Yukkuri nomi nasai!
Tarō (*Gabugabu nomu*)
Michiko Ara, mō nonjatta no? Mō ippai dō?
Tarō Mō ii kara, boku no heya ni kite yo.
Michiko Chotto matte ne, mazu toire ni iku kara . . .
Tarō Oi, hayaku shite yo.
(*pin-pon! – genkan no beru ga naru*)
Michiko Ara, mō irashita no kashira?
Tarō Masaka!
Michiko Yappari sō mitai da wa. Gomen nē, Tarō-chan, tetsudaitakatta no ni nē!
Tarō Dare ga shinjiru ka, sonna no! Nēsan mitai ni zurui yatsu mita koto nai yo. Nēsan no baka!
(*Futari wa naguriai ni nari-sō da ga, chōdo okāsan ga Hādo-san-tachi to issho ni heya ni haitte kuru*)
Minna Ara, dō shita no, kono futari? Māmā,. . .

[time] tats.u *[time] passes*
[sentence]-te morawanai to awanai *things will not match unless [sentence], this will only be squared if [sentence]* ● S5 on double negatives
a.u *to fit, match*
o-tsukare-sama *Thanks (for all your tiring work)* ● LS2
o-cha o ire.ru *to make tea*
nanka ● S4
Karupisu *'Calpis'*, brand name of a syrup of fermented milk, popular in summer for making cold drinks (marketed outside Japan as 'Calpico', not 'Calpis', for obvious reasons)
asedaku *dripping with sweat*
kōri *ice*
tekitō (na) *suitable, as one sees fit*
dai informal for **da** ● S1(*g*)
ē exclamation of surprise (rising intonation)
nan dai, kono koppu wa? = kono koppu wa nan dai? ● S1(*h*)
bakemono *monster*
mitai = yō da/sō da ● S1(*j*)
dekai (Eastern Japan dialect) **= ōkii** ● LS4
māmā *Calm down, there there* ● LS3
gabugabu nomu *to gulp down*
oi *hey!*
kono . . . *you . . .* (insult) ● LS1
pin-pon (sound of door chime)
beru *bell, chime*
masaka! *impossible!, surely not!*
shinji.ru *to believe*
zuru.i *crafty, cunning*
yatsu *fellow, person*
baka *idiot* ● LS1
naguri-ai *fight* (noun form of **naguri-a.u.** ● Unit 8 LS2)
nagur.u *to hit*

True or false?

3 Tarō wa o-cha o nomanakatta.
4 Karupisu no koppu wa chiisai.

Structures

1 *More on informal Japanese*

Informal language is used in a variety of situations between people of various relationships. It is very common between pupils at school, in the family (recall Unit 8) and between males (and, to a lesser degree females) who are engaged in informal types of work or are intimate. Apart from these reciprocal uses, there are also situations where it tends to be applied in one direction only, such as between customer and sales personnel (Unit 9), adult and child, superior and inferior (Unit 11, Tom and his secretary), and, with traditional-minded couples, husband and wife!

Characteristics of informal language include the omission of particles such as **o** and **wa**, and of **da** after **na** adjectives and **no (da)**, the use of contracted forms like **hōtt' oku** instead of **hōtte oku**, of certain sentence-final particles (**zo, ze, kai,** etc.), of informal or rough personal pronouns (**ore,** etc.), informal variants of **hai/iie**, the phrasing of questions without the final **ka?** and in inverted order, and the use of forms like **-ttara** and **mitai (da)**. Below, we will look at these phenomena one by one, while in Language and Society 1 and 4 there will be some information on insults and dialect forms, which are also occasionally found in informal language.

(*a*) *Omission of particles*

Refer back to Unit 8 Language and Society 3.

> Tabako katte kite. *Go and buy some cigarettes.* (Omission of **o**)
> Sore takai ne. *That's expensive, isn't it?* (Omission of **wa**)
> Nēsan sono aida nani suru n' da? *What are you going to do during that time?* (Omission of **wa** and **o**)
> Watashi iku. *I'll go.* (Omission of **wa**)
> Bā ikō ka? *Shall we go to the bar?* (Omission of **ni/e**)

O and **wa** are more likely to be omitted than other particles, especially in shorter sentences. Recall also (Unit 18 Structures 1(*e*)) that when announcing one's name on the telephone in formal situations **watakushi** is used without any particle.

(*b*) *Omission of* **da/desu**

In informal talk, this is often left out after **na** adjectives and **no,** especially by women (recall Unit 8 Language and Society 3):

Asoko wa totemo shizuka yo. *That place is very quiet.*
Anata kirai! *I hate you!*
Minna de iku no yo. *We are all going.*
Kono nekutai takakatta no yo. *This tie was expensive.*

(*c*) ***Contracted forms***

We have already seen examples of contracted forms in Unit 17 Structures 2 (**-te shimau** becoming **-chau/-jau**); a similar contraction is **jā/chā** instead of **de wa/-te wa** (Unit 15 Structures 7 and 8). For example, **[verb]-te oku/iku** is shortened to **[verb]-t' oku/iku**:

Hott' oite! *Leave me alone!*
Pan katt' oita. *I bought some bread.*
Tabet' ettara? *Why not eat before you go?*
Ano hito ga mott' etta. *He took it with him.*

Recall also that **-te iru** is often contracted to **-te 'ru** (Unit 11 Structures 2); similarly, **-te ita** often becomes **-te 'ta**:

Densha ga totemo konde 'ta yo! *The train was really crowded!*
Ama ga futte 'ta. *It was raining.*

Before **no/n'**, the **-ru** ending of verbs often becomes 'assimilated' to **n'**:

Nan ni su' n' no? *What will you have?*
Itsu owa' n' da yo?! *When are you going to finish?!*

Men and boys often contract the **-eba** form in the following way:

Verbs: **-eba** becomes **-yā**:

Ikyā yokatta no ni! *You should have gone!*
Takushī ni noryā hayai yo. *It'll be quick if you take a cab.*
Motto benkyō suryā yokatta. *I should have studied more.*

-i *adjectives*: **-kereba** becomes **-keryā** or **kyā**:

Kane ga nakeryā ikenai. *I can't go without money.*
Ikitakeryā ike! *Go if you want to!*
Sonna ni takakyā kaenai. *I can't buy it if it's that dear.*

Note that instead of **-kereba ikenai** (Unit 15 Structures 8) **-kyā** (or **-kereba**) is often used on its own:

Motto renshū shinakyā. *I/you must practise more.*
Mō kaeranakyā. *I must go.*

(*d*) ***The sentence-final particles* zo/ze/kai?**
These are mostly used by men, and convey the following shades of meaning:

Zo Emphasis (stronger than **yo**), ranging from approval through warning to threat.

Ii zo! *Great/You're doing fine!*
Futte kita zo! *It's started raining!*
Kyō kaeranai zo! *I'm not going home tonight!*
Naguru zo! *I'm going to hit you!*

Ze This is also a stronger version of **yo**, used when giving some sympathetic advice/warning about a proposed course of action, or alerting the listener about some situation, without any threatening overtones.

Mītingu (*meeting*) ni deta hō ga ii ze. *You'd better attend the meeting.*
Ano mise wa takai ze. *Be careful, that place is expensive.*
Samui kara, attakaku shit' oita hō ga ii ze. *It's cold, so you'd better put on something warm!* (**attaka.i = atatakai**)
Taihen datta n' da ze. *Let me tell you, this was no easy job.*

Kai? This is an intimate-sounding variant of **ka?**, used when asking permission or enquiring about others' intentions or feelings. It can have a slightly condescending ring, and is often used by men when talking to women, or adults to children.

Itte mo ii kai? *Is it all right if I come?*
Eiga wa omoshirokatta kai? *Did you enjoy the film?*
Kore katte hoshii kai? *Would you like me to buy it?*

(*e*) ***Informal expressions for 'I' and 'you'***
Boys and men use **boku** (Unit 1) or **ore** (Unit 19) in informal situations; the former is in fact acceptable in a variety of situations, for instance in classroom interaction between male pupil and teacher at school and university, whereas the latter is much more limited, being used by some men within the family, and more generally by

uneducated men (or by educated men in situations where they want to play up their masculinity). The word for *you* corresponding in level to **boku** is **kimi**, and to **ore**, **omae**. The former is often used by boys to address their girlfriends, the latter mainly by boys between themselves.

Boku wa kaeru kedo, kimi wa dō suru? *I'm going back – what about you?*
Omae no nōto kashite kure. *Let me borrow your notebook.*

Girls/women often use **atashi** for *I* in informal or intimate situations; for *you*, they will use mostly **anata**, but with many different kinds of intonation, ranging from cold to coquettish; older women sometimes use **anta**, which can sound rather angry or bossy.

Atashi ni mo tabesasete! *I want some too!*
Anata, kono yōfuku katte. *Darling, will you buy me this dress* (**yōfuku**)*?*
Anta, mata osoi no ne! *You are late again!*

You will also hear girls (and sometimes women) use their given name (sometimes in diminutive form) where English would use *I*:

Michiko mo ikitai! *I want to go, too!*
Junko mo issho ni tsurete 'tte! *Take me along, too!*
Jun-chan mo tabetai! *I want some too!*

A word that can used for *I* by either sex is **kotchi**, which originally (like the much more formal **kochira**) means *here*, and can be paired with **sotchi** for *you*:

Kotchi ni mo Karupisu tsukutte! *Make some Calpis for me, too!*
Sotchi wa sōji shit' oite! *You get the cleaning done!*

(*f*) *Informal variants of* **hai/ē** *and* **iie**

Instead of **hai** and **ē**, **un** and **ā** (male) are widely used, while instead of **iie** (and the less formal **ie**), **ūn** and **iya** (male) are common. **Un** and **ūn** are clearly distinguished by intonation: the former goes down as with **hai/ē**, and the latter down and up again as with **iie**. Note also that men often use **-n** instead of the plain negative ending **-nai**.

Taberu? – Un, tabetai wa!

Kono enpitsu karite mo ii? – Ā, ii yo.

Ashita no pāti iku? – Ūn, ikanai.
(Shashin] Kono hito shitte 'ru? – Iya, shiran.

(*g*) ***Questions without* ka? *and with* ka?/kai?**
Questions without **ka?** may end in plain forms of verbs or adjectives, or they may end in **no** (Unit 5 Language and Society 4). The latter gives the question a more familiar or insistent tone. Note that when questions end in verbs/adjectives, or **no**, rising intonation is normally used; when, however, question words such as **dō?** or **dare?** come at the end of the sentence, the intonation falls briefly and goes up again.

(i) Iku? *Will you go?*
Dare ga iku? *Who is going?*
Oishii? *Is it good?*
Mō kaeru no? *Are you leaving already?*

(ii) Kono shashin dō? *How is this photo?*
Mō ippai dō? *How about another?*
Kore dare na no? *Who is this?*
Kono shukudai dō na no? *How is this homework?*

After question words, **yo** can be used to finish a question; rising intonation makes for an emphatic question, but when falling intonation is used, the tone becomes impatient or aggressive:

(iii) Nēsan wa sono aida ni nani suru n' da yo? *What are **you** going to do during that time?*
Itsu gohan ga dekiru n' da yo! *When is dinner going to be ready?!*
Nani su' n' da yo! *What are you doing?!*

Ka/kai (with question intonation) can be attached to the end of the question in the (i) examples, **kai?** being the more intimate of the two.

In informal male conversation, **da/dai** (falling intonation) is often attached to the question, **dai** being the more intimate-sounding version. **Dai** can also be used in (iii) instead of **da**, with the effect of softening the tone.

(*h*) ***Questions in inverted order***
In Unit 5 Language and Society 2 we saw that statements can be inverted, with the information at the end being added in the form (and

with the intonation) of an afterthought. This is also common with questions. The raised question intonation is on the part where the question (a complete sentence) would normally end; the afterthought then follows in a lower tone:

(Sore wa itsu dasareta shukudai na no?) Itsu dasareta shukudai na no, sore (wa)?
(Kono koppu wa nan' dai?) Nan' dai, kono koppu wa?
(Ima sōji de isogashii n' da kara, dame yo!) Dame yo, ima sōji de isogashii n' da kara!
(Sonna no (wa), dare ga shinjiru ka?) Dare ga shinjiru ka, sonna no (wa)!
(Sonna no (wa), ya da yo.) Ya da yo, sonna no (wa).
(Ashita iku no ka?) Iku no ka, ashita?
(Mō kaeru no?) Kaeru no, mō?

Inversion is not restricted in use to the informal style only, but is not quite as often heard in the politer styles.

(*i*) *The use of* **-ttara**

This is distinct from the conditional **-tara**, and serves to reiterate a request or refusal. Another expression that can be used in this way is **-tte(ba)**; both are informal expressions.

Iranai-ttara! *I tell you, I don't want it!*
Kōri ga nai-ttara! *I tell you, there isn't any ice!*
Watashi wa ikanai-tte! *Don't you understand, I'm not going.*
Kaeru no ga ya da-tteba! *Can't you see, I don't want to go home!*

(*j*) *An informal variant of* **yō da/sō da: mitai (da)**

Mitai is widely used in colloquial Japanese (often without **da** in the present tense). It can replace **yō da** and **sō da** in all the uses that we saw in Unit 15 Structures 1 and 3, but note that it comes directly after **na** adjectives (without **na**), and that with past appearances the past tense generally comes before **mitai (da)**:

Michiko-san wa Ken-san ga suki mitai.
Tomu-san wa senshū byōki datta mitai.
Kinō Jiru-san wa tsukarete ita mitai.
Anzai-sensei wa ima taihen isogashii mitai.
Hādo-san no hisho wa totemo kirei mitai.
Kinō wa sugoi ame datta mitai.

Mitai acts like a **na** adjective in that it takes the form **mitai na** before nouns, and **mitai ni** before verbs and adjectives:

Kyō wa fuyu mitai na tenki da.
Kyōto mitai na furui machi ga suki.
Ken-san mitai na baka wa mita koto ga nai. *I've never seen a fool like* (i.e. *anyone as foolish as*) *Ken.*
Nēsan mitai ni zurui yatsu mita koto nai yo. *I've never seen anyone as crafty as you!/I've never seen such a cheat as you, sis!*
Kono koppu wa bakemono mitai ni dekai. *This glass is monstrously big.*
Kyō wa fuyu mitai ni samui. *It's as cold as winter today.*

2 *Relative clauses and the use of* jibun

In Unit 14 we saw an example of a relative clause involving **watashi**:

Kinō watashi ga katta hon o mimashita ka?

Naturally, it is also possible to have relative clauses involving the second or third persons (**anata**, **kare/kanojo**, etc.):

Anata ga/no kaita hon o yomimashita. *I read the book you wrote.*
Kanojo ga/no tsukutte kureta kēki wa totemo oishikatta. *The cake that she made was excellent.*

Now, in English it is possible to say things like *Tarō, who had been studying in his room . . .*, but in Japanese, **kare no** cannot be used in this case (unless **kare** refers to someone other than Tarō); when the meaning is *his/her* (*own*), **jibun no** must be used instead. Similarly, **jibun** must be used in relative clauses about first or second persons where the meaning is one of *self* (note that **jibun** has an honorific variant, **go-jibun**):

Jibun no heya de benkyō shite ita Tarō-kun wa shukudai ga umaku itte inai. *The homework of Tarō, who had been studying in his room, is not going well.* i.e. *Tarō had been studying in his room, but his homework is not going well.*
Jibun no ie de nete ita Tomu-san wa nyūin shimashita. *Tom, who had been in bed at home, was hospitalised.*

Watashi wa jibun de tsukutta kēki shika tabenai. *I only eat cakes that I have made myself.*
Kore wa (anata ga) go-jibun de kaita tegami desu ka? *Is this a letter that you wrote by yourself?*
Kanojo wa, jibun no o-kane de katta yōfuku ga daisuki desu. *She loves the dress she bought with her own money.*

The use of **jibun** depends on similar factors when used in other types of sentences:

Jibun no shukudai wa jibun de yarinasai! *It's your homework – do it by yourself!*
Jibun no o-kozukai de kaimashita. *I bought it from my pocket money.*
Kono kēki wa jibun de tsukutta n' desu ka? *Did you make this cake yourself?*

3 Kurai/gurai *after expressions not indicating amount* (*and more on* hodo)

Recall the following sentence from Unit 20:

Piano to tenisu gurai desu yo. *Just piano and tennis, no more.*

Here, **kurai/gurai** indicates a small degree; for this reason it is conveniently used in expressions of (real or feigned) modesty:

Gaikokugo ga takusan hanaseru deshō? *No doubt you can speak many foreign languages?*
Iie, Doitsugo to Furansugo to Supeingo gurai desu yo. *Oh no, just German and French and Spanish.*

In the **Kaiwa** example in the present unit, **kurai/gurai** indicates an implicit degree, too. Michiko is ***so*** busy that Tarō should be helping ***her***, rather than the other way around. Similarly, the following examples:

A O-kane o kashite kure.
B Kotchi ga karitai gurai da yo! (*I'm so short that*) *I'd like to borrow some* ***myself****!*
Nakitai gurai datta. (*I was so disappointed* etc.) *that I felt like crying.*

Kurai/gurai is also used in sentences indicating degree overtly:

Kare gurai Nihongo no jōzu na gaijin wa shiranai. *I don't know any foreigner who is as good at Japanese as he.*

In the last two sets of examples, **kurai/gurai** is interchangeable with **hodo**, which we saw in Unit 16 in idiomatic expressions such as **yama hodo** and **abiru hodo**:

Kare hodo Nihongo no jōzu na gaijin wa shiranai.

Hodo has a slightly more formal flavour than **kurai/gurai**. It has a similar effect when used instead of **gurai/kurai** after amounts:

Isshūkan hodo yasumimashita. *I took about a week off.*
Tomodachi o gonin hodo tsurete kimashita. *He brought along about five friends.*

Note that **hodo** cannot be replaced by **gurai** in expressions like **nochi hodo** or **ikahodo** (Unit 18), whereas it is possible to say **ikura gurai**:

Kono wanpisu wa ikura gurai shimasu ka? (*About*) *how much is this dress?*

4 *The use of* nante *and* nanka

Nante can be used to express disbelief, with expressions such as **jōdan jā nai** or **tonde mo nai** (here meaning *that's absurd*) normally implied after **nante**:

Sonna ni tōi tokoro made aruku nante . . . *What?! Walk that far?*
Zenbu taberu nante, jōdan ja nai yo. *What? Eat all of this? You must be joking.*

Both **nante** and **nanka** (and **nado**) are commonly used in expressions of modesty (when referring to oneself) or depreciation:

Watashi nanka, heta desu. *I am hopeless.*
Omae nanka ni wa dekinai yo. *You can't do it.*
O-kane nante, hoshiku arimasen. *I am not interested in money.*
Tōkyō nanka kirai da. *I hate Tokyo.*

5 *More on double negatives*

In Unit 15 Structures 8 you came across combinations like **nakute wa naranai/nakereba ikenai** expressing the idea of *must*. This type of expression in Japanese uses two negative forms, the first being a conditional, with the literal meaning of *it won't do if not/unless*. Double negatives are much more common in Japanese than in English, so it will be useful to look at some further examples:

Ashita ni naranai to wakarimasen. *I won't know until tomorrow.*
Kore wa supūn ga nai to taberarenai. *I can't eat this without a spoon* (**supūn**).
Kimi ga inai to ikite irarenai! *I can't live without you!*

6 *Formal/informal style conversations*

Let us look at some (slightly modified) **Kaiwa** sentences and consider what form they would take in more formal situations.

(Tarō to Michiko): Nēsan, chotto tetsudatte yo.
(Anzai to Tom): Hādo-san, chotto tetsudatte kudasai/itadakemasu ka?

(Tarō to Michiko): Nani suryā ii no kai?
(Anzai to Tom): Nani/donna koto o shitara ii n' deshō ka?

(Michiko to Tarō): O-cha ireru kara, yasunde ne.
(Tom to Anzai): O-cha o iremasu kara, dōzo, yasunde kudasai.

Using the reverse operation, let us look at some formal expressions from Unit 18 Structures and see what their informal equivalents might be. Naturally, there is a certain amount of variation in the informal equivalents depending on the speaker's sex (and other factors): for example, females are more likely to attach **no** to the end of a question or statement (although young men use **no** much more than older men), and to use the politer version where there are alternatives (recall Unit 5 Language and Society 4).

O-yakusoku itashimasu. – Yakusoku suru. (Unit 18 S1(*a*))
Mō o-kaeri ni narimasu ka? – Mō kaeru? (Unit 18 S1(*b*))
Go-chūmon ni narimasu ka? – Chūmon suru?

Suzuki-san o go-zonji desu ka? – Suzuki-san shitte 'ru? (Unit 18 S1(*c*))
Hai, zonjiagete orimasu. – Un, shitte 'ru (yo).
Kaimono ni itte mairimasu. – Kaimono ni itte kuru.
Hayaku kaette irasshai. – Hayaku kaette koi/kite.
Shujin wa mō yasumimashita. – Shujin wa mō neta no.
Chotto o-ukagai shitai desu ga . . . – Chotto kikitai n' da ga . . .
O-mie ni narimashita. – Irashita/kita.

Renshū

1 You (a male) are playing with the eight-year old child of a friend. Using **kai?** questions and the **-te** form as the imperative, change the italicised sections to produce informal/intimate style equivalents to the sentences below:
Rei: Kōen de sukoshi *asobimasu ka?* →asobu kai?

(*a*) Sanpo ni *ikimasu ka*?
(*b*) Aisukurīmu *tabemasu ka*?
(*c*) Hayaku *tabe nasai*!
(*d*) Bōru (ball) o *nagete* (throw) *kudasai yo*!
(*e*) Mō uchi ni *kaerimasu ka*?

2 At a low-life establishment, a male Japanese stranger of your age has started talking to you (male), using informal language. Using the hints, talk back to him in matching style. If possible, do this with a partner.
Rei: Doko kara kita no? (England)→Igirisu kara kita yo.

(*a*) Nihongo ga jōzu da ne! Daibu naratten' no? (about a year)
(*b*) Doko de benkyō shita? (in both England and Japan)
(*c*) Nihon no bīru oishii? (Yes, it's tasty)
(*d*) O-sake wa dame na no? (I don't drink it much – too sweet)
(*e*) Amakunai no mo aru yo. (but not in this place, I suppose)

3 A Japanese girl friend of your age is talking to you (Jane) after you saw a new movie together. Reply to her comments and questions in matching style, using the the English hints. If possible, practise this with a partner.
Rei: Zuibun hito ga haitte 'ta wa ne! (it was full)→Ē, ippai datta wa!

(*a*) Eiga wa dō omotta? (Hmm, not that interesting)
(*b*) Ara, dōshite? (Just lots of action (**akushon**), there seemed not much else)
(*c*) Jēn-san wa donna eiga ga suki na no? (Films with deeper meaning = **fuka.i**)
(*d*) Tatoeba (*for instance*) donna no? (For instance, films like Rashōmon)
(*e*) Furui ne (*how old-fashioned*)! Motto atarashii no de wa nani ga suki? (Among new films, there are hardly any good ones!)

4 Gossip is rife among Michiko's classmates concerning Ken and Michiko. Make sentences out of the hints, using **mitai**.
Rei: (Michiko likes Ken)→Michiko-san wa Ken-san ga suki mitai.

(*a*) (There aren't many boys who are handsome like Ken)
(*b*) (Michiko doesn't study much these days)
(*c*) (I'd like a boyfriend like Ken, too)
(*d*) (They went to see a baseball match together last month)
(*e*) (Michiko will go to England with Ken and his people)

Language and Society

1 *Insults*

Although Japanese has a rich vocabulary of slang, it lacks the abundance of insults that is found in many neighbouring countries. The most potent and widely used insult is **baka** (which can also be used as a **na** adjective *stupid*). Although this appears rather tame to us, it has been pointed out that in a country where academic performance is given enormous importance, it might be more insulting to impugn someone's intelligence than to call them all sorts of spicier names. **Kono yarō!** *You brute!* is also common, and there are various expressions coined by replacing **yarō**, which is not suitable for insulting women, with other nouns. **Kono . . .** can be used on its own, implying any suitable noun, while **yarō** can be attached to **baka** for a more emphatic version, **bakayarō**.

Instead of **kono baka**, the name or kinship term of the person addressed can also be included in the insult; this is done by joining the name or kinship term to **baka** etc. by means of **no**, in a similar way to

hisho no Kimura-san (Unit 11 Structures 4):

Tarō no baka! *Tarō, you fool!*
Nēsan no kechi! *You miser/how mean you are!*

2 O-tsukare-sama *and some other stock greetings*

You have already come across many of the greetings and stock phrases that are so important (and stereotyped) in Japan. Among others, Unit 2 gave everyday greetings, Unit 3 phrases used when entering/leaving people's homes, Unit 10 phrases used at table, Unit 13 congratulations, and Unit 18 phrases useful for the telephone.

Below are some phrases that are widely used at work and in everyday life.

O-tsukare-san/sama (desu) is used as a form of greeting after some work-type activity has been completed – it is ubiquitous among company workers at the end of their working day, performers and technicians etc. after a show or broadcast, or just to acknowledge that someone has done a job.

Go-kurō-san/sama (desu) (*thank you for your trouble*) is also sometimes used to acknowledge a well-done job, but unlike **o-tsukare-san** it can be used to greet someone who has just arrived for a meeting etc. Whereas **o-tsukare-san** is essentially an expression used among colleagues, **go-kurō-san** is typically used towards outsiders.

The above two expressions are often used instead of **konnichi wa, sayōnara** etc., although if you are leaving the workplace earlier than your colleagues, you will also use **o-saki ni (shitsurei shimasu)**. To thank someone for having done things for you, **o-sewa-sama** (*thank you for your help*) is often used (instead of **arigatō** etc.).

By way of reply to such greetings, **o-tsukare-san** is used both ways among colleagues, but **go-kurō-san** and **o-saki ni** are generally answered with **dōmo** (and/or a bow). Like other expressions of thanks, **o-sewa-sama** is often acknowledged with **iie** or **dō itashimashite**. The same goes for **o-machidō-sama deshita** (*sorry I've kept you waiting*).

3 *The use of* māmā

Calling someone names such as **baka** can easily lead to a fight, and in such situations it is common for third persons to intervene and try to stop people from attacking each other by saying, often repeatedly, **māmā!** The same expression is used to calm down someone who is overexcited, or about to burst into tears.

Māmā is also used when trying to prevent someone from doing something prematurely; it is used, for instance, to urge a guest who is trying to leave to stay a little longer, or a friend/guest who tries to imply that he has had enough food or sake:

A Sorosoro shitsurei shimasu. *I/we must be leaving soon.*
B Māmā, mada ii ja arimasen ka? *Come, come, surely it's still all right!*

Māmā, mō ippai gurai ii deshō? *Oh, do have another (bowl of rice/cup of sake etc.)*

4 *Informal speech and Tokyo dialect*

There is an abundance of dialects (**hōgen**) in Japan, ranging from Okinawa in the south to the dialects of North-Eastern Japan (Tōhoku) in the north. The northern island Hokkaidō itself has no specific Japanese dialect, having been colonised only around the end of the last century, mainly by people from the Tokyo and Tōhoku areas, so the dialects of these regions are heard there. (Hokkaidō also has a dwindling population of Ainu, whose language is unrelated to Japanese.) The major groups of dialects are those of Western Japan (Kansai, the old cultural centre including Osaka and Kyoto), of Eastern Japan (Kantō, including Tokyo), of Tōhoku and of the island of Kyūshū in the southwest.

The Tokyo dialect, which is one of the Kantō dialects, has some features distinguishing it from the standard language (**hyōjun-go**), and these are often heard as part of informal speech in Tokyo. Apart from vocabulary such as **dekai**, a major characteristic of Tokyo/Kantō dialects is the pronunciation of **ē** instead of standard **ai/ae**, so forms like **itē (itai)** and **omē** (**omae**) are typically heard as part of informal language, too.

Appendix 1: Numbers and counting

Counter	ichi	ni	san	shi	go	roku	shichi	hachi	kyū/ku	jū
fun (*minutes*)	ippun		sanpun	yonpun		roppun	nanafun	happun hachifun	kyūfun	juppun
hon (*bottles, etc.*)	ippon		sanbon	yonhon		roppon	nanahon	happon	kyūhon	juppon jippon
ko (*small things*)	ikko			yonko		rokko	nanako	hakko	kyūko	jukko jikko
mai (*flat objects*)				yonmai					kyūmai kumai	
nen (*years*)				yonen						
nichi (*days*)	ichinichi tsuitachi*	futsuka	mikka	yokka	itsuka	muika	nanoka nanuka	yōka	kokonoka	tōka
nin (*humans*)	hitori	futari		yonin						
pēji (*pages*)	ippēji			yonpēji		roppēji	nanapēji	happēji hachipēji	kyūpēji	juppēji jippēji
pondo (*lb. or £*)				yonpondo			nanapondo		kyūpondo	juppondo jippondo
satsu (*bound objects*)	issatsu			yonsatsu			nanasatsu	hassatsu	kyūsatsu	jussatsu jissatsu
shū (*weeks*)	isshū			yonshū			nanashū	hasshū	kyushū	jusshū jisshū
tō (*large animals*)	ittō			yontō			nanatō	hattō	kyūtō	juttō jittō
wa (*birds*)			sanba	yonwa						juppa jippa

*Only used in the meaning of *the first of the month*.

The above chart lists some common counters (See Unit 9 about use of counters) and the way they combine with numerals. Only those combinations which involve sound change, irregular formation, or involve only one of two regular ways of formation are listed (the remainder is predictable, consisting of the numeral (**ichi**, **ni** etc.) given at the top plus the form of the counter given in the vertical left column). Note, however, that the pronunciation, especially of the syllabic **n**, varies according to its phonetic environment; for instance, before **b** and **m**, it is prounounced as **m** (see Introduction, p. 8). Combinations with **nan-** *how many* are the same as those with **san** *three*.

With counters expressing time (**fun**, **nen** etc.), the suffix **-kan** can be added (optionally in the case of **byō**, **fun**, **nen**, **nichi** and **shū**) to indicate *duration of time*. For instance, **goji** on its own means *five o'clock*, whereas **gojikan** means *five hours*. Note, however, that whereas the months of the year (January–December) are counted **ichigatsu**, **nigatsu** etc., *one month* is **ikkagetsu**, to which **-kan** can be added. The days of the month from the 11th onwards are as follows, insofar as they are irregular:

14th jūyokka
19th jūkunichi
20th hatsuka
24th nijūyokka

Appendix 2: Basic noun and adjective forms (including **da** and **nai**)

	[noun] da	**na** *adjectives*	**-i** *adjectives*		
				i.i	**na.i (-nai)**[1]
sentence final *polite*					
present positive	kasa desu	genki desu	samu i desu	ii desu	
present negative	kasa de wa/ja arimasen	genki de wa/ja arimasen	samu ku arimasen samu kunai desu	**yo**ku arimasen/**yo**kunai desu	
past positive	kasa deshita	genki deshita	samu katta desu	**yo**katta desu	
past negative	kasa de wa/ja arimasen deshita	genki de wa/ja arimasen deshita	samu ku arimasen deshita/ samu kunakatta desu	**yo**ku arimasen deshita **yo**kunakatta desu	
sentence final *plain*[2]					
present positive[3]	kasa da	genki da	samu i	ii	
present negative	kasa de wa nai/ja nai	genki de wa/ja nai	samu kunai	**yo**kunai	nai
past positive	kasa datta	genki datta	samu katta	**yo**katta	
past negative	kasa de wa/ja nakatta	genki de wa/ja nakatta	samu kunakatta	**yo**kunakatta	nakatta
in front of nouns[4]	kasa no	genki na	samu i	ii	nai
in front of **darō/deshō**[5]	kasa	genki	samu i	ii	nai
in front of **no/n' da**[6]	kasa na	genki na	samu i	ii	nai
in front of **naru/suru**[7]	kasa ni	genki ni	samu ku	**yoku**	(-naku)
in front of **-sō da**		genki	samu -	**yosa-**	nasa-
-te/*conjunctive form*					
positive	kasa de	genki de	samu kute	**yo**kute	
negative	kasa de (wa)/ja nakute	genki de (wa)/ja nakute	samu kunakute	**yo**kunakute	nakute
-tara *form*					
positive	kasa dattara	genki dattara	samu kattara	**yo**kattara	
negative	kasa de nakattara	genki de nakattara	samu kunakattara	**yo**kunakattara	nakattara
-eba *form*					
positive	kasa de areba	genki de areba	samu kereba	**yo**kereba	
negative	kasa de nakereba	genki de nakereba	samu kunakereba	**yo**kunakereba	nakereba

[1] This column will also give you information about the behaviour of the negative plain form of verbs, and the base from which to construct the negative **-tara** and **-eba** forms of verbs.
[2] This is also the form found in front of **sō da**.
[3] This is also the form found in front of **to** meaning *when/if*.
[4] This is also the form found in front of **yō da, hazu da**. For past and negative endings, see the plain sentence final forms.
[5] This is also the form found in front of **ka mo shirenai/kashira**, **nara** and **rashii**. For past and negative endings, see the plain sentence final forms.
[6] This is also the form found in front of **no de** and **no ni**. For past and negative endings, see the plain sentence final forms.
[7] For adjectives, this is also the adverbial form.

Appendix 3: Basic verb forms (includes **aru**, **matsu**, **suru**, **kuru** and **nasaru**)

	polite	*plain* **-iru/-eru**[1]		**-u**[2]			*irregular*		
-masu base[4]		mi.ru mi-	tabe.ru tabe-	kak.u kaki-	aru ari-	matsu machi-	suru shi-	kuru ki-	nasaru[3] nasai-
sentence final									
present positive	-masu	mi ru	tabe ru	kak u	aru	matsu	suru	kuru	nasaru
present negative	-masen	mi nai	tabe nai	kak anai	**nai**	matanai	shinai	konai	nasaranai
past positive	-mashita	mi ta	tabe ta	kai ta	atta	matta	shita	kita	nasatta
past negative	-masen deshita	mi nakatta	tabe nakatta	kak anakatta	**na**katta	matanakatta	shinakatta	konakatta	nasaranakatta
imperative									
positive	-te kudasai	mi ro	tabe ro	kak e		mate	shiro	**koi**	**nasai (mase)**
negative	-naide kudasai	mi ru na	tabe ru na	kak u na		matsu na	suru na	kuru na	
-te *form*									
positive		mi te	tabe te	kai te	atte	matte	shite	kite	nasatte
negative		mi nakute/ naide	tabe nakute/ naide	kak anakute/ anaide	**na**kute	matanakute/ matanaide	shinakute shinaide	konakute konaide	nasaranakute nasaranaide
-tari *form*[5]		mi tari	tabe tari	kai tari	attari	mattari	shitari	kitari	nasattari
-tara *form*[5]	-mashitara	mi tara	tabe tara	kai tara	attara	mattara	shitara	kitara	nasattara
-eba *form*[5]		mi reba	tabe reba	kak eba	areba	mateba	sureba	kureba	nasareba
-(y)ō *form*	-mashō	mi yō	tabe yō	kak ō		matō	shiyō	koyō	
potential		mi rareru/ reru	tabe rareru/ reru	kak eru		materu	**dekiru**	korareru	
causative		mi saseru	tabe saseru	kak aseru		mataseru	saseru	kosaseru	
passive		mi rareru	tabe rareru	kak areru		matareru	sareru	korareru	
passive causative		mi saserareru	tabe saserareru	kak aserareru/ asareru		mataserareru/ matasareru	saserareru	kosaserareru	

[1]Includes all passive, potential, causative and passive causative forms.
[2]For the basic **-u** verb patterns (including **dasu** etc.), see Appendix 4.
[3]Also applies to **kudasaru**, **irassharu** (note alternative **irashita** etc.).
[4]This is also used with **-tai**, **-garu**, **-nagara**, **ni iku/kuru** and in making the regular honorific and humble forms.
[5]For negative forms, see **nai** column in Appendix 2.

Appendix 4: Basic **-u** verb patterns[1]

	-masu *base*	*plain present negative*	*past positive*[2]	(*passive causative*)
ka**k**.u	ka**ki**-	ka**k**anai	ka**it**a	
(ik.u)			**itta**	
oyo**g**.u	oyo**gi**-	oyo**g**anai	oyo**id**a	
yo**m**.u	yo**mi**-	yo**m**anai	yo**nd**a	
aso**b**.u	aso**bi**-	aso**b**anai	aso**nd**a	
to**r**.u	to**ri**-	to**r**anai	to**tt**a	
a.u[3]	**ai**-	a**w**anai	a**tt**a	
da**s**.u	da**shi**-	da**s**anai	da**sh**ita	**dasaserareru** only

[1]For verbs similar to **mats.u**, and for **ar**.u, see Appendix 3.
[2]Positive **-te**, **-tari**, and **-tara** can be worked out from this.
[3]Includes all **-u** verbs which have a vowel preceding **-u** (e.g. **i.u**, **ka.u**).

Key to the exercises

Unit 1

True or false? 1 T 2 F 3 F 4 F 5 F 6 T

1 (*a*) Furansujin (*b*) Doitsujin (*c*) Supeinjin (*d*) Itariajin (*e*) Chūgokujin.

2 (*a*) Furansugo no sensei (*b*) Doitsugo no sensei (*c*) Supeingo no sensei (*d*) Itariago no sensei (*e*) Chūgokugo no sensei.

3 (*a*) Hādo-san wa Eigo no sensei desu. Buraun-san mo Eigo no sensei desu. (*b*) Gurēza-san wa Doitsugo no sensei desu. Shumitto-san mo Doitsugo no sensei desu. (*c*) Santosu-san wa Supeingo no sensei desu. Toruresu-san mo Supeingo no sensei desu.

4 (*a*) doko (*b*) kore (*c*) Doitsu (*d*) no (*e*) are (*f*) no (*g*) de wa/ja arimasen (*h*) desu (*i*) mo (*j*) no (*k*) nan (*l*) ichigo no.

5 **Tomu:** Kore/Kochira* wa boku no Furansugo no sensei desu. **Misheru:** Bāru desu/to mōshimasu. Hajimemashite/Hajimete o-me ni kakarimasu. **Tanaka:** Tanaka desu/to mōshimasu. Hajimemashite/Hajimete o-me ni kakarimasu. **Tomu:** Tanaka-san wa Doitsugo no sensei desu. **Misheru:** Dōzo yoroshiku. *See Unit 2 Structures 4

Unit 2

True or false? 1 T 2 T 3 T 4 F

1 (*a*) C, D (*b*) J (*c*) F, A (*d*) H, B (*e*) E, G

2 (*a*) Sore wa shizuka na hoteru desu ka? Hai, taihen shizuka desu. Iie, amari shizuka de wa/ja arimasen. (*b*) Are wa furui Rōrusu-roisu desu ka? Hai, taihen furui desu. Iie, amari furuku arimasen/furukunai desu. (*c*) Koko wa yūmei na kissaten desu ka? Hai, taihen yūmei desu. Iie, amari yūmei de wa/ja arimasen. (*d*) Kore wa atatakai sūpu desu ka? Hai, taihen atatakai desu. Iie, amari atatakaku arimasen/atatakakunai desu. (*e*) Sore wa hayai kuruma desu ka? Hai, taihen hayai desu. Iie, amari hayaku arimasen/hayakunai desu.

3 (*a*) Kono bīru wa tsumetaku arimasen/tsumetakunai desu. (*b*) Kono Furansujin wa hansamu de wa/ja arimasen. (*c*) Kono kasa wa benri de wa/ja

arimasen. (*d*) Kono resutoran wa shizuka de wa/ja arimasen. (*e*) Kono kissaten wa kirei de wa/ja arimasen.
5 Tomu: Hoteru wa doko desu ka? **Suzuki:** Achira/Sochira desu. **Tomu:** Tōi desu ka? **Suzuki:** Iie, amari tōku arimasen/tōkunai desu. Eki no chikaku desu. **Tomu:** Yūmei na hoteru desu ka? **Suzuki:** Hai, taihen/totemo yūmei desu.

Unit 3

True or false? 1 F **2** F **3** T **4** F
1 (*a*) Hon wa koko ni arimasu. (*b*) Inu wa niwa ni imasu. (*c*) Watashi no shī dī wa soko ni arimasu. (*d*) Michiko-san wa doko ni imasu ka?
2 (*a*) Imasen; amari imasen; tomodachi ga amari imasen; otōto wa tomodachi ga amari imasen. (*b*) Arimasu; takusan arimasu; shī dī ga takusan arimasu; heya ni shī dī ga takusan arimasu. (*c*) Arimasu; nikai ni arimasu; heya wa nikai ni arimasu; watashi no heya wa nikai ni arimasu. (*d*) Imasu; niwa ni imasu; inu wa niwa ni imasu; ōki na inu wa niwa ni imasu.
3 (*a*) Koko ni o-kane ga arimasu. (*b*) Tabakoya wa koko ni arimasu. (*c*) Hon wa asoko ni arimasu. (*d*) Asoko ni inu ga imasu. (*e*) Michiko-san wa asoko ni imasu.
4 (*a*) **A:** Gomen kudasai! **B:** Hai! – A, Sumisu-san (*Smith-san*), konnichi wa. Dōzo, o-agari kudasai. **A:** O-jama shimasu. (*b*) **A:** O-jama shimashita. **B:** Mata dōzo. **A:** Arigatō gozaimasu. Ja, shitsurei shimasu. **B:** Sayōnara.

Unit 4

True or false? 1 T **2** F **3** F **4** T
1 (2) Terebi o mimashō. (3) Hanbāgā o tabemashō. (4) Tōkyō de kaimono shimashō. (5) Shinbun o yomimashō. (6) Umi de oyogimashō.
2 (*a*) de (*b*) o (*c*) de (*d*) o (*e*) de (*f*) ni (*g*) o (*h*) de/o.
3 (*a*) **A:** Kono bīru wa totemo tsumetai desu ne. **B:** Iie, sonna ni tsumetaku arimasen/tsumetakunai desu. (*b*) **A:** Michiko-san wa taihen kirei desu ne. **B:** Iie, sonna ni kirei de wa/ja arimasen. (*c*) **A:** Ken-san wa yoku benkyō shimasu ne. **B:** Iie, sonna ni benkyō shimasen. (*d*) **A:** Suzuki-san wa o-sake o takusan nomimasu ne. **B:** Iie, sonna ni nomimasen.
4 Tom: Sā . . . , kōhī demo nomimashō ka? **Suzuki:** Un, nomimashō. Doko ka ii tokoro ga arimasu ka? **Tom:** Ē, chikaku ni totemo ii kissaten ga arimasu. **Suzuki:** Ja, soko ni shimashō. **Proprietress:** Irasshaimase. **Tom:** Nan ni shimasu ka? **Suzuki:** Sō desu ne. Burendo o kudasai. **Tom:** Boku mo burendo da. **Proprietress:** Wakarimashita. Hai, dōzo.

5 **Tanaka:** Maiban Eigo o benkyō shimasu ka? **Yamamoto:** Iie, sonna jikan wa arimasen yo! **Jiru:** Doko ka ii nikuya ga arimasu ka? **Michiko:** Sakaya no tonari ni ii nikuya ga arimasu. **Ken:** Itsu ka aimashō. **Michiko:** Denwa bangō o oshiemashō ka?

Unit 5

True or false? 1 F 2 F 3 T 4 F

1 (*a*) de (*b*) e/ni; ikimashita (*c*) ni (*d*) o, misemashita (*e*) o; yomimashita; yomimasen deshita (*f*) no (*g*) ni; imashita (*h*) de (*i*) o; benkyō shimashita; benkyō shimasen deshita; asobimashita.

2 (*a*) Sashimi/sushi o tabeta koto ga arimasu ka? (*b*) O-cha o nonda koto ga arimasu ka? (*c*) Kyōto/Nara e/ni itta koto ga arimasu ka? (*d*) Nō/Kabuki o mita koto ga arimasu ka? (*e*) Ryokan ni tomatta koto ga arimasu ka?

3 (*a*) atte (*b*) ga (*c*) ga (*d*) mite (*e*) kaite.

4 (*a*) atsukunakatta desu (*b*) shizuka deshita (*c*) oishikatta desu (*d*) kirei de wa arimasen deshita (*e*) yoku arimasen deshita.

Unit 6

True or false? 1 F 2 F 3 T 4 F

1 (*a*) Rokuji juppun (*b*) hachiji nijūgofun (*c*) yoji gojūgofun/goji gofun mae (*d*) yoji yonjūgofun/goji jūgofun mae (*e*) shichiji gojuppun/hachiji juppun mae (*f*) jūniji sanjuppun/jūniji han.

2 (*a*) Iie, doko ni mo ikimasen deshita. (*b*) Iie, nani mo tabemasen deshita. (*c*) Iie, dare ni mo aimasen deshita. (*d*) Iie, nani mo kaimasen.

3 (*a*) Watashi no kuruma wa hayai deshō? (*b*) Watashi no heya wa ōkii deshō? (*c*) Watashi no burausu wa kirei deshō? (*d*) Watashi no jamu wa oishii deshō? (*e*) Watashi no inu wa kawaii deshō?

4 (*a*) O-kane ga atta kara kaimashita. (*b*) Ken-san ga itta kara, watashi mo ikimashita. (*c*) Yūbe hayaku neta kara, kesa hayaku okimashita.

Unit 7

True or false? 1 F 2 F 3 T 4 T

1 (*a*) Benkyō ga aru n' desu. (*b*) Jikan ga nai n' desu. (*c*) Mongen ga kuji-han na n' desu. (*d*) Pen ga nakatta n' desu! (*e*) Kirei datta n' desu. (*f*) Samukatta n' desu.

2 (*a*) Nomiya ni iku! (*b*) Eiga (o mi) ni iku! (*c*) Resutoran ni tabe ni iku! (*d*) Tomodachi no ie ni tomari ni iku!
3 (*a*) Shinjuku-eki kara depāto made takushī de ikimashita. (*b*) Niji kara depāto no resutoran de gohan o tabemashita. (*c*) Tomodachi no ie made aruite ikimashita. (*d*) Yoji kara tomodachi no ie de asobimashita. (*e*) Yoru no jūji kara jūniji made disuko de odorimashita.

Unit 8

True or false? 1 F **2** T **3** T **4** F
1 (*a*) Tēburu o dashimashō ka? Hai, dashite kudasai. Iie, dasanaide kudasai. (*b*) Kyabetsu o kirimashō ka? Hai, kitte kudasai. Iie, kiranaide kudasai. (*c*) Chīzu o kai ni ikimashō ka? Hai, itte kudasai. Iie, ikanaide kudasai. (*d*) Koppu o araimashō ka? Hai, aratte kudasai. Iie, arawanaide kudasai.
2 Tomu-san wa bīru ga suki desu; jūsu ga kirai desu; gitā ga tokui desu; ryōri ga nigate desu; sore kara se ga takai desu. Ken-san wa Michiko-san ga suki desu; benkyō ga kirai desu; yakyū ga tokui desu; ragubī ga nigate desu; sore kara karada ga ōkii desu. Michiko-san wa Ken-san ga suki desu; niku ga kirai desu; Eigo ga tokui desu; piano ga nigate desu; sore kara me ga kirei desu.
3 (Tom) Boku wa bīru ga/o nomitai desu; gītā ga/o hikitai desu. (Ken) Boku wa Michiko-san ni aitai desu/Michiko-san ni/to hanashitai desu; yakyū ga/o shitai desu. (Michiko) Watashi wa Ken-san ni aitai desu/Ken-san ni/to hanashitai desu; Eigo o/de hanashitai desu/Eigo no hon ga/o yomitai desu.
4 (*a*) Iie, kōhī yori bīru no hō ga suki desu. (*b*) Iie, ragubī yori yakyū no hō ga tokui desu. (*c*) Iie, Furansu yori Eikoku/Igirisu e ikitai desu. (*d*) Iie, yakyū yori tenisu ga/o mitai desu.
5 (*a*) **A:** Mainichi dono gurai benkyō shimasu ka? **B:** Sanjikan desu/benkyō shimasu. (*b*) **A:** Nanji ni Michiko-san ni aimasu ka? **B:** Goji ni aimasu/Goji desu. (*c*) **A:** Kudamono no naka de ringo ga ichiban suki desu. **B:** Boku/Watashi wa ringo yori orenji no hō ga suki desu. (*d*) **A:** Atatakaku narimashita ne! **B:** Shimoda ni kite yokatta deshō.

Unit 9

True or false? 1 T **2** F **3** F **4** T
1 (*a*) Kodomo ga sannin imasu. (*b*) Neko ga nihiki imasu. (*c*) Hon ga rokusatsu arimasu. (*d*) Tori ga ichiwa imasu. (*e*) Pen ga yonhon arimasu.

(*a*) Kodomo ga nannin imasu ka? (*b*) Neko ga nanbiki imasu ka? (*c*) Hon ga nansatsu arimasu ka? (*d*) Tori ga nanwa imasu ka? (*e*) Pen ga nanbon arimasu ka?

2 (*a*) Shinbun wa hitotsu ikura desu ka? (*b*) Kan-bīru; ippon. (*c*) Kōhī; ippai. (*d*) Kodomo no shatsu; ichimai. (*e*) Fuji-san no e-hagaki; ichimai. (*f*) Aka no enpitsu; ippon. (*g*) Neko; ippiki. (*h*) Kono manshon; hitotsu. (*i*) Furansugo no wa hitotsu sen-en desu. (*j*) Tsumetai no wa ippon roppyaku-en desu. (*k*) Itaria-sei no wa ichimai niman-en desu. (*l*) Chiisai no wa ichimai hyakunijū-en desu. (*m*) Sono genki na no wa ippiki ichiman-en desu.

3 (*a*) godai (*b*) jūmai (*c*) sansatsu (*d*) nimai; futatsu (*e*) ippai.

4 (*a*) Sumimasen ga, kamera uriba wa doko desu ka? (*b*) Renzu dake arimasu ka? (*c*) Kono chiisai no wa ikura desu ka? – Kore desu ka? Sanman gosen-en desu. (*d*) Ringo wa ikura desu ka? – Hitotsu gojū-en desu. (*e*) Sore ja, itsutsu kudasai. – Nihyaku gojū-en desu. (*f*) Kinō, Tarō-kun wa hanbāga o yottsu to aisukurīmu o muttsu tabemashita. Yūbe byōki ni narimashita.

Unit 10

True or false? 1 F 2 T 3 F 4 T

1 (*a*) Terebi demo mimashō ka? (*b*) Ginza e demo ikimashō ka? (*c*) O-sake demo nomimashō ka? (*d*) Yakyū demo mi ni ikimashō ka?

2 (*a*) Remon to orenji to painappuru to ichigo o kaimashita. (*b*) Zasshi ya shinbun o kaimashita. (*c*) Bīru mo wain mo uisukī mo igusuri mo kaimashita. (*d*) Tako ya sakana nado o kaimashita.

3 (*a*) wa (*b*) ga (*c*) wa; ga (*d*) wa; wa (*e*) wa; ga (*f*) wa; ga.

Unit 11

True or false? 1 F 2 T 3 F 4 F

1 (*a*) Tomu-san wa gitā o hiite imasu; Michiko-san wa tomodachi to asonde imasu; Tarō-kun wa terebi o mite imasu; Anzai-sensei wa uisukī o nonde imasu. (*b*) Tomu-san wa gitā o hiitari, uta o utattari shimashita; Michiko-san wa tomodachi to asondari, Tarō-kun to kenka shitari shimashita; Tarō-kun wa terebi o mitari, chokorēto o tabetari shimashita; Anzai-sensei wa uisukī o nondari, tabako o suttari shimashita.

2 (*a*) tsumetakute (*b*) yūmei de (*c*) ōkute (*d*) yokute (*e*) atsukunakute.

3 (*a*) Hai, mō shimatte imasu. (*b*) Iie, mada desu/akimasen. (*c*) Hai, mō kite imasu. (*d*) Iie, mada desu/demasen.

4 (*a*) yonde kara/yomi-nagara (*b*) hanashite kara/hanashi-nagara (*c*) musunde kara/musubi-nagara (*d*) mite kara/mi-nagara.

5 (*a*) **A:** Miura-san o shitte imasu ka? **B:** Hai, shitte imasu. Ginkō no tonari no manshon ni sunde imasu. (*b*) **C:** Kao-iro ga warui desu ne. **D:** Yūbe osoku made repōto o kaite imashita. Mada tsukarete imasu. (*c*) **E:** Kimura-san wa atama ga yokute kirei desu ga, kekkon shite imasen. **F:** Kekkon shitaku nai (no*) ka mo shiremasen. *explanatory **no da/desu** in front of **ka mo shiremasen**.

Unit 12

True or false? 1 F **2** T **3** T **4** F

1 (*a*) Watashi ga okoshita n' desu. (*b*) Michiko ga aketa n' desu. (*c*) Watashi ga hiyashita n' desu. (*d*) Michiko ga kowashita n' desu. (*e*) Michiko ga tometa n' desu.

2 (*a*) Kesa no shinbun ni kaite atta. (*b*) Nimotsu ga dashite aru. (*c*) Bīru ga reizōko ni irete aru. (*d*) Montō ga keshite aru. (*e*) Zenbu tabete aru.

3 (*a*) Bīru mo aru shi, wain mo arimasu. (*b*) O-sushi mo tabetai shi, sutēki mo tabetai desu. (*c*) Kono kodomo wa genki da shi, atama mo ii desu. (*d*) Michiko-san mo ikanai shi, Ken-san mo ikimasen. (*e*) Kono bīru wa yoku hiete iru shi, oishii desu.

4 (*a*) Sonna ni iyagaranaide kudasai. (*b*) hoshigaranaide (*c*) atsugaranaide (*d*) nomitagaranaide (*e*) kaeritagaranaide.

Unit 13

True or false? 1 F **2** F **3** F **4** T

1 (*a*) Shushō ga shinda to nyūsu de iimashita. (*b*) Koko no tako wa totemo oishii to Itariajin ga yorokobimashita. (*c*) Ken-san wa kyō konai to Michiko-san ga denwa de iimashita. (*d*) Anzai-sensei wa shinsetsu na ha-isha-san da to Tomu-san ga kotaemashita.

2 Maria to iu Itariajin ni atta koto ga arimasu ka? Okkusufōdo to iu machi ni tomatta koto ga arimasu ka? Mango to iu kudamono o yunyū shita koto ga arimasu ka? Mitsukoshi to iu resutoran ni/e itta koto ga arimasu ka?

3 Maria to iu Itariajin ni au koto ni shimashita/narimashita. Okkusufōdo to iu machi ni tomaru koto ni shimashita/narimashita. Mango to iu kudamono o yunyū suru koto ni shimashita/narimashita. Mitsukoshi to iu resutoran ni/e iku koto ni shimashita/narimashita.

4 (*a*) Kayōbi ni Ōsaka ni ikō to omoimasu. (*b*) Suiyōbi ni keiyaku o musubō to omoimasu. (*c*) Mokuyōbi ni Ōsaka kara kaerō to omoimasu. (*d*) Kinyōbi ni osoku made neyō to omoimasu.

5 (*a*) **A:** Sarada o wasurete dōmo sumimasen/wasuremashita ga, dōmo sumimasen. **B:** Ii desu. Sarada ga amari suki de wa/ja arimasen. (*b*) **C:** Ken-san wa byōki da to omoimasu. **D:** Dōshite desu ka? **C:** Nanimo tabetakunai to itte iru kara desu. (*c*) **E:** Kono denwa wa dame desu. **F:** O-kane o iremashita ka? **G:** Ireyō to shimashita ga, hairimasen deshita.

Unit 14

True or false? 1 F **2** F **3** F **4** F

1 (*a*) Watashi mo me no chiisai onna ga kirai da. (*b*)... kami no nagai onna ga suki da. (*c*) ... iro no kuroi onna. (*d*) ... ashi no futoi onna ... (*e*) ... zubon o haku onna ...

2 (*a*) Hon o motte kuru no o wasuremashita. (*b*) Michiko-san ga kuruma o unten suru no o mimashita. (*c*) Kyōto no natsu ga atsui koto o/wa shitte imasu. (*d*) Anzai-sensei ga utau no o kikimashita. (*e*) Anzai-sensei ga utau koto o kikimashita. (*f*) Watashi wa (hon o) yomu no ga hayai desu.

3 (*a*) Yasai o tabeta hō ga ii desu yo! (*b*) Arukōru o nomanai hō ga ii desu yo! (*c*) Hayaku neta hō ga ii desu yo! (*d*) Suwanai hō ga ii desu yo!

4 (*a*) Watashi wa kuruma no unten ga dekimasen. (*b*) Watashi wa Nihongo ga kakemasen. (*c*) Watashi wa tako ga taberaremasen. (*d*) Watashi wa oyogemasen. (*e*) Watashi wa tenisu ga dekimasen. (*f*) Watashi wa sake ga nomemasen.

Unit 15

True or false? 1 T **2** F **3** F **4** T

1 (*a*) oishii yō desu (*b*) konakatta yō desu (*c*) benri na yō desu (*d*) shachō no yō desu.

2 (*a*) oishii sō desu (*b*) konakatta sō desu (*c*) benri da sō desu (*d*) shachō da sō desu.

3 (*a*) Hiru-gohan no toki; Nihongo o benkyō suru mae ni (*b*) Genki na toki ni; Terebi o mite iru aida (ni) (*c*) Shigoto no mae ni; hataraite iru aida (ni) (*d*) Tsukarete iru toki; shigoto ga owatte kara.

4 (*a*) Maiban terebi o mite mo ii deshō ka? Iie, mite wa ikemasen/dame desu. (*b*) Atsui o-furo ni haitte mo ii deshō ka? Iie, haitte wa ikemasen/dame desu. (*c*) Hanbāgā o tabete mo ii deshō ka? Iie, tabete wa ikemasen/dame desu. (*d*) Yoru osoku made hon o yonde mo ii deshō ka? Iie, yonde wa ikemasen/dame desu.

5 (*a*) Ginza de Tanaka-san ni awanakute mo ii deshō. Iie, awanakereba/

awanakute wa narimasen/ikemasen/dame desu/awanai to ikemasen/dame desu. (*b*) Kaimono ni ikanakute mo ii deshō. Iie, ikanakereba/ikanakute wa/ikanai to (etc). (*c*) Ban-gohan o tsukuranakute mo ii deshō. Iie, tsukuranakereba/tsukuranakute wa/tsukuranai to (etc). (*d*) Ashita dekakenakute mo ii deshō. Iie, dekakenakereba/dekakenakute wa/dekakenai to etc).
6 **A:** Suzuki-san wa doko deshō ka? **B:** Juppun mae ni denwa o kakemashita/shimashita ga, chōshi ga amari yokunai sō desu. **A:** Sō desu ka? (O-)isha(-san) ni mite moratta hō ga ii ka mo shiremasen. **B:** Tonikaku, ano repōto o owaranakereba/owaranakute wa narimasen/ikemasen/dame desu/owaranai to ikemasen/dame desu.

Unit 16

True or false? 1 F 2 T 3 T 4 F
1 (*a*) kure (*b*) age (*c*) morai (*d*) morat (*e*) age (*f*) kure.
2 (*a*) Haha ga asa-gohan o amari takusan taberu na to/tabenai yō ni iimashita. (*b*) Haha ga daidokoro de tetsudae to/tetsudau yō ni iimashita. (*c*) Sensei ga nōto o wasurenaide kure to/wasurenai yō ni iimashita. (*d*) Tarō ga motto nome to/nomu yō ni iimashita. (*e*) Tarō ga mada kaeranaide kure to/kaeranai yō ni iimashita.
3 (*a*) onīsan; ani (*b*) haha; onēsan (*c*) Otōto-san; otōto (*d*) Obāsan; sobo; sofu.

Unit 17

True or false? 1 F 2 T 3 F 4 T
1 (*a*) Raishū iku tsumori desu. (*b*) Eiga o miru tsumori desu. (*c*) Iie, Michiko-san ni au tsumori desu. (*d*) Iie, hon o yomu tsumori desu.
2 (*a*) **A:** Bīru o zenbu nonde shimaimashita! **B:** Katte kimashō ka? (*b*) Sukiyaki o uchi de tsukutte mitai desu. (*c*) Yamada-san wa mainichi eki made aruite ikimasu. (*d*) Hādo-san wa mō hikōki ni notte shimaimashita. (*e*) Kore kara dandan samuku natte iku deshō.
3 (*a*) nijūkunichi no hazu desu (*b*) oishii hazu desu (*c*) shizuka na hazu desu (*d*) mitsukatta hazu desu (*e*) raishū no hazu desu.
4 (*a*) Kinō nan-bon nonda ka oboete imasen. (*b*) Michiko-san ga mada matte iru ka dō ka shitte imasu ka? (*c*) Sukiyaki ni satō o ireru ka dō ka wasuremashita. (*d*) Hikōki wa nanji ni tsuku ka shirabemashō. (*e*) Hādo-san ga tabako o yameta ka dō ka wakarimasen.

5 (*a*) tsukawanakute (*b*) watasanaide (*c*) hikanakute (*d*) konakute (*e*) kaeranaide.
6 (*a*) Tanaka-san wa amari genki de wa/ja nasa-sō desu/genki-sō de wa/ja arimasen. (*b*) Tanaka-san wa kao-iro ga amari yokunai rashii desu. (*c*) Tanaka-san wa saikin naki-sō ni narimashita. (*d*) Tanaka-san wa yūbe nerarenakatta rashii desu. (*e*) Tanaka-san wa itsumo kanashi-sō desu.

Unit 18

True or false? 1 F 2 F 3 T 4 T
1 (*a*) Moshi-moshi, Tanaka-san no o-taku desu ka? – Hai, Tanaka de gozaimasu. (*b*) Watakushi [*your surname* (without **-san**!)] to mōshimasu ga, Yōji/Yōko-san irasshaimasu ka? – Hai, shōshō o-machi kudasaimase. (*c*) Osoreirimasu. (*d*) Moshi-moshi, Yōji/Yōko desu ga. – [*your first name* (without **-san**!)] desu. Konnichi wa. O-hima deshitara, doyōbi ni issho ni eiga o mi ni ikimasen ka? (*e*) Arigatō gozaimasu. Chotto techō o mite kimasu kara, sukoshi o-machi kudasai. (*f*) Moshi-moshi, o-matase shimashita, Doyōbi wa zannennagara aite inai n' desu ga . . . (*g*) (Sō desu ka . . .) Ja, Nichiyō wa ikaga deshō? – Nichiyōbi nara hima desu. (*h*) Sore ja, Nichiyōbi ni goji ni o-taku made mukae ni ikimasu ga, ikaga desu ka? – Hai, o-machi shite imasu. (*i*) Sore ja, shitsurei shimasu. – Sayōnara.
2 (*a*)haiken shimashita (*b*) go-zonji desu (*c*) Bēkā to mōshimasu (*d*) irasshaimasu.
3 (*a*) . . . tsutomeru tame desu./. . . tsutomeru tame ni Nihongo o narau n' desu. (*b*) O-kane ga ii tame desu./O-kane ga ii tame ni, . . . tsutometai n' desu. (*c*) . . . sunde iru tame desu./. . . sunde iru tame ni . . . kita n' desu. (*d*) . . . miru tame desu./. . . miru tame ni . . . okiru n' desu. (*e*) . . . nonde ita tame desu./. . . nonde ita tame ni . . . osokatta n' desu. (*f*) Urusai tame desu!/Urusai tame ni hanashitagaranai n' desu!
4 1(*b*) 2(*c*) 3(*e*) 4(*a*) 5(*d*).

Unit 19

True or false? 1 T 2 F 3 F 4 F
1 (*a*) iku to; takai desu (*b*) kiku to; oshiete kuremasu (*c*) aru to; benri desu (*d*) nomu to; shitsurei desu (*e*) au to, akushu shimasu.
2 (*a*) 1 kaitara; okutte moraimasu 2 okutte morattara; tabemasu 3 tabetara; ikimasu 4 kaette kitara; shimasu 5 shitara; kaerimasu. (*b*) 1 meshiagareba/agareba 2 o-yame ni nareba 3 nasareba 4 irasshareba/o-ide ni nareba.

3 (*a*) iku to (*b*) yokereba/yokattara (*c*) kakeru nara (*d*) hansamu dattara/nara (*e*) ittara/ieba/iu nara.
4 (*a*) Supōtsu ga jōzu dattara/de areba, gakkō de ninki ga atta no ni. (*b*) Daigaku de motto benkyō sureba, yokatta no ni. (*c*) Terebi ga motto omoshirokattara/omoshirokereba, maiban nomiya de o-sake o nomanai no ni. (*d*) Kanai ga itsumo monku bakari iwanakereba, ii no ni.
5 (*a*) bakari (*b*) dake (*c*) shika (*d*) dake/bakari (*e*) shika.

Unit 20

True or false? **1** T **2** F
1 (*a*) Imōto ni kai ni itte moratta. (*b*) Katei kyōshi ni shite moratta. (*c*) Otōto ni katte kosaseta. (*d*) Otōsan ni kaite moratta. (*e*) Tomodachi ni arawaseta.
2 (*a*) Mainichi sanpo sasete (saseru yō ni shite) kudasai. (*b*) Tabako o suwasenaide (suwasenai yō ni shite) kudasai. (*c*) Amai mono o tabesasenaide (tabesasenai yō ni shite) kudasai. (*d*) Yasai ya sakana o yoku tabesasete (taberu yō ni shite) kudasai. (*e*) Asa made terebi o misasenaide (misasenai yō ni shite) kudasai.
3 (*a*) Ashita no asa hayaku okiru yō ni shite kudasai. (*b*) Ojīsan ga yoku/takusan taberu yō ni narimashita. (*c*) Nihongo ga sukoshi hanaseru yō ni narimashita. (*d*) Konban osoku naranai yō ni shite kudasai. (*e*) Rōrusu-roisu ga kaeru yō ni naritai desu.

Unit 21

True or false? **1** F **2** F **3** F
1 (*a*)yonde/yomarete (*b*) mite/mirarete (*c*) kakete/kakerarete (*d*) ite/irarete (*e*) suwatte/suwararete.
2 A + U arimasen deshita kara; nakatta kara/no de; B + Y benri desu kara; benri da kara/na no de; C + Z futte imasu/iru kara; E + V oishii (desu) kara; F + W tabemasu kara; taberu kara/no de.
3 (*a*) 1 hatarakaseraremasu/hatarakasaremasu 2 yomaseraremasu/yomasaremasu 3 tsukawaseraremasu/tsukawasaremasu 4 kisaseraremasu; 5 saseraremasu. (*b*) 1 hatarakanakereba/hatarakanakute wa/hatarakanai to ikemasen (etc.) 2 yomanakereba/yomanakute wa/yomanai to ikemasen (etc.) 3 tsukawanakereba/tsukawanakute wa/tsukawanai to ikemasen (etc.) 4 kinakereba/kinakute wa/kinai to ikemasen (etc.) 5 shinakereba/shinakute wa/shinai to ikemasen (etc.)

4 (*a*) tsukawasete moraimashita (*b*) misasete moraimashita (*c*) kikasete moraimashita (*d*) torasete moraimashita.
5 (*a*) Suzuki-san wa kasa ga arimasen deshita kara/nakatta kara/no de, ame ni furaremashita/furarete shimaimashita. (*b*) Tarō-kun wa (o-)isha(-san) ni nigai kusuri o nomaseraremashita/nomasaremashita. (*c*) Jiru-san wa Eigo dake de (wa)/ja naku(te), Doitsugo mo oshiemasu.

Unit 22

True or false? 1 F **2** F **3** T **4** F
1 (*a*) iku kai? (*b*) taberu kai? (*c*) tabete! (*d*) nagete! (*e*) kaeru kai?
2 (*a*) Ichinen gurai naratte 'ru n' da. (*b*) Igirisu de mo benkyō shita shi, Nihon de mo benkyō shita. (*c*) Un, oishii. (*d*) Ama-sugiru kara amari nomanai. (*e*) Demo, koko ni wa nai darō ne.
3 (*a*) Sō ne, amari omoshirokunakatta wa. (*b*) Akushon bakkari de, ato wa nani mo nakatta mitai. (*c*) Motto fukai eiga ga ii wa. (*d*) Tatoeba, Rashōmon mitai na eiga. (*e*) Atarashii no de wa, nakanaka ii no ga nai wa yo!
4 (*a*) Ken-san mitai ni hansamu na otoko no ko wa sukunai (ne). (*b*) Michiko-san wa konogoro amari benkyō shinai mitai. (*c*) Watashi mo Ken-san mitai na bōifurendo ga hoshii (wa). (*d*) Sengetsu, issho ni yakyū o mi ni itta mitai. (*e*) Michiko-san wa Ken-san-tachi to Igirisu ni iku mitai.

Hints for further study

The best way in which to build upon this book is through constant practice and revision. Do not worry about making mistakes; the Japanese whom you encounter will be only too pleased that you are making the effort to learn their language. The next obvious step is to start learning the written language. Although this requires much time and a high degree of motivation, it will make life in Japan easier, and more enjoyable. In addition, it will often help the learning of vocabulary items, since you will recognise the basic meanings of the **kanji** with which they are written.

To learn the **hiragana** and **katakana** syllabaries, we would recommend P. G. O'Neill's *Kana Workbook* (Kodansha), which should be readily available both in Japan and elsewhere, and is admirably suited to self-teaching. If you are actually in Japan, a book such as Michael Pye's *Everyday Japanese Characters* (Hokuseido) will give you a useful introduction to the sort of **kanji** which you are likely to see in street signs etc. We would also recommend P. G. O'Neill's *Essential Kanji* (Kodansha) or W. Hadamitzky and M. Spahn's *Kanji & Kana* (Tuttle), which are more comprehensive, but less concerned with everyday survival. They present the **kanji** recognised for use in modern Japan in a way which makes them fairly accessible to the determined and methodical learner, and can also be used as **kanji** dictionaries. They do not, however, provide any reading practice. In fact, we are not aware of any up-to-date book which actually aims to teach someone working by him/herself how to read Japanese.

English-Japanese and Japanese-English dictionaries tend to be very expensive, particularly outside Japan. With the exception of the one mentioned below, they are produced with the needs of the Japanese student of English in mind, and are therefore of limited use to the learner of Japanese anyway. If you are in Japan, or have friends there, we would suggest *The Japan Foundation Basic Japanese-English Dictionary* (Bonjinsha).

Finally, we will be only too pleased to receive your queries and comments. You may not get an immediate reply, but we will endeavour to respond before too long.

INDEX

U: Unit; K: **Kaiwa**; S: Structures; R: **Renshū**; LS: Language and Society notes

1 Vocabulary (words)

Where no straightforward English-language equivalent exists, we refer you straight to the relevant part of the text; even if we are able to give an English equivalent, you should go back to the text to check usage. Where necessary, intransitive verbs are identified as **vi**, and transitive verbs as **vt**.

datta *past form of* **da** U5 K, S2
dattara *in that case* U22 K
datte *you see* U20 K
de [*instrument*] U4 K, S3; [*number*] U9 S6; U19 S3; [*passive agent*] U19 S1; [*place*] U4 K, S3; [*reason*] U16 K; [*vehicle*] U16 K; **de ii** U9 S9
de [sentence] *and so* [*sentence*] U6 K
de gozaimasu =*formal* **desu** U9 K, LS2; U18 S2
de wa [sentence] *well then/if that's so* [*sentence*] U2 K
de wa arimasen *negative of* **desu** U1 K, S1
de wa nakute U13 K; U17 S5
dekake.ru *to set/go out* U7 K; U11 S2
deki.ru *to be made, prepared* U11 S2; *to be good/excel at* U14 K, S5, LS1
dekiru dake *as much/far as possible* U15 K
demo [noun] *or something* U4 K; U10 S3
demo [sentence] *but, however* [*sentence*] U2 K; U5 S4
denki (*electric*) *power/lights* U17 S2
densha (*commuter*) *train* U5 S7
denwa (suru) *telephone* U13 K; U17 S2
denwa bangō *telephone number* U4 K
depāto *department store* U9 K
de.ru *to come/go out, leave* U9 S1; U11 S2; *to graduate* U15 K; *to take part in* U21 K
deshō U6 K, S2
desu *is* U1 LS1
disuko *disco* U7 K
dō? *how?* U5 S3
dō yatte? *how?/in what way?* U16 K
dochira? *which way?* U2 S4
Doitsu *Germany* U1 LS4
doko? *where?/what place?* U1 K; U2 S4; U4 K, S8; U6 S8
doko ka *somewhere* U4 K, S8
dōmo *thanks* U1 K; *sorry* U6 LS1; *somehow* U15 K
donna? *what sort of?* U4 S6
dore? *which?* U8 K
dōro *road* U7 K
dorobō *burglar* U21 K
dōshite? *why?* U7 S5
dōshitemo *inevitably* U15 K
dōsō-kai *class reunion, alumni meeting* U18 K
doyō(bi) *Saturday* U6 LS2
dōzo *please* (*take*) U4 K, S3; U16 LS2

e *to, in the direction of* U5 K, S1
e *picture* U9 R2
ē *exclamation of surprise* (*rising intonation*) U22 K
ē *yes* (*informal*) U2 K
eiga *film* U6 S7
Eigo *English* (*language*) U1 K, LS3
Eikoku *Britain* U1 LS3
eki *station* U2 R5
en *yen* U9 K
enpitsu *pencil* U2 R4
erab.u *to choose, select* U21 K

fue.ru *to increase* (**vi**) U12 K, S1
fujin *lady, woman* U21 LS
fuk.u *to blow* U19 LS1
fuk.u *to wipe* U12 K
fuka.i *deep* U22 R3
fukuro *bag* U8 K
fukuzatsu na *complicated* U21 R3
Furansu *France* U1 K, LS3
furo *bath* U6 K
fur.u *to fall* (*rain, etc.*) U19 LS1
furu.i *old* U2 S1; U8 S1
fushigi na *mysterious* U12 S4
futari *two persons, the two* U6 K; U9 S7

fūtō *envelope* U9 K
futo.i *fat* U14 R1
futor.u *to become fat* U11 S2
fuya.su *to increase* (**vt**) U12 S1
fuyu *winter* U6 S7

ga U3 K, S2; U8 S4, 6; U10 S3; U14 S1, S5
ga *but* U1 K; U5 S4
gaijin/gaikokujin *foreigner* U1 LS4
gaikoku *foreign country* U1 LS4
gakkari suru *become disappointed* U19 K
gakki (*academic*) *term* U11 S3
gakkō *school* U12 S4
gakusei *student* U17 S7
-gar.u *to feel, show signs of* U12 K, S4
-gatsu *month* U6 LS2
genkan U3 K, LS3
genki na *healthy, well* U2 K; *cheerful* U17 S7
geri (suru) *diarrhoea* U15 LS
getsuyō(bi) *Monday* U6 LS2
ginkō *bank* U11 S2
gitā *guitar* U8 R2
-go *language* (*of country*) U1 LS3
go- *honorific prefix* U2 LS1
gochisō (suru) *to treat* (*to a meal*) U16 K; U10 LS1
gogo *p.m.* U6 S6; *afternoon* U10 K
gohan (*cooked*) *rice, meal* U2 LS1
go-ran ni nar.u =*honorific* **mi.ru** U18 S1*c*
goro *about* U6 K, S6; U18 LS2
gozaimasu =*formal* **ar.u** U9 K; U18 S2
gozen *a.m.* U6 K, S6
gurai *about* U8 S8; *just* U20 K; U22 S3
gurīn *green* U9 K, S2
gyūnyū *milk* U20 R1

ha *tooth* U1 K
hae.ru *to grow, sprout* (**vi**) U19 K
hagaki *postcard* U9 R2
haha (*my*) *mother* U16 K, LS1
hai *yes* U1 K; U9 LS3, LS5; *at your service, sir/madam* U9 K, LS5
haiken suru =*humble* **mi.ru** U18 S1*c*
hair.u *to enter* U6 K; U11 S2
ha-isha *dentist* U1 K
haishaku suru =*humble* **kari.ru** U18 S1*c*
haiyū *actor/actress* U17 S6
hajimar.u *to begin* (**vi**) U11 S2
hajime.ru *to begin* (**vt**) U12 S1
hajimete *for the first time* U19 K
hakar.u *to measure* U15 K
hakkiri *clearly* U12 LS; U18 K
hak.u *to put on, wear* U11 S2
han *half* (*past*) U6 K, S6
hana *nose* U14 K
hanashi *talk, conversation* U2 LS1; U21 K, S6; *proposal* U14 K
hanashia.u *to discuss* U8 LS2
hanas.u *to speak, talk* U4 S1
hanbāgā *hamburger* U9 R4
hansamu na *handsome* U2 S1
hara.u *to pay* U20 S1
haru *spring* U8 S2
hashir.u *to run* U14 S2
hataraki-sugi *over-work* U11 K
hatarak.u *to work, labour* U4 K
-hatsu (*train/bus*) *leaving at/starting from* U8 K
haya.i *quick, early* U2 S1; U8 S1; U14 K
hazu da *should/is likely to* U17 K, S3
hazukashi.i *to feel ashamed* U18 K
hazus.u *to take off, unfasten* U14 K
hē *exclamation indicating surprise* U7 K
Heisei U6 LS2
hen na *strange* U2 K; S1, S2
heta na *bad at* U8 S6

heya *room* U3 K
hi *day* U7 K
hido.i *terrible* U21 K
hie.ru *to become cool* U12 S1
hikōki *aeroplane* U17 K
hik.u *to catch* (*a cold*) U5 K; *to play* (*piano, violin, etc.*) U8 R3
hiku.i *low* U8 S6; *flat* U14 K
hima na *leisure* (*time, etc.*) U15 S4
hinichi *date* U18 K
hiru *noon/daytime/lunch* U13 K
hiru-gohan *lunch* U13 K
hiruma *daytime/during the day* U4 K
hirune (suru) *nap* U11 R1
hisashiburi da/ni *after an interval* U2 K, LS2; U18 K, LS2; U21 K
hisho (*personal*) *secretary* U11 K
hito *person* U2 S3
hitori de *by oneself/on one's own* U19 K, S3
hitoyasumi (suru) *little rest* U10 K
hitsuyō (na) *necessary* U20 K
hiyas.u *to cool* U12 S1
hō U8 K, S7; U14 K, S4
hodo *about* U22 S3
hoka ni *apart from this, in addition* U3 K
hoka no [noun] *other* [*noun*] U20 K
hokōsha *pedestrians* U7 K
home.ru *to praise* U21 S1
hōmu *platform* U8 K
hon *book* U2 LS1
Honkon *Hong Kong* U17 K
hon no *just* (*a little, etc.*) U20 K
hontō na *true* U2 S1
hontō ni (honto ni) *really* U3 K
hora! *look!* U1 K
hōridas.u *to throw down* U22 K
hōr.u *to throw* U22 K
hoshi.i (*I*) *want* U8 K, S6; U12 S4; U22 K
hotondo [negative] *hardly at all* U15 K
ichiban *most, -est* U8 S7
ichido *once, one day* U17 S2
ichigo *strawberry* U1 K
ichinenjū *all through the year/all year round* U19 K
ichiō *for the time being, tentatively* U18 K, LS2
ie *house* U3 K
ie/īe *no* U1 K, S4; U9 LS3
Igirisu *Britain* U1 K, LS4
igusuri *digestive pills* U6 K
i.i *good, all right* U2 S1, 2; U9 S4, S9; *indicating choice/preference* U8 K; U9 S4
ik.u *to go* U5 K; U7 S1; U11 S2; U17 S2
ikaga? =*formal* **dō** U2 K; U18 S2*b*
ikena.i *it won't do* U15 S7
ikura? *how much?* U4 LS
ikura ka *a little, somewhat* U19 K
ima *now* U3 K
inu *dog* U3 K
irassharu =*honorific* **ik.u, i.ru, kuru** U10 K; U11 K; U18 S1*c*
ire.ru *to put in, insert* U10 K
iro *colour* U9 S2
iroiro *various, all sorts of* U5 K
i.ru *there is* (*animate*) U3 K, S1; *to stay* U4 S1; -te iru U11 S2
ir.u *to need* U6 K; U10 S3*c*
isha *doctor* U1 K; U15 K, LS
isogashi.i *busy* U4 K; U10 K; U12 S4
isog.u *to hurry* U8 K
issho ni *together* U6 K; U7 K; U8 S3
isu *chair* U6 K
itadak.u =*humble form of* **mora.u, nom.u, tabe.ru** U6 K; U18 S1*c,d*
ita.i *painful* U11 K; U12 S4
Itaria *Italy* U1 LS4
itas.u =*humble* **suru** U18 K, S1*c*
itete *ouch* U6 K
itsu? *when?* U4 K, S8
itsu mo *always* U6 S8; U7 K

i.u *to say* U13 K, S1
iya *no* (*male*) U22 S1*f*
iya na (*I*) *hate* U8 S6; U12 S4
iyā ne *oh no/dear me* (*fem.*) U10 K
izure ni shite mo *either way/in any case* U19 K
izure (wa) *anyhow, some day, in due course* U20 K

ja/jā [sentence] *well then/if that's so* [*sentence*] U2 K
ja arimasen *negative of* **desu** U1 K, S1
ja nakute U12 K; U17 S5
jamu *jam* U1 K
-ji *o'clock* U6 K, S6
jibun *oneself* U13 S7; U22 S2
jikan *time* U4 K
-jikan *counter for hours* (*duration*) U8 K, S8
jimusho *one's place of work, office* U11 K
-jin *person* (*of country*) U1 LS3
jīnzu *jeans* U9 S7
jisho *dictionary* U9 K
jitsu wa *actually, in fact* U14 K
jiyū ni *freely* U21 R4
jiyūseki *unreserved seat* U8 LS1
jōbu na *strong, robust* U17 S7
jōdan *joke* U13 K
josei *woman, the female sex* U13 S3
jōshaken (*bus/train*) *ticket* U8 LS1
jōzu na *good at* U8 S6
jūsho *address* U2 LS1

ka *or* U20 K
ka? U1 K, S2
ka dō ka *whether or not* U17 K, S4
ka na? =*informal* **kashira?** U9 K
ka mo shirenai *may, perhaps* U6 K, S3
kachō *section head* (also *address/reference*) U11 LS
kaeri ni *on the way home/back* U21 K
kae.ru *to change* (**vt**) U12 S1; U14 K
kaer.u *to go/come back, return* (*home, etc.*) U5 K; U17 S2*c*
kaette *on the contrary, in fact* U11 K
-kai *counter for storeys, floors* U9 K, LS1
kai *meeting* U18
kai? =**ka?** (*informal*) U22 S1*d,g*
kaidan *stairs* U17 S2
kaifuku (suru) *recovery* U15 LS
kaigai *abroad* U20 K
kaigi *conference* U17 K
kaimono (suru) *shopping* U4 S1
kaisatsuguchi *ticket barrier* U8 K
kaisha *company/the office* U4 K
kaiwa *dialogue* U1 K
kaji *housework* U21 K
kakar.u *to last* (*of time*) U8 K; *to hang* (**vi**) U12 S1
kake.ru *to hang* (*up*) (**vt**) U12 K S1; U13 K; *to put on* (*glasses*) U14 K
kak.u *to write* U4 S1
kakunin (suru) *confirmation* U18 K
kakure.ru *to hide* (**vi**) U12 S1
kakus.u *to hide* (**vt**) U12 S1
kamawana.i *to not care* U19 S4
kami *hair* U8 R2
kami *paper* U9 S7
kanai (*my*) *wife* U1 K, LS2
kanari *fairly, quite* U17 S6
kanashi.i *sad* U17 S7
kanben (suru) *to spare, let off* U16 K
kane *money* U2 LS1
kanemochi *rich man, rich* U19 R4
kangae.ru *to think, consider* U13 K, S5, 7
kangofu *nurse* U15 LS
kanji *feeling* U14 K
kanjō *bill* U4 LS
kankei *relation, connection* U11 K
kanojo *she* U3 S4

kanpai! *cheers!* U4 K
kantoku (suru) *supervision* U22 K
kao *face* U13 K
kao-iro *facial colour/complexion* U11 K
kara *after* U11 K, S2; *from* U5 K, S1; U7 S3; U9 S1; U16 S1
kara *and so* U6 K, S4
karada *body* U8 R2
kare *he* U13 K, S7
karē *curry* U11 R1
kari.ru *to borrow* U18 S1
kasa *umbrella* U1 K
kaseg.u *to earn (money), work (for money)* U19 K
kashira? *I wonder? (fem.)* U5 K; U6 S3
kas.u *to lend* U16 S1
kata =*honorific* **hito** U14 K; U18 S2*c*
katamichi *one way (trip)* U8 LS1
katei *household, home* U20 K
ka.u *to buy* U4 S1
kawai.i *lovely, cute* U3 K
kawakas.u *to dry* (**vt**) U12 S1
kawak.u *to become dry* U8 K; U11 S2
kawar.u *to change* (**vi**) U12 S1
kayō(bi) *Tuesday* U6 LS2
kayo.u *to visit regularly, commute to* U20 K
kaze *wind* U19 LS1
kaze *(a) cold* U5 K
kazoku *family* U10 K
kechi (na) *mean, stingy* U22 K, LS1
kedo =*informal* **keredomo** U14 K
kega *injury* U21 K
keisatsu *police* U21 K, LS
keiyaku *contract* U11 R2
kēki *cake* U4 S3
kekka *results* U15 K
kekkon (suru) *marriage* U11 S2; U13 K
kekkon-shiki *wedding (ceremony)* U14 K
kekkyoku *eventually, finally* U14 K
ken *ticket* U8 LS1
ken =*formal* **koto** U18 K, S2c
kenbutsu (suru) *sightseeing* U4 S1
kenka (suru) *quarrel* U11 R1
kensa (suru) *check-up* U15 K
keredo =**keredomo** U14 K
keredomo *but, however* U8 K
kesa *this morning* U5 K
kes.u *to switch off* (**vt**) U6 K
ketsuatsu *blood pressure* U15 K
ketsueki *blood* U15 K
ki o tsuke.ru *to be careful, pay attention* U12 K
ki o ushina.u *to faint* U19 S1
kie.ru *to go out, be extinguished* U12 S1
kiiro.i *yellow* U9 S2
kik.u *to ask, hear* U13 S1
kimar.u *to be decided* U18 K
kime.ru *to decide* U14 K
kimi (intimate) *you (male)* U1 LS2; U19 K; U22 S1*e*
kimochi *feeling, inclination* U7 K
kinchō (suru) *stress, tension* U15 K
kinjo *neighbourhood* U20 K
kinō *yesterday* U5 S6
kinyō(bi) *Friday* U6 LS2
kioku *memory* U10 K
kippu *ticket* U7 K; U8 LS1
kirai na *(I) hate* U8 K, S6
kirei na *pretty, clean, neat* U2 S1
ki.ru *to put on, wear* U11 S2; U17 S2
kir.u *to cut* U4 S1
kisha *(long distance) train* U8 K, LS1
kissaten *coffee-shop* U2 S5
kitana.i *dirty* U15 S7
kitchin-taoru *wiping-up cloth* U12 K

kitte *(postage) stamp* U9 R3
kitto *no doubt, certainly* U9 K
ko *child* U20 K
kō *this way, like this* U7 K, S6
kōban *police box* U21 K
kochira *this way* U2 S4; U18 K
kodomo *child* U9 R1
koe *voice* U19 K
kōfun (suru) *excitement* U19 K
kōgi *lecture* U9 S7
kōhī *coffee* U4 LS
kōjō *factory* U21 R4
koko *here* U2 S4
kōkōsei *high-school student* U17 S3
kōkū-binsen *air (mail) letter-paper/pad* U9 K
kokusai *international* U17 K
komaka.i *detailed, small (change)* U9 K
komar.u *to get into difficulties* U6 K; U13 S4
kon- *this* U5 S6
konban *this evening/night* U2 LS; U20 S2
kondo *this time* U4 K
kondo no [noun] *next/this coming [noun]* U19 K
kongetsu *this month* U5 S6
konkai *this time* U18 K
konna *this sort of* U4 S6
kono [noun] *this [noun]* U2 K, S3
konogoro *recently* U15 K
konshū *this week* U5 S6
kontakuto (renzu) *contact lenses* U14 K
koppu *glass (for drinking from)* U8 R1
kore *this* U1 K, S5
kore kara *after this, now* U8 K
kōri *ice* U22 K
kōshite *in this way* U12 K
kotae.ru *to reply* U13 S1
koto *(abstract) thing* U5 K, S3; U14 S2, S5; *about* U17 K
koto ga aru U5 K, S3
koto ni naru *to be decided to* U13 K, S3
koto ni suru *to decide* U13 K, S3
kotoshi *this year* U5 S6
kotowar.u *to refuse* U13 S1
koware.ru *to break* (**vi**) U12 S1
kowas.u *to break* (**vt**) U12 S1
kozukai *pocket money* U12 K
kudamono *fruit* U8 R5
kudasai *please (give me) [noun]* U4 K, S3; *[verb]* U8 K, S5; U16 S2
kudasaru *to give* U16 S2; U18 S1*d*
kūkō *airport* U17 K
-kun *form of address/reference* U1 LS2
kuni *country* U15 S1; U22 K
kurai *about* U8 S8; *if anything, rather* U22 K, S3
kurasu-kai *class reunion* U18 K
kure *please [verb]* U16 K, S2
kure.ru *to give* U16 S1
kuro.i *black* U9 S2
kuru *to come* U4 S1; U7 S1; U11 S2; U17 S2
kuruma *car* U2 R2
kushami (suru) *sneeze* U16 K
kusuri *medicine* U15 K
kyaku *guest* U18 S1*c*
kyasshu kādo *cash card* U21 K
kyō *today* U5 S6
kyōiku *education* U20 K
kyonen *last year* U5 S6
kyōshi *instructor, teacher* U20 K

mā *well* U4 K
ma ni au *to be in time* U8 K
machi *town* U13 R2
machiawase *meeting, rendezvous* U17 K
mada *still/(not) yet* U11 K, S6
made *until* U4 K, U7 S3; *even* U16 K
mado *window* U19 K
mae *in front* U2 S5; *before* U6 S6; U15 K, S5

noriokure.ru *be late for* (*train, etc.*) U8 K, LS2
nor.u *to get on* (*train, etc.*) U8 K; U12 S1; *to get excited* U20 K
nose.ru *to place on/load* U8 K; U12 S1
nōto *notebook* U16 R2
nug.u *to take off* U15 K
nuke.ru *to come/fall out* U12 S1
nuk.u *to pull out* U12 S1
nusum.u *to steal* U21 K
nyūgaku (suru) *to enter school/university* U13 LS2
nyūin (suru) *to enter hospital* U15 LS
nyūsu *news* U4 S3

o U4 K, S3; U7 K, S4; U9 S1
o- *honorific prefix* U2 LS1
o-cha (*Japanese*) *tea* U5 R2; U22 K; *the tea ceremony* U20 K
o-hana *flower arranging* U20 K
o-hiru *lunch, lunchtime* U6 K
o-ide ni naru =*honorific* **ik.u/kuru/i.ru** U18 S1*c*
o-mawari-san *policeman* U21 K
o-mizu (*cold*) *water* U4 LS
o-naka *stomach* U11 K, S1; U15 K
o-negai shimasu U16 LS2
o-taku *your house* U3 K; U20 LS2
obasan *aunt/middle-aged woman* U14 K
oboe *memory, recollection* U18 K
oboe.ru *to learn, memorise* U11 S2
ochi.ru *to fall, fall off* U6 K; U11 S2; U12 S1
ochitsuk.u *to settle down, calm down* U16 K
odor.u *to dance* U7 K
ōfuku *return* (*trip*) U8 LS1
oi *hey!* U22 K
ō.i *many* U8 K, S6; U19 K
oishi.i *delicious/*(*of restaurants, etc.*) *good* U2 K
ojōsan (*your*) *daughter* U20 K, LS1
okāsan *mother* (*address/reference*) U3 K; U16 LS1
ōki na/ōki.i *big* U2 S1, 2
oki.ru *to get up* U6 K; U12 S1
okor.u *to get angry* U13 S1
okos.u *to rouse* U12 S1
ōku *most/the majority* U8 S1
ok.u *to put, place* U12 K; U16 S4
okure.ru *to fall behind/be late for* U20 K
okusan (*your/his*) *wife* (*address/reference*) U1 K, LS2
omae *you* (*male*) U1 LS2; U22 S1*e*
omoidas.u *to remember* (*something forgotten*) U5 K; U8 LS2
omoshiro.i *interesting* U13 S5
omo.u *to think, feel* U8 LS2; U13 K, S5, S7
onaji *same* U15 K, S2
onēsan (*elder*) *sister* (*address/reference*) U16 LS1
onna *woman, female* U19 K
onna no ko *girl, young woman* U19 K
or.u =*humble* **i.ru** U11 K; U18 S1*c*; U21 S1
ore *I* (*male*) U19 K; U22 S1*e*
orenji *orange* U8 K
ori.ru *to climb down, get off* (**vi**) U9 K; U12 S1
oros.u *to take off/down, unload* U8 K; U12 S1
osae.ru *to hold down* U6 K
ōsetsu-shitsu *reception room* U11 K
oshie.ru *to teach, inform* U4 K
oso.i *slow, late* U2 S1
osoku made *until late* U8 S1
ossharu *honorific* **i.u** U18 S1*c*
Ōsutoraria *Australia* U1 LS4
oto *noise* U19 R1
otoko *man, male* U12 K
otoko no ko *boy, young man* U12 K
otoko no hito *man* U21 K

undō (suru) *exercise* U15 K
unten (suru) *driving* U14 S5*b*
unzari (suru/da) *to be disgusted, fed up* U12 K, LS
ura *reverse/other side, behind* U2 S5
ureshi.i *happy* U17 S7
uriba *sales counter, section* U9 K
urusa.i *annoying; choosy* U14 K; U18 R3
ushina.u *to lose* U19 S1
ushiro *back, behind* U2 S5
uta *song* U11 K
uta.u *to sing* U11 K
utsur.u *to spread; be infected* (**vi**) U16 K

wa U1 K, S1; U3 K, S1, 3; U4 K, S5; U8 K, S4, 6; U10 S3
wa (*sentence ending*) U5 K, LS4
waka.i *young* U2 S1
wakar.u *to understand* U4 S1; U10 S3*c*
wan *woof* U3 K
wāpuro *word processor* U21 R3
wara.u *to smile, laugh* U11 S1
ware.ru *to break, get broken* (**vi**) U12 K
war.u *to break* (**vt**) U12 K
waru.i *bad* U2 S1; (*of illness*) *serious* U15 K
wasuremono *something forgotten/left behind* U21 K
wasure.ru *to forget* U10 K
watakushi =*formal* **watashi** U18 K, S2*c*
watar.u *to cross* U17 S2
watashi *I* (*male and female*) U1 K
watas.u *to hand over* U16 K

ya *and* U7 K; U10 S1
-ya *shop, etc.* (*dealing professionally in*) U2 K, LS3
yahari *after all/just as I thought* U8 K
yaku ni tatsu *to be a help/useful* U21 K
yakusoku (suru) *promise, appointment, date* U16 K
yakuza *gangster* U21 LS
yakyū *baseball* U7 K
yakyū-bu *baseball club* U21 K
yama *mountain, hill* U7 K; U16 K
yama hodo *heaps* U16 K
yame.ru *to give up, cease* (**vt**) U13 K
yam.u *to stop, cease* (*rain, etc.*) (**vi**) U19 K, LS1
yappari =**yahari** U17 K
yar.u =**suru** U16 K; U18 S1*d*; *to live* U20 K
yasai *vegetable* U14 R3
yase.ru *to become thin* U11 S2
yasu.i *cheap* U8 S7
yasumi *holidays* U11 LS
yasum.u *to rest, take time off work* U16 K; *euphemism for* **ne.ru** U18 S1*c*
yatsu *fellow, person* U22 K
yatto *finally, at length* U6 K
yō da *it seems that* U15 K, S1
yō ni U16 K, S3
yō ni nar.u U20 S2
yō ni suru *to make a point of doing* U20 K, S2
-yō(bi) *-day* (*of the week*) U6 LS2
yobidas.u *to call, summon* U14 K
yob.u *to call, invite* U5 S2
yōfuku *dress* U22 S1*e*
yōi (suru) *preparation* U10 K
yōji *things to do* U16 K
yokatta *past form of* **ii** U5 K, S5
yoku *well, often* U4 R3; *miraculously, luckily* U16 K
yokuna.i *negative form of* **ii** U2 S2
yom.u *to read* U4 S1
yori *than* U8 K, S7
yorokob.u *to rejoice* U13 S1
Yōroppa *Europe* U5 K
yoroshi.i =*honorific* **i.i** U19 S1*e*
yoru *night-time/at night* U4 K
yor.u *to be based upon* U15 K, S3

2 Vocabulary (expressions)

Where no straightforward English-language equivalent exists, we refer you straight back to the relevant part of the text; even if we are able to give an English equivalent, you should go back to the text to check usage.

apologising U6 LS1
congratulating U13 LS2
eating/drinking U4 LS; U10 LS1; U14 LS2
giving/receiving U5 LS1; U6 LS1
greetings U2 LS2; U3 LS1; U22 LS2
illness U15 K, LS
insults U22 LS1
introductions and meeting people U1 LS1
police U21 LS
shopping U9 K, LS6
telephone U18 K
travel U8 K, LS1; U17 K, LS
weather U19 LS
work U11 LS
(see also Section 3, under *speech*)

arigatō (gozaimasu) thanks U3 LS2
boku mo bīru da that'll be beer for me too U4 K
boku no pen de dōzo please (write it) with my pen U4
chōdo itadakimasu thank you, sir/madam U9 K
chotto o-negai shimasu excuse me, please U4 LS
chotto sumimasen excuse me, please U4 LS
dō itashimashite don't mention it U11 K
dō shita n' deshō I wonder what's happened U10 K
dochira-sama desu ka? who is speaking? U2 S4
dōmo (arigatō [gozaimasu]) thanks U1 K; U5 LS1
dōmo (sumimasen) sorry U6 LS1
dore, dore! let's see! U14 K
dōzo U16 LS2
dōzo yoroshiku pleased to meet you U1 K, LS1
ē, chotto . . . I am afraid not U9 K, LS4
ēto . . . let me see . . . U5 K
go-busata shite orimasu U18 K, LS2
gochisōsama deshita U10 LS1
go-kurō-sama thank you for your trouble U22 LS2
gomen kudasai! U3 LS2
gomen nasai I am/we are sorry U6 K, LS1
hai, dōzo here you are U4 K

hajimemashite/hajimete o-me ni kakarimasu how do you do U1 K, LS1
ichiman-en de o-tsuri o kudasai Please give me change from ¥10,000 U9 K, S6
ii kagen ni shi nasai yo! behave yourselves! U8 K
ikemasen ne that won't do (an expression of sympathy) U15 K
irasshaimase U4 K, LS
itadakimasu yes please U6 K; U10 LS1; U18 S1*c*
itte (i)rasshai U3 LS1
itte kimasu/mairimasu U3 LS1
jitsu o iu to . . . to tell the truth . . . U21 K
jōdan ja nai you must be joking U22 K
kashikomarimashita very well, sir/madam U5 LS3; U9 K, LS2
kochira ni narimasu this is it U9 K
konban wa good evening U2 LS2
konnichi wa hello/good day U2 K, LS2
kore wa shitsurei shimashita I am so sorry about this U10 K
kyō wa ii/iya na o-tenki desu ne! what lovely/horrible weather it is today U19 LS1
maido arigatō gozaimasu thank you, sir/madam U9 K
māmā desu it's so-so U4 K
[*name*] *to mōshimasu* my name is [name] U1 K, LS1; U13
nani ka atta no? is something wrong? U16 K
nan/nani ni shimasu ka? what will you have? U4 K
nanmei-sama desu ka? how many are you? U4 LS
nannen umare desu ka? when were you born? U15 K
natsukashii wa this brings back memories U5 K
[*noun*] *wa ikaga desu ka?* how about/would you like [noun]? U2 K
o-agari kudasai please come in U3 K, LS1
o-azukari shimasu U9 K, LS6
o-genki desu ka? how are you? U2 K, LS1
ohayō (*gozaimasu*) good morning U2 LS2
o-hisashiburi desu ne it's a long time since we met U2 K, LS2; U18 K, LS2
o-jama shimasu U3K, LS2
o-kaeri nasai! welcome back U3 K, LS1
o-kage sama de thanks for asking U2 K
o-machi shite imasu we will be waiting for you U10 K
o-matase (*ita*)*shimashita* I'm sorry to have kept you waiting U9 K; U20 S1
o-medetō (*gozaimasu*)*!* congratulations U13 K, LS2
o-negai shimasu please/excuse me, please U4 K, S3, LS; U16 LS2
o-saki ni U22 LS3
o-sewa-sama thank you for your help U22 LS3
osoreirimasu I would be much obliged U18 K, LS2
o-tsukare-sama thanks (for all your tiring work) U22 K, LS2
sekkaku desu ga . . . that's very kind of you but . . . U7 K
shibaraku desu ne it's a long time since we've met U1 K; U2 LS2
shikata ga arimasen there's no alternative/it's inevitable U4 K

3 Structures

We have arranged this in a way which we hope will aid speedy reference, even if it is slightly unorthodox. For verb forms, etc., also see **Appendices.**